A Feast of Wonders: Sergei Diaghilev and the Ballets Russes

A Feast of Wonders

Sergei Diaghilev and the Ballets Russes

edited by
John E. Bowlt
Zelfira Tregulova
Nathalie Rosticher Giordano

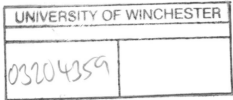
Cover
Léon Bakst, costume design for Ida Rubinstein in the "Dance of the Seven Veils," *Salomé*, 1908
Watercolor, gouache, bronze and silver paint and graphite pencil on paper, 47 × 30.2 cm
STG (5444)

Back cover
Giorgio de Chirico, design for the cover of the souvenir program of Sergei Diaghilev's Ballets Russes for the 1929 season in Monte Carlo and Paris
Graphite pencil, tempera and watercolor on paper, 27.5 × 20 cm
WA (1933.438) The Ella Gallup Sumner and Mary Catlin Sumner Collection Fund

Page 2
Léon Bakst
Portrait of Sergei Diaghilev and His Nanny, 1904–06
Oil on canvas, 161 × 116 cm
SRM (Zh-2117)

Art director
Marcello Francone

Graphic project
Luigi Fiore

Editorial coordination
Eva Vanzella

Copy editor
Emanuela Di Lallo

Layout
Antonio Carminati
Serena Parini

Translations
Mark Berelekhis and Paul Metcalfe on behalf of *Scriptum*, Rome

First published in Italy in 2009 by
Skira Editore S.p.A.
Palazzo Casati Stampa
via Torino 61
20123 Milano
Italy
www.skira.net

Printed and bound in Italy.
First edition

ISBN: 978-88-572-0371-3 ("Ekaterina" Cultural Foundation)
ISBN: 978-88-572-0090-3 (Skira)

Distributed in North America by Rizzoli International Publications, Inc., 300 Park Avenue South, New York, NY 10010, USA.
Distributed elsewhere in the world by Thames and Hudson Ltd., 181A High Holborn, London WC1V 7QX, United Kingdom.

The Principality of Monaco
Under the presidency
of H.R.H. the Princess
of Hanover

Étonne-moi! Serge Diaghilev et les Ballets Russes

Monaco, Villa Sauber, 9 July – 27 September 2009
Monaco, Salle des Arts du Sporting d'Hiver, 9 July – 30 August 2009

Videnie tantsa: Sergei Diaghilev i Russkie baletnye sezony

Moscow, State Tretyakov Gallery, 27 October 2009 – 25 January 2010
With the support of the "Ekaterina" Cultural Foundation, Moscow

This exhibition is jointly organized by the Nouveau Musée National de Monaco, under the direction of Marie-Claude Beaud, with the support of the government of the principality, the "Ekaterina" Cultural Foundation, Moscow, chaired by Ekaterina and Vladimir Semenikhin, and the State Tretyakov Gallery, Moscow, under the direction of Valentin Rodionov.

Scientific curators
John E. Bowlt
Zelfira Tregulova

Associate curators
Nathalie Rosticher Giordano, Curator of the Nouveau Musée National de Monaco
Lidia Iovleva, First Deputy General Director of the State Tretyakov Gallery, Moscow

General supervision
Emmanuelle Capra, Nouveau Musée National de Monaco
Vera Glushchenko and Alexandra Kharitonova, the "Ekaterina" Cultural Foundation, Moscow

Iconographic research for the catalogue
Christine Loiseau

Exhibition in Monaco

Artistic director
Pierre Passebon

Lighting design
Dominique Drillot

Sound and animated images
Vincent Vatrican, Laurent Trancy, Roger Badot, Sylvie Primard, Audio-Visual Archives of Monaco

Costume mounting
carried out by Anne-Sophie Loussouarn under the direction of Carmen Lucini

Graphic design
Luc Clément, Outremer agency

3D images
Frédéric Maurel

Painted decoration
Arnaud Rolland

Supervisor at Villa Sauber
Béatrice Blanchy

Administration, management and secretarial services
Danièle Batti Nocentini, Mélanie Crozet

Technical direction
Daniel Montuori, Jean-Michel Bianchi

Supervisors for inventory, organization and restoration
Angélique Malgherini, Emilie Tolsau

Restoration
Blandine Durocher (graphic arts), Claude Wrobel (painting), Lucille Dessennes (models)

Lighting of scenery models
Vincent Farelly, restorer

Trainee
Ilena Ojog

Communication, press and public relations
Anne-Gaëlle Bernardet, assisted by Hannen Sayhi

Parisian and international press
Emmanuelle Toubiana, Tambour Major

Cultural mediation
Elodie Cabrera, Coline Landucci

Visitor services assistants
Robert Pelazza, Gérard Angibeau, Henri Cavandoli, Florentin Certaldi, Yves Chemol, Lucien Zambelli

Institutional Partners Monaco

Committee for the Centenary of the Ballets Russes
chaired by Jean-Charles Curau, Director of the Monaco Directorate of Cultural Affairs, and Françoise Gamerdinger, Vice-director

Les Ballets de Monte-Carlo
Jean-Christophe Maillot, Director and choreographer

Monaco Dance Forum
Josu Zabala, Assistant to the Artistic Direction

Directorate of Tourism and Conventions
Michel Bouquier, Executive officer
Jean-François Gourdon, Press and public relations

Press Office
François Chantrait, Director
Jean-Pierre Doria, Press attaché

Audio-Visual Archives of Monaco
Vincent Vatrican, Director

Private Partner Monaco

Groupe Monte-Carlo SBM
Jean-Luc Biamonti, President
Bernard Lambert, General manager

Exhibition in Moscow

Curators
Evgenia Iliukhina, Irina Shumanova

Organization
Nina Divova

Design
Gennadii Sinev
Graphic Design: Stanislav Grandov, Prodesign Studio

Conservation of costumes
Emilia Gertz, Natalia Fedorova

Restoration and preparation of works
Alina Teys, Irina Bykova, Raisa Puchkova, Inna Solovova, Anna Isaikina (drawings); Andrei Golubciko, Ekaterina Volkova (paintings)

Preparation of archival materials
Tamara Kaftanova, Olga Zabitskaia

Photography
Aleksandr Sharoukhov

Photographic and video material
Aleksandr Dibin

Three-dimensional installations
Vizualnie innovatsii

Technical equipment
Prodesign Studio

Project coordination
Tatiana Gubanova, Ekaterina Semenova, Maria Shelkova (for meetings outside Russia); Olga Polianskaya (for meetings in Russia)

Electronic version of the exhibition
Sofiia Petrikova, Zoya Shergina, Elena Terkel, Irina Lodigina, Anna Uriadnikova

Press
Eleonora Tyan

Institutional Partners Russia

Gosudarstvennyi Russkii Muzei (State Russian Museum), director Vladimir Gusev

Sankt-Peterburgskii Gosudarstvennyi Muzei teatralnogo i muzikalnogo iskusstva (St. Petersburg State Museum of Theater and Music), director Natalia Metelitsa

Gosudarstvennyi Tsentralny Muzei im. A. A. Bakhrushin (State Bakhrushin Theater Museum), director Dmitrii Rodionov

Gosudarstvennyi Akademicheskii Bolshoi Teatr (Museum of the Bolshoi Theater), director Anatoli Iksanov

The exhibition in Moscow is carried out with the financial support of

Mister Anatolii Novikov

Public and Private Institutions

Bibliothèque nationale de France, Musée de l'Opéra, Paris (MO)
"Constantine" International Charity Foundation, St. Petersburg (CICF)
Curatorial Assistance, Los Angeles (CALA)
Dansmuseet, Stockholm
Fine Arts Museums of San Francisco, Theater and Dance Collection (FAMSF)
Legion of Honor Museum of the Fine Arts Museums of San Francisco (FAMSF)
Les Ballets de Monte-Carlo, Monaco
Los Angeles County Museum, Los Angeles (LACMA)
Marion Koogler McNay Art Museum, San Antonio (MKMAM)
The Metropolitan Museum of Art, New York
Musée des arts décoratifs, Paris
Musée d'Orsay, Paris
Musée National d'Art Moderne, Centre Georges Pompidou, Paris
Museum of the Bolshoi Theater, Moscow (MBT)
National Pushkin Museum, St. Petersburg
Nouveau Musée National de Monaco (NMNM)
Palais Princier, Monaco
Ravenscourt Galleries, London
Société des Bains de Mer, Monte Carlo (SBM)
State Bakhrushin Theater Museum, Moscow (SBTM)
State Museum of Theater and Music, St. Petersburg (SPSMTM)
State Russian Museum, St. Petersburg (SRM)
State Tretyakov Gallery, Moscow (STG)
Theatre Museum of the Victoria and Albert Museum, London (TML)
Thyssen-Bornemisza Collections

Wadsworth Atheneum, Hartford, Connecticut (WA)

Private Collectors

Claudine Boni
Andrei Cheglakov
Nicolas and Pierre Constantinowitz
Nilufer Dobra
Pierre Lacotte
Nina Lobanov-Rostovsky
John Neumeier
Ekaterina and Vladimir Semenikhin

Acknowledgments

Many people and institutions have rendered invaluable assistance in the organization of the exhibition and the publication of the catalog. All of them are warmly thanked for their efforts.

A sincere appreciation goes to our authors who not only contributed original and informative essays to the catalog, but also shared of their knowledge and judgment in matters of cultural and historical research. They are Oleg Brezgin, Elena Fedosova, Vadim Gaevsky, Lynn Garafola, Evgenia Iliukhina, Jean-Claude Marcadé, Nicoletta Misler, Sjeng Scheijen, and Alexander Schouvaloff

Thanks are also due to the many other curators, scholars and administrators who, as we assembled the exhibition, helped us resolve issues of access, selection and attribution.

In particular:
Helen Adair, Oleg Antonov, Anastasia Antonova, Debbie Armstrong, Mark Armstrong, Elena Barkhatova, Kit Smyth Basquin, Gabriella Belli, Jody Blake, Ludmila Bobrovskaia, Maksim Bokser, Karin Breuer, Clarenza Catullo, Christiane Cane, Ekaterina Churakova, Guy Cogeval, Nicolas Constantinowitz, Pierre Constantinowitz, Annick Daniel, Maria De Peverelli, Margherita de Pilati, Marina Elzesser, Véronique Fabre, Sarah Gage, Renate Gallois-Montbrun, Elena Grushvitskaia, Tatiana Gubanova, Vladimir Gusev, Shannon Haskett, Yvon Hivet, Gordon Hollis, Axel Hoppenot, Graham Howe, Hervé Irien, Mikhail Kamensky, Anne and Jérôme Kaplan, Lidia Kharina, Mark Konecny, Elena Kordik, Heather Lammers, Régis Lecuyer, Sergei Levitin, Nikita Lobanov-Rostovsky, Nina Lobanov-Rostovsky, Isabelle Lombardot, Charlotte Lubert, Olga Machroff, Jean-Christophe Maillot, Natalia Marisova, Geoffrey Marsh, Caroline Mathieu, Irina Menchova, Elizabeth Meshkvicheva, Natalia Metelitsa, Olga Michasova, Oleg Minin, Sarah Moon, Eric Naslund, Sergei Nekrasov, Mykia Omphroy, Alfred Pacquement, Evgenia Petrova, Galina Pogodina, Amy Porter, Jane Pritchard, Maria Reilly, Samantha Rippner, Dmitrii Rodionov, Valentin Rodionov, Guillaume Rose, Linda Roth, Raymond Sarti, Irina Shumanova, Yulia Solonovich, Kaye Spilker, Tatiana Sventorzhetskaia, Elena Terkel, Gary Tinterow, Alexandre Vassiliev, Jeroen Verbruggen, Tatiana Vlasova, Anna Winestein, and Eric Zafran.

And also to the following institutions:
Albert and Elaine Borchard Foundation, Los Angeles
Astrakhan State Picture Gallery, Astrakhan
Fulbright Hayes Program, Washington, DC
Getty Research Institute, Los Angeles
Institute of Modern Russian Culture, Los Angeles
International Research and Exchanges Board, Washington, DC
University of Southern California, Los Angeles

Sarah Moon
Triptych

Costume for a Brigand after
a design by Léon Bakst,
Daphnis et Chloé, 1912
NMNM (2006.27.3)
Toned vintage silver
gelatin print, 60 × 40 cm
Jeroen Verbruggen,
dancer with the Ballets
de Monte-Carlo
Production NMNM 2009

Costume for a Béotien after
a design by Léon Bakst,
Narcisse, c. 1911
NMNM (2006.27.1)
Toned vintage silver
gelatin print, 60 × 40 cm
Jeroen Verbruggen,
dancer with the Ballets
de Monte-Carlo
Production NMNM 2009

Costume for a Brigand after
a design by Léon Bakst,
Daphnis et Chloé, 1912
NMNM (2006.27.2)
Toned vintage silver
gelatin print, 60 × 40 cm
Jeroen Verbruggen,
dancer with the Ballets
de Monte-Carlo
Production NMNM 2009

The Nouveau Musée National de Monaco is embarking upon one of the most significant events in the cultural and artistic history of the principality.

Monte Carlo was a particularly important place of artistic invention for Sergei Diaghilev. It was here, between 1911 and 1929, that he created *Le Spectre de la Rose*, *Narcisse*, *Daphnis et Chloé*, *Les Noces*, *La Chatte*, *Le Bal*, and other productions that were to change the world of ballet definitively. What remains most extraordinary is Diaghilev's success in bringing together figures as renowned as Stravinsky, Massine, Bakst, Picasso, Goncharova, Fokine, Benois, Satie, Nijinsky, Chanel, Larionov, Cocteau, de Chirico, Pavlova, Chaliapin, Lifar, Balanchine, Kochno, Serov, Karsavina, and Roerich over a span of two decades. Just reading these names gives some idea of what an incredible feat it was to persuade these artists from different universes to work and create together. The quest for total art is and will remain the hallmark of Diaghilev's achievements.

In accordance with our desire to make the setting of this exhibition at the Villa Sauber, an architectural gem of the Belle Époque, as intimate and evocative as possible, we called upon the talents of an unclassifiable figure, namely Pierre Passebon, an inspired interior decorator, tireless collector, gallery owner with a passion for the decorative arts, and eclectic publisher. The design thus developed will provide visitors with insight into the endless connections between the arts.

I am particularly fond of dance. My grandmother, Princess Charlotte, had a genuine passion for ballet. She took private lessons with Lubov Tchernicheva and never missed a rehearsal of the Ballets Russes. My mother, Princess Grace, invited Balanchine and Nureyev on a regular basis in the 1960s. It was her dream to see a ballet company set up in Monaco once again, and this was accomplished in 1985, initially under the direction of Ghislaine Thesmar, then Jean-Yves Esquerre, and finally Jean-Christophe Maillot since 1993. The company does not of course confine itself to an established repertoire but, faithful to the spirit of Diaghilev, draws upon a constantly renewed range of creative talents spanning all horizons in its response to the great impresario's magical exhortation: "Astound me!"

Caroline

H.R.H. Princess of Hanover

Sarah Moon
Diptych

Costume for Gérard Mulys
playing the Blackamoor
in *Petrouchka* after a design
by Alexandre Benois, 1943
On permanent loan to SBM
at the NMNM (D. 2002.3829)
Toned vintage silver
gelatin print, 60 × 40 cm each
Jeroen Verbruggen,
dancer with the Ballets
de Monte-Carlo
Production NMNM 2009

When we are assigned to a new position and take over a project begun by a predecessor, we often have some pleasant surprises. The exhibition "A Feast of Wonders: Sergei Diaghilev and the Ballets Russes" is one of those pleasures you could not have imagined or hoped for. Everything has come together in a way that will make this project an unforgettable event for the Principality.

Pierre Passebon has designed the exhibition layout in the wonderful Villa Sauber, the ideal setting in which to celebrate the genius of Diaghilev, in association with Nathalie Rosticher Giordano, Curator at the Nouveau Musée National de Monaco, working in close collaboration with the "Ekaterina" Cultural Foundation in Moscow.

The whole team at the Nouveau Musée National de Monaco has made an intensely concerted effort in record time to devise the concept and make the preparations for this exhibition, supported by the scientific expertise of John E. Bowlt and Zelfira Tregulova. Almost three hundred items from all over the world will be on display to relate the dazzling adventure that was the story of the Ballets Russes and Diaghilev (1909–1929). Twenty years that have gone down in history to ensure that this dance legacy will live on in Monaco and the world at large.

As part of the Ballets Russes centennial celebrations, the exhibition will make the Principality throb for over a year to the rhythm of the dramatic arts. Sketches, costumes, scale models, stage sets… will open up this period to the world, offering visitors a glimpse of a vibrant creativity that has never been equalled: those days of the Ballets Russes.

That the creativity of this period has never been equalled is perhaps not entirely true, but in another way and at another time, since the only comparison I can possibly think of is those years between 1934 and 1957 in the United States, and the incredible artistic flowering that centered on Black Mountain College, with leading figures like John Cage, Merce Cunningham, Josef Albers and Willem de Kooning, which led to the creation of the New York School with Bob Rauschenberg, Trisha Brown, Terry Riley, and many others.

But that is another story… one which Jean-Christophe Maillot et Les Ballets, and the Nouveau Musée National de Monaco are preparing for 2010.

Marie-Claude Beaud
Director of the Nouveau Musée National de Monaco

Sarah Moon
Costume for Tony Gregory
playing the Magician in
Petrouchka after a design by
Alexandre Benois, 1943
On permanent loan to SBM
at the NMNM (D. 2002.5262)
Toned vintage silver gelatin
print, 60 × 40 cm
Jeroen Verbruggen, dancer
with the Ballets de Monte-Carlo
Production NMNM 2009

The exhibition project, "A Feast of Wonders: Sergei Diaghilev and the Ballets Russes," marks a second stage in the cultural cooperation between the "Ekaterina" Cultural Foundation of Moscow and the Principality of Monaco. The auspicious beginning of this cooperation came with the exhibition devoted to the avant-garde painters of the Knave of Diamonds group held on the Quai Antoine Premier in 2004. Following its venue in Monaco, the "Knave of Diamonds" was hosted in Moscow by the State Tretyakov Gallery, with which we have now partnered for the Diaghilev exhibition. In the fall of 2008, the Foundation also hosted "The Grace Kelly Years, Princess of Monaco" in Moscow, the first major event in Russia dedicated to the history of Monaco's ruling dynasty. Attracting some sixty-five thousand visitors, it was a triumphant celebration.

2009 marks the centennial of the first Russian ballet seasons in Paris and we think it only natural that one of the most significant exhibitions dedicated to this important date is taking place in Monaco and Moscow. For eighteen years, the Principality of Monaco served as the headquarters of Diaghilev's company; it was virtually a laboratory where the Ballets Russes created and honed many of its productions, and, indeed, it was at the Opéra de Monte Carlo built by Charles Garnier that many of them were first shown publicly. After Diaghilev's death in 1929, his company continued its work in Monaco, staging performances for decades to come, while preserving the visual texture and emotional ambiance of the legendary original productions.

Monaco bears many traces of Diaghilev's spirit: in 1959, in the presence of Princess Grace, a monument to this outstanding individual was unveiled near the Opéra, and a variety of cultural and archival institutions in the Principality continue to preserve—and to acquire—models, sketches, and costumes from the Diaghilev era.

One goal of our exhibition, open at the Villa Sauber—a Belle Époque building reminiscent of Garnier's masterpiece—is to reconstruct the atmosphere of the historic performances created under Diaghilev's stewardship. Visitors will have a chance to see diverse artistic and documentary materials such as costume and set designs by great Russian and European artists, as well as props, original costumes, vintage photographs, and posters. Visitors will also appreciate the highly decorative nature and luxury of the early spectacles, which so shocked and delighted European audiences, and the radical avant-gardism of the later productions.

Notwithstanding the challenges raised by the uncertainties of the current economic climate, for us to witness the implementation of this exhibition is a very exciting moment. In turn, we are delighted to be paying homage to the outstanding personality of Sergei Diaghilev, through whose tireless efforts the international community has come to admire the Russian genius.

Ekaterina and Vladimir Semenikhin
Co-founders of the "Ekaterina" Cultural Foundation

Sarah Moon
Costume for Marcelle Cassini
playing the Ballerina in
Petrouchka after a design
by Alexandre Benois, 1943
On permanent loan to SBM
at the NMNM (D. 2002.3823)
Toned vintage silver
gelatin print, 40 × 60 cm
Model Avril
Production NMNM 2009

The name of Sergei Diaghilev means much to Russian art and culture. At the turn of the twentieth century, Russia faced serious economic, social, political, and cultural change. The dominant traditions of Russian Realism, rooted, first and foremost, in social ideals, could no longer satisfy the younger generation of Russian artists who longed for fresh imagery and new styles, seeking a stronger rapprochement with European movements. Prior to the avant-garde explosion of the early 1910s, retrospective interludes of the Gothic and Classical techniques and of Symbolist visions had been typical of a Russian aesthetic language which was striving to reinvent itself. It was against this background that Sergei Diaghilev, an individual of extraordinary verve, came forth, eager to revive Russian art—and his advance was a welcome and timely event on the cultural horizon. Educated in the European manner and a graduate of Law School at the University of St. Petersburg (a fashionable academic department in late-nineteenth-century Russia), Diaghilev wore many hats: he was an art critic, a music and art historian, and, above all, a brilliant promoter of a new type of literary and art magazine (such as *Mir iskusstva* [The World of Art], 1898–1904) and of grand exhibitions (such as the so-called "Tauride" exhibition of historical Russian portraits of 1905 or the large retrospective displays of Russian art in Paris, Berlin and Venice in 1906–07).

It was Diaghilev's wish to integrate Russian and European art that led him to the idea of establishing a cycle of "Russian seasons" in Paris, the cultural capital of Europe, in 1908. Their overwhelming and rapid success made Diaghilev world famous as an impresario and, at the same time, brought wide acclaim to the new Russian art—including music and the theater, which were of primary interest to Diaghilev and which are now the subject of this exhibition.

Diaghilev's artistic energy manifested itself primarily in St. Petersburg, Paris, and Monte Carlo. Thus, it is only natural that museums in these cities are among the first contributors to this exhibition. However, Diaghilev also turned his attention to Moscow, for he was interested — and on occasion directly involved in—the exhibitions, museums, art schools and theaters of the ancient Russian capital. Even though Moscow, in all fairness, may not be called a "Diaghilev" city, some of its institutions maintain priceless evidence of Sergei Pavlovich's fervent activity such as the State Bakhrushin Theater Museum and our main Moscow museum—the State Tretyakov Gallery.

It is, indeed, a great honor and a rare delight for the State Tretyakov Gallery to participate in, and host, this unique exhibition and to commemorate the ballet seasons which Diaghilev organized in Paris and Monte Carlo a century ago.

Lidia Iovleva
First Deputy General Director,
the State Tretyakov Gallery

Aleksandr Golovin
Design for the Theater Wings
L'Oiseau de Feu, 1910
Watercolor, Indian ink,
pen and whitening on paper
29.9 × 39.8 cm
SPSMTM (GIK 6087/5
OR 10000)

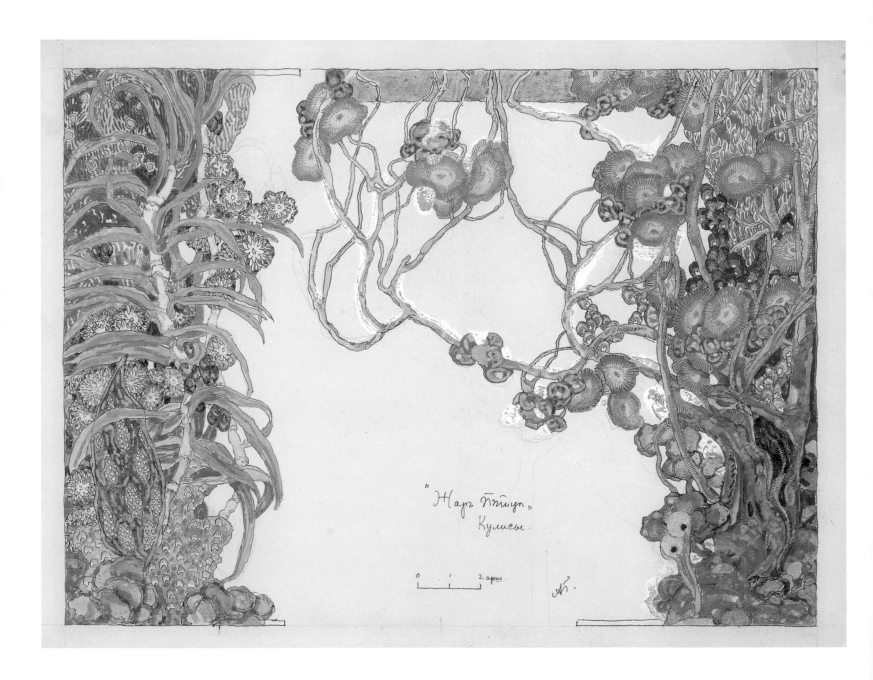

Contents

Note to the Reader

It is inevitable that, with an enterprise of this magnitude, one with complex itineraries and schedules involving international loans of precious works of art, the exhibitions at the two respective venues in Monte Carlo and Moscow cannot be identical. Although the items in the checklist correspond to the designs, pictures and objects on display, some pieces may be present at the one venue, but absent at the other, and we apologize for any inconvenience which this discrepancy may create.

Transliteration System for the English Language Edition

The transliteration of Russian words modifies the Library of Congress system, whereby the soft and hard signs have either been omitted or rendered by an "i" (e.g., "Grigoriev"). This system is also used throughout the footnotes and the bibliographical data where references involve Russian language sources.

Many Russian dancers, artists, and writers spent part of their lives in Europe or the USA and often their names received various, sometimes contradictory, transliterations from the original Russian into the language of their adopted home. For the sake of uniformity, names have been transliterated in accordance with the above system, except when a variant has long been established, e.g. Alexandre Benois (not Aleksandr Benua), Vaslav Nijinsky (not Vatslav Nizhinsky).

Times and Places

In most cases, dates referring to events in Russia before January 1918, are in the Old Style. Consequently, if they are in the nineteenth century, they are twelve days behind the Western calendar, whereas if they are between 1900 and 1918 they are thirteen days behind.

The city of St. Petersburg was renamed Petrograd in 1914, Leningrad in 1924 and then St. Petersburg again in 1992. However, both the names Petrograd and Petersburg continued to be used in common parlance and in publications until 1924. As a general rule, however, Petrograd has been retained here as the official name of St. Petersburg for the period 1914–24.

Titles of works of art, books, catalogs, journals and newspapers are italicized; titles of articles, manuscripts and exhibitions are in quotation marks.

Unless stated otherwise, day, month and year refer to the date of Diaghilev's first production or intended production. For a full list of the Diaghilev productions see L. Garafola, *Diaghilev's Ballets Russes* (New York: Oxford University Press, 1988), pp. 393–415.

All dimensions are in centimeters, height before width.

John E. Bowlt, Zelfira Tregulova

A Feast of Wonders[1]

John E. Bowlt
Zelfira Tregulova

The Ballets Russes (1909–1929) of Sergei Pavlovich Diaghilev (1872–1929) marked a veritable renaissance in the Russian performing and visual arts. Not only did his enterprise impact critical and public perceptions of the dance in particular, but it also accommodated the new Russian culture within the broader arena of Europe and America, underscoring the essential, interdisciplinary commitment of the new ballet to painting, music, poetry, photography, cinema, plastic movement, *haute couture*, literary criticism, and many other media.

Even though the principal stars of the Ballets Russes hailed from the Russian Empire (Diaghilev himself, Léon Bakst, Alexandre Benois, Tamara Karsavina, Serge Lifar, Léonide Massine, Vaslav Nijinsky, Igor Stravinsky), the company also attracted foreign celebrities, particularly in the late 1910s and 1920s—from Giorgio de Chirico to Claude Debussy, from Pablo Picasso to Erik Satie and from Juan Gris to Lydia Sokolova (stage name of the Englishwoman Hilda Munnings). Like the original "Mir iskusstva" (World of Art) group, in many ways, the intellectual and aesthetic genesis of the Ballets Russes, Diaghilev's company was, as Benois might have said, "not this, that or the other in isolation, but everything together."[2]

Since 1954, the year of Richard Buckle's pioneering "Diaghilev Exhibition" in Edinburgh and London,[3] there has been an ever increasing public recognition of the Diaghilev epoch. Artistic and documentary materials are numerous and much research has been conducted on the great dancers and choreographers, such as Michel Fokine, Karsavina and Nijinsky, the patrons such as Gabriel Astruc, the designers, especially Bakst and Benois and, of course, on Diaghilev himself. Naturally, after twenty years of the most diverse repertoires, casts and

tours, the Saisons Russes left behind a huge corpus of extremely varied materials and the primary recipients of this inheritance—such as the Library and Archive of the Lincoln Center in New York City, the Musée de l'Opéra in Paris, the Nouveau Musée National de Monaco, the Robert Tobin Collection at the Marion Koogler McNay Art Museum in San Antonio, Texas, the St. Petersburg State Museum of Theatrical and Musical Art, the Société des Bains de Mer in Monte Carlo, the Theatre Museum of the Victoria and Albert Museum in London and the Wadsworth Atheneum in Hartford, Connecticut—continue to guide historians in their endeavors to reassess the Golden Age of the Russian ballet—not least, the recent studies by some of our catalog essayists, particularly, Oleg Brezgin, Lynn Garafola, Sjeng Scheijen and Alexander Schouvaloff.[4]

The "Sergei Diaghilev and the Ballets Russes" exhibition marks the centennial anniversary of the Ballets Russes, one of the most dazzling cultural enterprises of the twentieth century. Founded by Diaghilev in Paris in 1909, the Ballets Russes or, as Diaghilev used to call the company, "Le Ballet Russe," amazed the world with its radical concepts of dance, choreography, scenography, and music. The Ballets Russes gratified and provoked, enticed and repelled, and became a legend in its own lifetime. This exhibition explores the vitality and prescience of that legend.

There have been a number of shows devoted to the accomplishments of Diaghilev, his dancers, designers and musicians.[5] This year alone, a century since the first productions of *Le Pavillon d'Armide* and *Cléopâtre* in Paris, witnesses at least ten other exhibitions devoted to the Ballets Russes, strong testimony to the enduring legacy that Diaghilev left behind. Without the luminaries of his

Alexandre Benois
A Venetian Feast in the Sixteenth Century, set design for *Fêtes Veniciennes* (unrealized), 1912
Tempera and pencil on paper on canvas, 65.7 × 102 cm
STG (1599)

Léon Bakst
Madame Ida Rubinstein
c. 1910
Watercolor, gouache
and pencil on paper mounted
on canvas, 128.3 × 69.2 cm
Signed on the left
The Metropolitan Museum
of Art, New York, The Chester
Dale Collection, Bequest of
Chester Dale (1962. 64.97.1)

Vaslav Nijinsky dancing
the Siamese Dance in
Les Orientales, 1910
Photograph by Karl Fisher
Original print
SPSMTM (GIK 10883/22)

Tamara Karsavina
in *Giselle*, 1910
Photograph by Auguste Bert
Original print
SPSMTM (GIK 15715/28)

company—Bakst, Benois, Adolph Bolm, Georges Braque, Fokine, Natalia Goncharova. Karsavina, Mikhail Larionov, Bronislava Nijinska, Nijinsky, Picasso, Maurice Ravel, Stravinsky and many others, the history of the modern performing and visual arts, in particular, would be unthinkable. Our exhibition pays tribute to their many accomplishments, placing a special focus on Monte Carlo which, from 1911 onwards, became the cornerstone for Diaghilev's administration of the Ballets Russes.

The exhibition is intended not only to celebrate the glory of the Ballets Russes at the equinox of European Modernism, but also to position that enterprise within a broader cultural framework. On the one hand, it observes a traditional presentation, moving by chronological sequence according to premieres of productions (from the opera *Boris Godunov* on May 19, 1908, and *Le Pavillon d'Armide* on May 19, 1909, in Paris, to *Le Bal* on May 9, 1929 in Monte Carlo). Grouped under the rubric of each production are references to the set and costume designs, material costumes, maquettes, prints and documentary photographs relating to that production. On the other hand, we have made every effort to enhance the sequence by adding ancillary items in the form of portraits, dramatic landscapes, theatrical evocations, and personal possessions which enliven and amplify the history of a particular scenic episode. From the very beginning, the catalog of the exhibition has been considered as an integral and permanent part of the project, inasmuch as its authors, distinguished specialists in the performing, visual and literary arts of Russia, explore many paths of enquiry, some centered on the actual ballet productions, others on parallel and comparative subjects.

Inevitably, this exhibition does not carry references to the entire repertoire of the Ballets Russes. Not all the productions were equal in their innovative force—some were artistic triumphs, others failed; sometimes movement, image and sound integrated totally, at other times there was acute disparity. In other words, the course of Diaghilev's ballet company was uneven, affected by financial, technical, artistic, geographical and even political forces, so that a prestigious venue, a generous subvention or lavishness of production were not always synonymous with aesthetic innovation, the 1921

Sleeping Princess being a case in point. All this is to say that some of the Saisons Russes were more clement than others and that certain ballets such as *Petrouchka*, *Le Sacre du Printemps* and *Ode* deserve permanent attention for their radical artistic and technical devices, whereas others such as *Midas* and *Les Biches* seem to be paler and less innovative. Although we wished to provide as extensive a survey as possible, our choice of objects for the exhibition was informed by these considerations and, of course, by conditions beyond our control such as issues of physical accessibility, fiscal limitations, conservation and transportation: because of their fragility a few works can be shown only at one of the two venues.

[1] "A Feast of Wonders" translates "La Fête Merveilleuse," the title of a ballet, based on Peter Tchaikovsky's *Sleeping Beauty* and re-orchestrated by Igor Stravinsky, which Diaghilev commissioned from Juan Gris (designs) and Bronislava Nijinska (choreography). The ballet was produced as a fund-raising gala in the Hall of Mirrors at Versailles on June 30, 1923, by the Ballets Russes; see L. Garafola, *Diaghilev's Ballets Russes* (New York: Oxford University Press, 1989), p. 119. The "Etonne-moi!" in the French title of our exhibition ("Etonne-moi! Serge Diaghilev et les Ballets Russes") refers to a conversation between Diaghilev and Jean Cocteau after a ballet production in Paris in 1912: "Le premier son de cloche d'une période qui commence en 1912 et ne se terminera qu'avec ma mort, me fut sonné par Diaghilev, une nuit, place de la Concorde. Nous rentrions

de souper après le spectacle. Nijinsky boudait, à son habitude. Il marchait devant nous. Diaghilev s'amusait de mes ridicules. Comme je l'interrogeais sur sa réserve (j'étais habitué aux éloges), il s'arreta, ajusta son monocle et me dit: 'Etonne-moi.' L'idée de surprise, si ravissante chez Apollinaire, ne m'était jamais venue." J. Cocteau, *La Difficulté d'Etre* (Paris: Du Rocher, 1983; first edition 1947), pp. 39–40.
[2] A. Benois, *Vozniknovenie "Mira iskusstva"* (Leningrad: Komitet populiarizatsii khudozhestvennykh izdanii, 1928), p. 6. Benois was describing the World of Art group.
[3] R. Buckle (ed.), *The Diaghilev Exhibition*, catalog of the exhibition at the Edinburgh Festival, Edinburgh, and Forbes House, London, 1954.
[4] See, for example, Garafola, *Diaghilev's Ballets Russes*, 1989; L. Garafola and N. van Nor-

man Baer, *The Ballets Russes and Its World* (New Haven: Yale University Press, 1999); A. Schouvaloff, *The Art of Ballets Russes. The Serge Lifar Collection of Theater Designs, Costumes and Paintings* (New Haven: Yale University Press, 1998).
[5] See Oleg Brezgin's bibliographical survey in this catalog for a list of relevant exhibitions. Among the more comprehensive shows special mention should be made of "Les Ballets Russes de Serge de Diaghilev, 1909–1929" held at the Ancienne Douane, Strasbourg, May–September 1969; "Diaghilev. Les Ballets Russes" at the Bibliothèque nationale de France, Paris, May 1979; "Diaghilev. Creator of the Ballets Russes. Art, Music, Dance" at the Barbican Art Gallery, London, January–April 1996; "Working for Diaghilev" at the Groninger Museum, December 2004 – March 2005.

Que reste-t-il de nos amours?

Nathalie Rosticher
Giordano

On June 16, 1980,[1] Serge Lifar wrote to Prince Louis de Polignac, President of the Société des Bains de Mer, concerning the "Diaghilev–Lifar collection" which he proposed to donate on condition that a foundation be created in the Principality of Monaco. Maurice Rheims was asked to provide an expertise; the introduction to the inventory established that the collection of pieces from the Ballets Russes was exceptional due to the fact that they were among the last available for purchase; a unique reflection of the art of ballet and musical taste of the period, the collection would constitute the heart of a museum entirely dedicated to Dance.

The assembly of materials includes preparatory sketches for stage sets and theater costumes, many of which were created at Monte Carlo by Alexandre Benois, Léon Bakst, Georges Braque, Jean Cocteau, Giorgio de Chirico, André Derain, Max Ernst, Naum Gabo, Natalia Goncharova, Juan Gris, Mikhail Larionov, Henri Laurens, Marie Laurencin, Juan Miró, Pablo Picasso, Pedro Pruna, Georges Rouault, Maurice Utrillo, as well as leading representatives of Russian Modernism such as Ivan Bilibin, Konstantin Korovin, Aleksandr Golovin, Dmitrii Stelletsky, and Pavel Tchelitchew. The listing also includes original handwritten musical scores by Claude Debussy, Francis Poulenc, Sergei Prokofiev, Erik Satie, and Igor Stravinsky, a reference bibliography, and, of special note, various issues of the famous *Mir iskusstva* (World of Art) journal and other, equally important historical documents such as photographs, commemorative objects, and correspondence between celebrities of the Ballets Russes such as Sergei Diaghilev, Tamara Karsavina, Henri Matisse, and Maurice Ravel.

Strange as it may seem, the collection of the would be Monaco foundation was never purchased. What is even more regrettable is that over the years a large amount of the artistic memorabilia so carefully

collected by Lifar has become dispersed. In a recording preserved in the Audiovisual Archives of Monaco, Lifar emotionally recalls his arrival in Monte Carlo in 1922 after the horrific ordeals experienced during his escape from Russia.[2] In this "paradise," as he liked to call it, in this icon of the Ballets Russes, Lifar dreamed of creating his foundation.

After the triumph of his first seasons at Théâtre du Châtelet, Diaghilev transformed his transitory troupe into a permanent dance company and, beginning in 1911, he organized a season each spring in Monte Carlo. After 1922, the company remained several months every year in this hospitable region where it found a permanent space to keep all their stage costumes and scenery in safety.[3] This would seem to indicate that a certain number of the original pieces belonging to the Ballets Russes still existed and were still located in the Principality. Unfortunately, this is not the case.

Miraculously, the Société des Bains de Mer, which produced all the performances between 1879 and the 1940s, managed to conserve its own collection of historical costumes. In the early 2000s the State of Monaco agreed to take a part of the costumes into storage and to conduct an inventory of all the items. An initial classification had already been made in 1978 by Philip Dyer,[4] nominated by the Société des Bains de Mer to evaluate the whole collection, according to the wishes of Princess Grace who intended to create a museum in the Principality devoted to theater costumes and dance. After selecting the most important items, Dyer was appointed to commission an auction at Sotheby's in 1980 of the items in the collection which were not to be kept.[5] It is likely that costumes of great historical interest disappeared at that time.[6]

Between June and October 2002, specialists examined the 30,000 theater costumes held by the Société des Bains de Mer,[7] and during an initial survey were

South-east facade of the Opéra
Garnier under construction,
Monte Carlo, 1878
Photograph by Louis-Émile
Durandelle
Original silver albumen print
33.4 × 42.3 cm
Archives NMNM (2003.1.2)

able to identify approximately 600 items[8] from the main body of the collection, called "Russian collection, repertoire of the Ballets Russes, successors to Diaghilev." It was thought that the superb corpus of Russian opera costumes had been created during Diaghilev's first seasons: several publications devoted to the Ballets Russes[9] describe the opera costumes of the 1909 season, which were most certainly used later by Raoul Gunsbourg for his own production of *Ivan the Terrible* in 1911, with Fedor Chaliapin in the title role.

Interior of the Opéra Garnier, Monte Carlo, 1910
Photograph by Joseph Enrietti
Original silver albumen print
13 × 18 cm
Archives NMNM (2003.1.3)

Lynn Garafola, historian of the Ballets Russes, had spoken to Francis Rosset, founder of the Service du Patrimoine historique of the Société des Bains de Mer, about the existence of a contract[10] signed between Gabriel Astruc, one of Diaghilev's financiers for the 1909 season, and Raoul Gunsbourg, director of the Monte Carlo Opéra between 1893 and 1951. If the fourth Russian season in Paris had been an unprecedented artistic success, the production was a considerable financial loss for Diaghilev. Apparently, Gunsbourg bought the main costumes and stage sets of *Ivan the Terrible*, *Cléopâtre*, *Le Pavillon d'Armide*, *Les Sylphides*, *Le Festin*, *Ruslan and Liudmila*, and *Prince Igor* for 20,000 francs.

On further examination, today it would seem that this information is highly improbable. In Gunsbourg's presentation of *Ivan the Terrible*, the costumes designed by Bakst figured in the 1911 program. The painter is said to have provided three original watercolors for the costumes and sets designed by Alphonse

Visconti for the premiere at Monte Carlo,[11] as reported in the newspaper *Le Petit Monégasque* on March 3, 1911 after the performance at the Opéra Garnier: "The three stage sets devised by Mr. Visconti recreate to perfection in color, design, and minutest detail, the three scale models painstakingly created by the famous Russian painter Bakst based on authentic documents, on commission for the new work by Mr. Raoul Gunsbourg. ... The public particularly admired the magnificent red velvet cloaks decorated with golden braid, and gowns and head-dresses in pearl-studded white satin worn by the Boiarynias, or aristocratic women, in the last act. These luxurious costumes brought from Russia are authentic masterpieces of art and opulence."

In the catalog of the exhibition devoted to the Opéra de Monte Carlo at the Musée d'Orsay in 1990,[12] the wonderful red velvet cloak worn by the Boiarynia (as reported by the *Le Petit Monégasque*) is no longer included among the anonymous costumes, even though the 1990 catalog entry states that "this is probably one of the antique original costumes brought to Paris by Diaghilev for his lyric operas in 1908 and 1909."[13] However, all evidence seems to indicate that the costumes were actually created for the occasion by Gunsbourg.

Why are the collections which are reputed to have been bought from Astruc no longer to be found in the Principality?[14] The agreement stipulated that if Diaghilev repaid all his debts within the established date, the costumes and stage sets would have been returned to him, so we can assume that this is what happened.

Certain performers from the Ballets Russes also contributed to the lyrical opera program in Monte Carlo which included parts for dancers. George Balanchine was the ballet-master for *Ivan the Terrible* in 1927 and for *Turandot* in 1930. He also choreographed the ballets for *L'Enfant et les Sortilèges*, the highlight of the 1925 season in Monte Carlo, with music by Ravel, based on a libretto by Colette (Sidonie-Gabrielle Colette). The collection includes thirty-two costumes. As for Léonide Massine, he was featured on the programs for *Valse de Vienne* in 1933 and *Contes d'Andersen* in 1938.

After Diaghilev's death, several attempts were made to perpetuate the memory of the Ballets Russes. One of these was *L'Amour sorcier* produced in 1932 by the "Ballets Russes de Monte-Carlo" (1932–35) under the direction of Colonel Wassily de Basil and René Blum.

Casse-Noisette was also created in 1926 under the sole direction of Blum, with costumes made by

© ARCHIVES MONTE-CARLO SBM

Barbara Karinska, the famous costumier of the Ballets Russes, based on gouache sketches by Alexei Alexeieff, which were acquired by Jean-Michel Bouhours on behalf of the Nouveau Musée National de Monaco in 2004. Groups of costumes produced later demonstrate that the repertoire of the Ballets Russes was maintained during the seasons performed by the Nouveaux Ballets de Monte-Carlo under the direction of Marcel Sablon. If fourteen costumes from *Schéhérazade* come from productions whose origins are uncertain, it is beyond any doubt that one costume does date from the Diaghilev period, as it bears the name of Stanislas Idzikowski, a dancer with the Ballets Russes, and was included in the *Schéhérazade* program of 1921. The forty-eight costumes for *Petrouchka* were re-created in 1944 based on the sketches by Benois taken from his original models of 1912,[15] while the costumes of the *Danses Polovtsiennes* in 1943 were made from the original drawings by Léon Zack.

Between 1945 and 1947, while director of what was called at that time "Les Ballets Russes de Monte-Carlo," Lifar produced three magnificent performances: *Dramma per Musica*, *Chota Roustavelli* and *Salomé*. The installation of the costumes was enriched during the various exhibitions by the other collections still conserved by the Société des Bains de Mer: photographs, performance programs and models of the sets which were more than probably designed by Georges Reinhard for the repertoire of the Ballets Russes, created from the original gouache drawings.

In 1974 a donation by Simone Del Duca permitted the State of Monaco to purchase certain works from the Lifar collection: sketches of the costumes for *La Belle au bois dormant* by Bakst, for *Petrouchka* by Benois, a study for a set of *Prince Igor* by Korovin, and a model built by André Derain for *Jack-in-the-Box*. Other purchases made at auctions (Gilberte Cournand sale in 1995) added further pieces to the Ballets Russes collection. In 1991 the Principality purchased seventy pieces from the Boris Kochno estate, including some important documents from the Diaghilev period and materials relating to artistic activities in the 1930s at the Théâtre des Champs-Elysées in Paris (works by Christian Bérard, Cocteau, Derain, Picasso…). Last, but not least, certain very important, previously unpublished documents which had belonged to Lifar were purchased in London in 2002. Works of the Ballets Russes had become too rare or too expensive, so acquisition policy was redirected towards other theatri-

Sarah Moon
"Mi-faune mi-esclave favori": trousers for Stanislas Idzikowski in *Schéhérazade*
1921
On permanent loan to SBM at the NMNM (D. 2002.5182)
Toned vintage silver gelatin print, 60 × 40 cm
Jeroen Verbruggen, dancer with the Ballets de Monte-Carlo
Production NMNM 2009

alongside the finished costume as well as the photo taken on stage; the gouache of a scene placed for comparison next to a three-dimensional model, together with a painting of the set; the transparency of an animated image or the fragment of a voice represent changes in scale and material, evanescent visions and unexpected presences which fire the imagination as to how the monumental effect must have looked.

But all this required a setting that had far more atmosphere than straightforward museum environment. The Villa Sauber and the Salle des Arts at the Sporting d'Hiver immediately immerse the visitor in the period of the Ballets Russes, from the Belle Époque to Art Deco—two perfect settings for displaying scenes from opera and ballet. In the Villa Sauber the visitor wanders through a nineteenth-century Salon, and whether through Classical mythology or the iconography of Russian folklore rediscovers a golden age in the art of Bakst and Benois, in Vaslav Nijinsky as the Faun, in the Opéra de Monte-Carlo of yesteryear… The turning point of the Great War abandoned the world of the past, and the transition toward the avant-garde drew inspiration from industry and its new materials.

To ensure that this heritage does not perish, it must be constantly given a new breath of life. The idea of taking photographs and re-setting the stage using the costumes from our collection (allowing just enough time to take a few pictures) had been at the back of our minds for some time. Thus, Sarah Moon, a timeless artist, entered into the spirit of the Ballets Russes costumes with her "half-faun, half-favorite slave," an image borne away in a state of artistic grace.

For the fleeting moment of a single summer in Monaco, the museum of Serge Lifar's dream has come true.

cal avant-gardes: even thirty years had not been enough to try and gather together what Lifar had proposed.

Why did it take so long for an art museum to become established in Monaco? Perhaps because the most accredited historical collections—from an artistic point of view—are those which are no longer used in the theater and belong to a domain which museums have only come to recognize relatively recently. From the perspective of museums, recreating scenes of theatrical performances is, surely, one of the most difficult tasks.

How can traces of fleeting magic be exhibited? Pitfalls can occur through pastiche or the temptation to reconstruct. We have chosen a different route, that of subtle evocation: an itinerary punctuated here and there with colorful quotes and references, an invitation to enter an illusion. The preparatory sketch placed

[1] Archives of the Nouveau Musée National de Monaco.

[2] This episode in the life of Serge Lifar is described by J. Kessel in his *La Rage au ventre* (Paris: Editions Eos, 1927).

[3] See Lynn Garafola, "Workshop of the Muses: Sergei Diaghilev and Monte Carlo" in this catalog, pp. 33–43.

[4] Consultant for the Theatre Museum, Victoria and Albert Museum, London.

[5] *Catalogue of Costumes from The Monte Carlo Opera House, sold by order of The Société des Bains de Mer*, Sotheby's, London, November 16, 1980, p. 7.

[6] Out of the 238 lots placed for auction, 51 were sold under the title "various pieces" without any description of their origin. Today

it is known that certain costumes by Bakst were sold among these group lots.

[7] See the report by D. Pinasa and N. Rosticher Giordano, *L'expertise scientifique de la collection de costumes de la Société des Bains de Mer*, December 2002.

[8] Collections belonging to the following performances: *Boris Godounov, Ivan the Terrible, Prince Igor, Petrouchka, Schéhérazade, L'Enfant et les Sortilèges*…

[9] L. Garafola, *Diaghilev's Ballets Russes* (New York: Oxford University Press, 1989), p. 178; A. Schouvaloff, *Léon Bakst* (Paris: Scala, 1991), annexe 1, p. 237; R. Buckle, *Diaghilev* (Paris: Lattès, 1980), p. 182.

[10] Archives Gabriel Astruc, artistic agent, New York Public Library, Lincoln Center.

[11] The performance was at the Théâtre de la Monnaie in Brussels in December 1910 with the authorization of Prince Albert I.

[12] J.-M. Nectoux (ed.), *L'Opéra de Monte-Carlo au temps du Prince Albert Ier de Monaco*, catalog of the exhibition at the Musée d'Orsay, Paris, March 13 – June 10, 1990, Les Dossiers du Musée d'Orsay, no. 38 (Paris: Réunion des Musées Nationaux, 1990).

[13] Ibid., p. 72.

[14] Today most of these collections are preserved in the National Gallery of Australia, Canberra.

[15] The complete collection is preserved by the Service du Patrimoine historique of the Société des Bains de Mer.

ARCHIVES MONTE CARLO S

Workshop of the Muses:
Sergei Diaghilev and Monte Carlo

Lynn Garafola

Monte Carlo occupied a special place in Diaghilev's heart. It was here in 1911 that he founded his Ballets Russes as a permanent company, premiered some of its most iconic works, and beginning in 1922, wintered for several months each year. Thanks to the generosity of the reigning Grimaldi family and the famed Casino that made its largesse possible, Monte Carlo became Diaghilev's creative workshop of the 1920s. In its rehearsal halls, which shared quarters with the Casino and Garnier's jewel-like opera house, were born Bronislava Nijinska's *Les Noces*, George Balanchine's *Apollon Musagète*, and other great works. Former Imperial ballerinas, now permanently exiled from Russia, passed on their secrets to Diaghilev's rising emigré stars, while Diaghilev himself, a sorcerer of the ephemeral, tried to conjure into being a museum of the arts embodied in multiple forms of performance. Although what he ultimately achieved fell short of his vision, it was in Monte Carlo that he succumbed one last time to the Wagnerian dream of his youth—of a life devoted wholly to art.

Although ballet was no stranger to Monte Carlo, the arrival of the Ballets Russes in 1911 opened a new chapter in Monte Carlo ballet history. Here it made its debut as a permanent company and returned every spring, ceasing to be a seasonal phenomenon descending periodically from the steppes, but a year-round entity headquartered in the West itself. This Western face of the company's identity was underscored by Diaghilev's decision to open the first Monte Carlo season with *Giselle* (1841), a ballet revered in Russia but long forgotten in Paris, its birthplace. This was not the only occasion when the novelty of the Monte Carlo repertoire rested solely on its unfamiliarity. In 1912 Diaghilev presented the first of multiple, variously abbreviated

Swan Lakes. (This one, in two acts, eliminated all of Act I, most of the character dances of Act III, and most of Act IV.) For this Monte Carlo premiere he engaged Mathilde Kschessinska, the Maryinsky's *prima ballerina assoluta*, who, in true diva fashion, arrived with an entourage of grand dukes, attracting a public whose elegance, even for Monte Carlo, was "quite exceptional."[1]

Of course, most of the repertoire was given over to Michel Fokine's "new ballets." In short order, Monte Carlo witnessed the triumphs of Diaghilev's first Paris seasons, exotic works like *Schéhérazade* (1910), *Cléopâtre* (1909), and the Polovtsian dances from *Prince Igor* (1909), which electrified audiences with their hot colors, throbbing rhythms, and a constellation of themes drawn from Symbolism, decadence, and the iconography of the fin de siècle— all new to ballet. Also in the repertoire were works that mined Fokine's neo-Romantic vein, such as *Les Sylphides* (1909), a homage to *Giselle* that did away with plot and pantomime; *Carnaval* (1910), an intimate *fête galante* that Antoine Watteau might have imagined; and *Le Spectre de la Rose* (1911), a piece of inspired whimsy for Vaslav Nijinsky and Tamara Karsavina, the company's great stars, that became the first Diaghilev work to receive its premiere in Monte Carlo. In 1912 Monte Carlo audiences witnessed the first innovative ballets of Igor Stravinsky, *L'Oiseau de Feu* (1910) and *Petrouchka* (1911), and the following year, Nijinsky's path-breaking *L'Après-midi d'un Faune* (1912).[2]

Important though Monte Carlo was as a performance site, it was even more significant to Diaghilev as a rehearsal venue. Indeed, with the shift of his headquarters to the West, it replaced St. Petersburg during the all-important months leading up to the Paris and London seasons, the high points of the company's yearly performance calendar. Bronislava Nijinska remembered her first stay in Monte Carlo as a "happy milestone," a time for young dancers like herself "to grow and develop." "As we performed in new ballets and created new roles we acquired new artistic techniques, distinguishing us as *Diaghilev artists*," she wrote in *Early Memoirs*.[3] The growing repertoire made rehearsal time and studio space increasingly necessary both to keep older works in shape and to create new ones. Nijinska recounts how she assisted Fokine in rehearsing a number of his ballets, including *L'Oiseau de Feu*, during the winter and spring of 1912. "When we began our rehearsals of *L'Oiseau de Feu* in Monte Carlo we found that few of the artists from the 1910 season were still dancing with us. And Fokine himself had difficulties remembering his own choreography."[4] During these same months Nijinsky was creating *Faune*, and people whispered that Fokine was about to be supplanted. Company members would peek into the studio where Nijinsky was working, puzzled by what they saw, while the choreographer, bristling at criticism from members of Diaghilev's entourage, swore over lunch that he would never change a single measure of his ballet, no matter what they thought of it.[5] *Faune* proved to be a triumph, launching Nijinsky as a choreographer. Within months he was back in Monte Carlo working with his sister on the first sketches for *Jeux* (1913), a ballet at least partly inspired by the tennis matches they observed on nearby courts. For Nijinska, their morning practice sessions were just as memorable as the rehearsals for *Jeux*. "Nijinsky did not have any regular pupils," she later wrote, "but he liked to work with me, so I was both his pupil and his assistant, the human material for his choreographic experiments and research for new forms of dancing and artistic expression."[6] A little more than a decade later, in those same studios, she would choreograph her masterpiece, *Les Noces* (1923).

World War I interrupted this cosy relationship with Monte Carlo. Not once but twice during the war years the Ballets Russes hovered on the brink of collapse. That the company did not fail, but even flourished creatively, is testimony to Diaghilev's indomitable will and unquenchable desire to make art. But the company that returned to Monte Carlo in 1920 differed markedly from its predecessor.

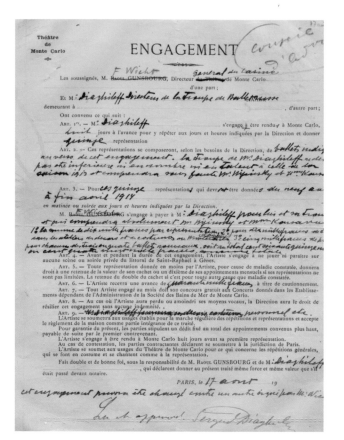

Original contract between the Théâtre de Monte-Carlo and Sergei Diaghilev regarding productions by the "troupe du Ballet Russe" for the 1913–14 season in Monte Carlo. The contract, dated 17 August [1913], stipulates that the program should include performances by Vaslav Nijinsky and Tamara Karsavina. Diaghilev founded the "Ballet Russe de Diaghileff" formally in 1911
27.7 × 21.7 cm
Archives SBM

Most of the old dancers were gone. Some had returned to Russia; others had settled in America; Nijinsky was in the Steinhof Asylum in Vienna. As for Diaghilev, he had found in Léonide Massine both a lover and a choreographer, a willing instrument of his imagination and the architect of a new repertoire. The ballets that Diaghilev brought to Monte Carlo in 1920—*The Good-Humoured Ladies* (1917), *La Boutique Fantasque* (1919), and *Le Tricorne* (1919)—revealed the new orientation. They were modernist in style, contemporary in energy, and infused with irony and high comedy. Moreover, with designs by Pablo Picasso (*Tricorne*) and André Derain (*Boutique*), music by Domenico Scarlatti (*Ladies*), Gioacchino Rossini (*Boutique*), and Manuel de Falla (*Tricorne*), and subjects inspired by Carlo Goldoni (*Ladies*), Pedro de Alarcón (*Tricorne*), and the old Viennese ballet *Puppenfee*, they were identified in almost every way with the West.

Nevertheless, the Russian theme did not altogether vanish from the Diaghilev repertoire. Indeed, a number of works, including *Soleil de Nuit* (1915) and *Contes Russes* (1917), which the Monte Carlo public also saw in 1920, revealed a new, highly stylized way of treating Russian folk material.

Conceived during the war years, the two ballets were designed by Mikhail Larionov, with assistance from another Moscow avant-garde painter, Natalia Goncharova. Both had joined Diaghilev's wartime artistic "laboratory," often traveling with him and working closely with Massine during what amounted to his choreographic apprenticeship. The emphasis in their work on weight, volume, and angularity left a deep mark on Massine's choreography, even though the radicalism of their approach was mitigated by the folkloric subject and the "national" sound of the music (by Nikolai Rimsky-Korsakov for *Soleil de Nuit* and Anatolii Liadov for *Contes Russes*). Some ballets, moreover, had a Russian subtext. *Le Astuzie Femminili* (1920), an eighteenth-century Italian opera-ballet by Domenico Cimarosa, "had its origin," as Diaghilev explained in an interview with *The Observer*, "in the composer's experiences in Russia." In fact, the opera ended with "a Russian ballet" in which Cimarosa inserted

> a tune called "Kamatinskaya," a dance which no doubt he saw the peasants dance at weddings in Russia. Forty years later Mikhail Glinka, the father of modern Russian music, used the same tune for an orchestral fantasy that is looked upon as the starting-point of the modern Russian school.[7]

Olga Spessivtseva as Aurora
in *The Sleeping Princess*, 1921
Photograph by E. O. Hoppé
Vintage gelatin silver print
CALA (15481-0002)

In 1924 Diaghilev presented this "Russian ballet" in Monte Carlo as *Cimarosiana*.

Unlike his predecessors, Léonide Massine responded to the intellectual springs of Diaghilev's experimentalism. He sought a theoretical basis for this in texts that predated the revolution of romanticism and thus challenged the equating of ballet with the classicism elaborated in Russia during the late Imperial period. He called for "emancipation from the classic school," insisting that its focus on the feet, legs, and arms caused it to ignore numerous movement possibilities. "Our bodies," he declared, "have an orchestra of thirty different instruments, each of which is duplicated, and each of which is capable of being brought into play. From that you can gather the potential wealth of choregraphy [sic]."[8] He spoke of the need to "synthesize movement and form ... choreography and plastic art," and expressed the belief that "the most important collaboration is that of the choreographer, and of the designer of the scenery and costumes," with each developing the idea or plot "in the plane of his own art." Finally, he defined the relationship between music and dance not as one of correspondence, in which the two were analogous—the approach of both Fokine and Nijinsky—but rather of counterpoint in the musical and choreographic design.[9] These ideas anticipated key elements of the Cunningham–Cage aesthetic.

In 1921 Diaghilev staged *The Sleeping Beauty* in London. Re-titled *The Sleeping Princess*, it was an ambitious undertaking, a magnificent, full-evening production of Marius Petipa's most celebrated ballet. The costs, underwritten by Sir Oswald Stoll on behalf of the Alhambra Company Ltd., ballooned. The ballet opened to mixed reviews, and audiences soon fell off. Stoll had the sets and costumes impounded, and Diaghilev, with little more than a skeleton company, fled across the Channel. For the third time in less than a decade, the Ballets Russes was on the verge of collapse. In the postwar economic order, it needed the safety net of public subsidy to survive.

Diaghilev's arrangement with the Théâtre de Monte-Carlo in the autumn of 1922 was nothing short of providential. Engineered by the Princesse Edmond de Polignac *née* Winnaretta Singer, an heiress to the sewing machine fortune and one of

Diaghilev's most generous patrons, it offered him the luxury of working at least part of the year in a subsidized environment. For the next seven years, Monte Carlo became the hub of Diaghilev's operations, his winter capital and creative workshop. It was here that the company stored its hundreds of costumes and scenic properties; where the young George Balanchine, hired by Diaghilev in 1924, created dozens of dances for operas; where the dancers, for the first time, enjoyed months of guaranteed employment, and a lucky few even had apartments of their own. Well might Serge Grigoriev, the company's *régisseur* throughout the whole of its peripatetic existence, breathe a sigh of relief: "And so the Ballet at least acquired a permanent base."[10]

The one complication, as Diaghilev hastened to point out, was that the Casino management had already engaged an Italian ballet company for the upcoming season. But to Grigoriev the inconvenience was minor; he was all too happy to work with M. Belloni, the in-house Italian ballet-master— or even the Devil, he wrote in his memoirs, "if only this excellent plan could be realized."[11] Hence, the oddity of the ballet programming during the initial months of Diaghilev's new arrangement, the incongruous mix of names, the old-fashioned choreographic credits, and, most of all, the repertoire weighted with "old ballets," such as the *Coppélia* (1870) "arranged by Monsieur J. Belloni," with Vera Nemtchinova as Swanilda, Stanislas Idzikowski as Franz, and Messrs. Belloni and Baglioni as Doctor Coppélius and the Burgomaster, respectively. Ballets Russes dancers took most of the solo roles in *La Korrigane*, which Belloni also "arranged," and the leading roles in *Les Deux Pigeons*, which may have been the old Giorgio Saracco version, although it was uncredited. Occasionally Fokine's *Le Spectre de la Rose* served as a curtain raiser (with *Coppélia*); in one of the most incongruous bills of all it followed Mme Stichel's *Hagoromo ou La Robe de plume* (1922), a "lyrical ballet in one act," with costumes by Léon Bakst, and Belloni's "arrangement" of the "Walpurgisnacht" ballet from *Faust*. The company danced in galas, in operas such as *Aida*, and in the "Theatrical Matinees" at the Palais des Beaux-Arts, where they performed brief excerpts from the repertoire along with concert numbers.[12]

Meanwhile, the dancers were hard at work in the studio, where in the spring of 1923 Nijinska was choreographing one of Diaghilev's greatest works, *Les Noces*. The earliest photographs of the ballet, familiar from the company's souvenir programs, were taken on the roof of the theater, where the dancers, dressed in uniform practice wear, recreated Nijinska's architectural groupings. In his memoirs, Serge Lifar vividly recalled Stravinsky banging out the rhythms of his complicated score during rehearsals:

> To begin, he would only indicate roughly what was meant, but soon he was angrily gesticulating, and then, thoroughly aroused, would take off his coat, sit down at the piano and, reproducing all the symphonic sonority of the work, begin singing in a kind of ecstatic, but terrible voice, which carried so much conviction … Often he would go on in this way till he was completely exhausted. But still, a new life would have been infused into the rehearsal, and the whole company would start dancing for all it was worth.[13]

For the wealthy, Monte Carlo was a winter playground, with golf, tennis, opera, concerts, dances,

Natalia Goncharova
Portrait of Sergei Prokofiev
early 1920s
Oil on canvas, 61 × 50 cm
STG (Zh-1651)

horse shows, flower shows, de luxe dog shows, picture exhibitions, regattas, Mardi Gras pageants, pigeon shooting, and ballet.[14] Diaghilev's dancers, however, had little time—or energy, one suspects—for pleasure-seeking. Nicolas Kremnev was an assistant *régisseur* during this period, and his notebooks, now in the Serge Lifar Papers at the Archives de la Ville de Lausanne, give a day-to-day picture of the company life while *Les Noces* was in preparation. Referring to the schedule for the four-week period from April 17 to May 14, Drue Fergison writes:

> The most impressive thing … is how hard the dancers worked. The daily norm was either three rehearsals or two rehearsals and a performance. A typical day might include a morning rehearsal from ten to twelve or one, possibly beginning with a class conducted by Nijinska, an afternoon rehearsal from two-thirty to five, and an evening performance at nine. On Sundays, a matinee at three might be followed by an evening rehearsal from nine to eleven. … Although the dancers had an occasional

morning, afternoon, or evening free, they did not have a single full day off during the entire four-week period.[15]

By 1923, when *Les Noces* came to the stage, the Ballets Russes was a haven for Russian emigrés. Not all had fled the 1917 Revolution. Like Diaghilev himself, some had worked for years outside Russia, their exile chosen rather than imposed. Now they were being joined by a flood of stateless refugees. Ninette de Valois, who joined the Ballets Russes in 1923, recalled parties with "vodka, caviar and Russian folk songs, Russian toasts and Russian jokes," but also the "fatalistic helplessness" of "mortal beings engulfed in a whirlwind that was not of their making."[16] This sense of loss and helplessness was something they shared with the broader emigré community, including members of the former Imperial elite who had settled in Monte Carlo and its environs, sometimes in villas acquired before the Revolution. To some extent Diaghilev catered to this elite. His company danced for its most glamorous benefits, such as the brilliant affair in Monte Carlo in 1923 for Russian refugees in France and the "magnificent" 1925 performance in Cannes on behalf of the Franco–Russian Children's Home, one of the many emigré charities to which the Princesse Héritière gave her blessing.[17]

Monte Carlo never saw Diaghilev's production of *The Sleeping Princess*. However, it did witness a revival of *Swan Lake* with the former Imperial ballerina Vera Trefilova in the dual role of Odette–Odile. Diaghilev had coaxed her out of retirement in 1921 to appear as one of his four Auroras in *The Sleeping Princess*. Now, in 1923, he engaged the forty-eight-year-old ballerina, a "dancing Stradivarius" in André Levinson's phrase,[18] for a series of performances in her most celebrated role. "She amazed everyone at Monte Carlo by her extraordinary *fouettés*," Grigoriev commented laconically.[19] "She had remained extraordinarily young," observed Mathilde Kschessinska, a one-time rival, who was now living with Grand Duke André and their son in nearby Cap d'Ail.

> [W]e were all struck by her stylish entry, her classical curtsy and the amazing ease of her movements, gestures and stage

presence. The mark of our school was everywhere visible—in her noble movements, her elegant attitudes, all showing the class which had not been seen for a long time in Western Europe and which people had ceased to expect.[20]

In *The Dancing Times* critic Valerian Svetlov, whom Trefilova married in emigration, spoke of her Odette almost as an act of memory, unlocking the past and sharing its tragedy with the present:

Once again we saw that romantic Queen of the Swans, ethereal as a vision, and at the same time so human in her sadness. The theatre "listened" with strained attention, in the throes of an emotion that seized upon all, to the fairy-tale told by Trefilova not in words, and not by the movements of her body, legs and arms, but by her whole bewitched soul, the invisible emanation of which carried over the footlights and gripped the attention of all present.[21]

Two years later Diaghilev revived *Swan Lake* for Vera Nemtchinova, a classicist he had nursed to ballerina status, and brought in Kschessinska to coach her. Kschessinska also coached the fifteen-year-old Alicia Markova, who performed her first Odette wearing Trefilova's costume, dancing the Act II adagio in one of the signature roles of her later career.[22] In other words, Diaghilev proved that it was possible to pass on Imperial performance traditions, to transmit them to dancers who were not necessarily Russian or trained in Russian schools.

Together with *Aurora's Wedding*, the one-act "reduction" of *The Sleeping Princess* choreographed by Nijinska in 1922, Diaghilev's *Swan Lake* established a model for incorporating abbreviated versions of late Imperial works into a modernist repertoire dominated by one-act ballets. He took what might be termed an adaptive rather than restorative approach to the problem of staging, stressing theatrical viability rather than historical fidelity. And he established the primacy of the Peter Tchaikovsky ballets—as opposed to those by Léon Minkus, Cesare Pugni, and even Aleksandr Glazunov—by im-

posing the musical standards of a twentieth-century high modernist on works by "specialist composers" who adhered to the conventions of the late Imperial period. With *Aurora's Wedding* and *Swan Lake*, Diaghilev initiated the process of reinventing the late Imperial legacy as a Western tradition.

This process was one part of a much broader effort on Diaghilev's part to construct a postwar Russian identity. He told the young emigré composer, Vladimir Dukelsky—better known as Vernon Duke—that "he wanted a ballet combining classicism with Russian overtones—tutus with *kokoshniks*," an idea that eventually became the ballet *Zéphyr et Flore* (1925), a contemporary fable of Olympian marriage. There wasn't a Russian headdress in sight. But that wasn't the point. As Duke explains, the key to the ballet's Russianness lay in its imaginative origin, in the Russian "classical" painting of the eighteenth and early nineteenth centuries that Diaghilev loved and in Russian serf theaters, where the "rustic charms" of a landowner's favorite acquired the "godlike attributes of a Flora or Psyche."[23] Diaghilev's effort to distinguish between Russianness and folklore was evident even in the case of Russian-themed works such as *Chout* (1921). Here, Diaghilev told an interviewer, Sergei Prokofiev's music was "of the highest modernity and entirely in keeping with Russian characteristics, [but] without the musical themes being derived from folk-lore."[24] Diaghilev struck a similar note in an interview published in response to the first, disastrous reviews of *Les Noces* in London. Calling the ballet the "unrealised dream of Mussorgsky," he insisted that "nothing represents Russia more completely than this work. After all, I am a Russian myself, and I know what I am saying; and it is possibly not for nothing that the work is dedicated to me."[25] Here he echoes a statement of nearly thirty years earlier: "The only possible nationalism is the unconscious nationalism of the blood."[26]

Ode (1928) was another deracinated work of the late 1920s that emerged from Diaghilev's emigré atelier in Monte Carlo. The ballet had music by another of his young emigré discoveries, Nicolas Nabokov, a cousin of the novelist and a distant cousin of Diaghilev as well, and like *Zéphyr et Flore* it also had a Russian connection. "The subject of the ballet," Nabokov wrote, "was taken from a poem—an 'Ode to the Majesty of God on the Occasion

of the Appearance of the Great Northern Lights'—
by the eighteenth-century court-poet … Mikhail
Lomonosov. …Written in the flamboyant and archaic
Russian of that period, it represents a thinly
veiled allegory on the enthronement of Empress
Elizabeth—the Aurora Borealis of the poem."[27] Like
so many before him, Nabokov took the night train
from Paris to Monte Carlo. He arrived to find
arrangements for *Ode* in disarray, with Boris Kochno,
the librettist, at loggerheads with Massine, and
bedeviled by the Surrealist-influenced experiments
of the designer, Pavel Tchelitchew. By accident, he
walked in on a rehearsal of Stravinsky's *Apollon
Musagète* (1928), which Balanchine was choreographing.
It was Nabokov's first glimpse of the
"slight and incredibly young-looking" choreographer,
even then hailed as Diaghilev's "new choreographic
genius," and of the ballet's celebrated "sunburst"
pose:

> Diaghilev couldn't see me; his back was
> turned, and he seemed absorbed by what
> was going on on the stage. There, in the
> centre … Lifar knelt between … three
> ballerinas, who were in an arabesque
> figure; each had one leg up in the air; their

bodies dipped forward and their necks
stretched upward so that they looked like
three drinking swans whose precarious
balance was maintained by a trembling
hand firmly clutching Lifar's shoulder …
Diaghilev turned around, … pointed at
Balanchine and said, "What he is doing
is magnificent. It is pure classicism, such
as we have not seen since Petipas [sic]."[28]

In 1917 the Revolution had split Russian ballet
culture in two. In the aftermath of that conflagration,
many looked to Diaghilev, because of his
unique position as founder and director of the Ballets
Russes, to undertake, as Levinson wrote of *The
Sleeping Princess*, "the task of bringing to the European
stage such splendid echoes of a departed glory."[29]
This Diaghilev refused to do. By contrast,
throughout the 1920s he struggled to maintain the
vitality of the Ballets Russes as a creative organization:
his goal was a living art, contemporary in form
and experimental in outlook, a diasporic art engaged
with the present. His new works may have held particular
resonance for Russian emigré audiences, but
like *Ode*, *Les Noces*, or *Apollon Musagète* they were
as much French—or Western European—as Russian.

Serge Lifar as Borée
in *Zéphyr et Flore*, 1925
Original print, 8.7 × 13.5 cm
Archives NMNM
(2002 7 12 C 37 07 0004)
Serge Lifar Collection

Naum Gabo and Anton Pevsner
Décor design for *La Chatte*,
1927
Photograph by Henri Manuel
Reprint
Archives SBM (1927 01 58)

And whatever nostalgia the aging Diaghilev may have personally harbored, his repertoire did not trade on it. When it did look to the past (as in the case of *Ode*, *Le Astuzie Femminili*, or *Zéphyr et Flore*), it did so obliquely, and nearly always through a lens of irony. The past, like the present, fed his restless spirit, but it was never a surrogate home.

Nevertheless, Monte Carlo stirred atavistic memories in him. It resurrected dreams of Imperial grandeur and tempted him to make one last bid for the portfolio of fine arts denied him years before in Russia. His notes for the 1922–23 season, preserved at the Opéra library in Paris,[30] record the ambitious sweep of his vision: the plans for festivals and exhibitions, operas and ballets he saw as transforming the staid landscape of the resort into one of artistic ferment and discovery. At various moments of his life Diaghilev yielded to the passion for list making. But unlike the Black Notebook of 1910 or the "workbook" he kept in 1918–19,[31] his Monte Carlo jottings make no reference to

casting, cost, or repertory. Rather they trace the amblings of Diaghilev's mind down forgotten byways of the musical past.

Other notebooks, once in the collection of Serge Lifar, flesh out Diaghilev's plans. For the 1923–24 season he contemplated not only the major festival that took place in Monte Carlo but also festivals in Austria, Italy, and Spain, and another in honor of Stravinsky. (Although none of these were realized, the 1923 Paris season, with performances of *Les Noces* and *Le Sacre du Printemps*, had a strong Stravinsky flavor.) For Monte Carlo he planned seasons of grand opéra, concerts, a chamber music series, a festival of Russian music, and exhibitions devoted to portraiture, French and Spanish painting, fashion, and the art of the Ballets Russes—a curatorial tour de force. He noted the titles of old and more recent French ballets, such as Edouard Lalo's *Namouna* (1882), Maurice Ravel's *Ma Mère l'Oye* (1911), Daniel Auber's *Marco Spada* (1857), Etienne Nicolas Méhul's *Persée et Andromède* (1810) and *La Dansomanie* (1800), and even *Giselle*, imagining it designed by André Derain. According to Lifar, Diaghilev spent hours studying old scores in the Paris Opéra library; he had ordered music catalogues and manuscript copies of old music, and consulted numerous authorities, all as part of his research.[32] The result was the 1924 "Festival Français" (as it was called in the official Monte Carlo program) that included Charles Gounod's mid-nineteenth-century operas *La Colombe* (1924), *Le Médecin malgré lui* (1858), and *Philémon et Baucis* (1860), and Emmanuel Chabrier's somewhat later *L'Education manquée* (1879); revivals of Ravel's *Daphnis and Chloe* (1912), Claude Debussy's *L'Après-midi d'un Faune*, and Gabriel Fauré's *Las Meninas* (1916), choreographed by Fokine, Nijinsky, and Massine, respectively; and three newly minted ballets, all by Nijinska—Michel Montéclair's *Les Tentations de la Bergère* (1924), Francis Poulenc's *Les Biches* (1924), and Georges Auric's *Les Fâcheux* (1924). Here was the blueprint for the diasporic art about to emerge from his company's Monte Carlo workshop.

No choreographer was more deeply affected by Diaghilev's diasporic milieu than Balanchine. Joining the Ballets Russes in late 1924, he remained with the company until 1929, when Diaghilev died and the company disbanded. These were the years of Balanchine's apprenticeship, when he honed his craft and refined his taste. He choreographed scores of dances in those five years—nearly a dozen ballets and dances in nearly forty operas. He met collaborators who would strike a deeply sympathetic chord in his imagination and play a vital role in his life for decades. Foremost among them was Stravinsky, whom Diaghilev first teamed with Balanchine in 1925 in a choreographic remake of *Le Chant du Rossignol*. But the group embraced most of Diaghilev's musical protegés, his librettist Boris Kochno, and both Tchelitchew and Derain among his designers.

When Balanchine joined the Ballets Russes, he came with the baggage of a young Russian dance artist. In his imagination lived Petipa's magnificent legacy as well as the ballets that Fokine had created for the former Maryinsky company, and the even newer works by Fedor Lopukhov, such as *Dance Symphony*, a plotless work in which Balanchine himself had danced. With Diaghilev, now, he discovered the repertoire of Western ballet modernism.

He played the monster Kashchci in the revival of Fokine's *L'Oiseau de Feu* and Eusebius in his *Carnaval*. He discovered Nijinsky's *Faune* and Nijinska's *Noces* and *Biches*, and numerous ballets by Massine, including *Parade* and his version of *Le Sacre du Printemps*. Thanks to Diaghilev, Balanchine entered this Russo–Western line of descent, taking his place in a new historical succession that came into being with the Ballets Russes. This succession reached back to Russia. But it belonged to the West, a peculiarly deracinated West, one that mirrored the stateless identity of most of Diaghilev's dancers and the cultural hybridity of most of his works. Not until the 1940s, in New York, would Balanchine find an artistic habitat as congenial as the cosmopolitan world of the Ballets Russes.

In 1925 Raoul Gunsbourg, Diaghilev's archrival for control of Monte Carlo's cultural resources, staged the premiere of Ravel's *L'Enfant et les Sortilèges*, a "lyric fantasy" with a libretto by Sidonie-Gabrielle Colette. The choreography, by Balanchine, was his first major assignment as a member of the Ballets Russes, and with Ravel at his side the rehearsals were an unforgettable experience.[33] In other respects the experience must have been trying, given Diaghilev's efforts to wreck the production in his struggle with Gunsbourg. (In 1924 Prince Pierre had rescinded Gunsbourg's contract, leaving the way open for Diaghilev to lay claim to control of the Monte Carlo opera house.) Eight days before the opening, Diaghilev ordered his dancers pulled from the production,[34] then sent an attorney to René Léon, the Société des Bains de Mer's Managing Director, directing him to look for Ravel. Then, wrote Léon,

I had another surprise. As I left the
restaurant of the Hôtel de Paris, a
steward (!) handed me a letter in which you
advise that you decline all responsibility for
the perfect execution of the dance parts
that your contract obliges you to provide for
the operas in general, and Mr. Ravel's opera,
in particular. ... As to your statement that
the ballet piano parts ... were sent to
you too late and that Mr. Ravel's music
seems very complicated, it is truly curious
that these difficulties only became apparent

some hours after an incident you seem to have had with Mr. Ravel in the lobby of the Hôtel de Paris, and after which you were heard by several witnesses to declare, "I will never let them dance in his opera."[35]

The premiere took place without apparent mishap. But the *affaire* had not ended. At a later performance five of the ten dancers in the first-act pastorale failed to appear, and when Guns-bourg, incensed, demanded an explanation, Nico-las Kremnev, the Ballets Russes *régisseur*, told him to talk to Diaghilev. "This organization," Guns-bourg declared to Léon, "is a veritable hindrance to my immense labors." Léon now wrote to Di-aghilev saying that he could not, in good con-science, support his candidacy for the following year.[36] One can only imagine what Balanchine thought of this power play.

Thus ended Diaghilev's grand Monte Carlo dream. He had just turned fifty-three and lost the chance of a lifetime. He would never direct an opera house or set the artistic policy of a State, even one as diminutive as Monaco. He was fated to remain what he had become—an alchemist and power bro-ker within the specialized domain of ballet. What impelled him to act so rashly? So irresponsibly? How could he be so petty? Finally, why did he choose Ravel, France's greatest living composer and the most gentle of men, to victimize? The answers re-main unknown.

Arnold Haskell, who visited Monte Carlo around this time, seems to have been oblivious to what was taking place. In *Balletomania*, a book that enchanted a generation of ballet lovers, he devotes a chapter to his stay in "Mecca." It was Diaghilev's last "truly brilliant year, just before the transition and the gradual waning":

Nemtchinova and Dolin [were] at the very top of their form, … dancing in nearly every ballet; Tchernicheva contributing the finish and perfection of the early years; Doubrovska, about to be discovered as the perfect instrument for modernist experiment; Sokolova, most Russian and biggest personality of them all, favoured artist of the great man himself; … and Serge

Savelii Sorin
Portrait of Fedor Chaliapin
1931
Oil con canvas, 93 × 77 cm
Collection du Palais Princier
(P 000801)

Grigorieff, the backbone, with every ballet and lighting cue in his head, a big Russian Bear but a hundred per cent efficient. There was young Sergė Lifar at the very beginning … Markova just thirteen, in socks, but learning her very own Stravinsky ballet … and Nikitina and Danilova, the great hopes, whose fate was then being decided at the Hôtel de Paris, where Diaghileff sat with his cabinet—Poulenc and Auric, Boris Kochno, Picasso, Stravinsky, Pruna, Dukelsky and Edwin Evans.[37]

Haskell was in paradise. Less enchanted eyes might have discerned beneath the gaiety at the luncheon table an undercurrent of loss, of con-tained possibility, of talents untapped and ways not taken. To outsiders Monte Carlo summoned im-ages of cosmopolitan pleasure; to Haskell it evoked the magic and madness of ballet. To the artists and artisans of the Ballets Russes, who ate at modest eateries between rehearsals and returned to rent-ed rooms at night, Diaghilev's Monte Carlo work-shop lightened the burden of political and cultur-al statelessness, by offering a site for the forging of a diasporic identity that would serve them well in the years to come.

1 M. Kelkel, "Le Ballet à Monte-Carlo," in J.-M. Nectoux (ed.), *L'Opéra de Monte-Carlo au temps du Prince Albert Ier de Monaco*, Les Dossiers du Musée d'Orsay, no. 38 (Paris: Réunion des musées nationaux, 1990), p. 48; M. Kschessinska, *Dancing in Petersburg*, trans. A. Haskell (Garden City, New York: Doubleday, 1961), pp. 133–35, 138–39.

2 For the dates, cast lists, and program notes of Diaghilev's Monte Carlo premieres, see G. Detaille and G. Mulys, *Les Ballets de Monte-Carlo 1911–1944* (Paris: Editions Arc-en-ciel, 1954).

3 B. Nijinska, *Early Memoirs*, trans. and ed. I. Nijinska and J. Rawlinson, introd. A. Kisselgoff (New York: Holt, Rinehart & Winston, 1981), p. 332.

4 Ibid., p. 417.

5 Ibid., pp. 427–31.

6 Ibid., 442.

7 "Cimarosa at Covent Garden. Italian Opera and Russian Ballet. M. Diaghileff's Theory of Acting," in *The Observer*, London, June 20, 1920, p. 10.

8 "Massine's Ballets. Emancipation from the Classic School. Body Dancing," in *The Observer*, July 27, 1919, p. 6. Recently introduced into English, the word "choreography" was spelled in a number of different ways during this period.

9 L. Massine, "On Choreography and a New School of Dancing," in *Drama*, 1, no. 3, London, December 1919, pp. 69–70.

10 S. L. Grigoriev, *The Diaghilev Ballet 1909–1929*, trans. and ed. V. Bowen (London: Constable, 1953), p. 180.

11 Ibid., p. 180.

12 Playbills, November 1922 to April 1923, Société des Bains de Mer Archives (hereafter SBM). The Ballets Russes season opened on April 19, 1923. For the postwar Monte Carlo ballet repertoire, see Kelkel 1990, pp. 50–51. I am grateful to the SBM for copies of playbills and reviews in their collection. Mme Stichel was the professional name of Louise Manzini.

13 Serge Lifar, *Serge Diaghilev: His Life, His Work, His Legend* (New York, 1940; reprint New York: Da Capo, 1976), p. 255.

14 "Riviera Season: Calendar of Social and Sporting Events," in *The Times*, London, December 11, 1922, p. 15. See also "Programme Général de la Saison de Monte-Carlo 1923–1924," The Bancroft Library, University of California, Berkeley.

15 D. Fergison, "Bringing *Les Noces* to the Stage," in L. Garafola and N. van Norman Baer (eds.), *The Ballets Russes and Its World* (New Haven: Yale University Press, 1999), p. 179.

16 N. de Valois, *Come Dance With Me: A Memoir 1898–1956* (Cleveland and New York: World Publishing Company, 1957), p. 87.

17 "Figaro aux pays du soleil," in *Le Figaro*, Paris, March 23, 1923, p. 6; "Le Monde et la Ville," in *Le Figaro*, April 2, 1925, p. 2. Princess Charlotte was an ardent balletomane who studied ballet privately with Lubov Tchernicheva and sat in on the company's rehearsals. Diaghilev's Monte Carlo seasons took place under her patronage.

18 A. Levinson, "Le Retour des 'Ballets Russes,'" in *La Danse au Théâtre: Esthétique et actualité mêlées* (Paris: Bloud et Gay, 1924), p. 35.

19 Grigoriev 1953, p. 191.

20 Kschessinska 1961, p. 216.

21 V. Svetloff, "The Recent Creations of Vera Trefilova," in *The Dancing Times*, London, January 1929, p. 518.

22 For Nemtchinova, see Kschessinska 1961, p. 219; for Markova, see N. de Valois, *Invitation to the Ballet* (London: John Lane, 1937), p. 56; A. Dolin, *Markova: Her Life and Art* (London: W. H. Allen, 1953), p. 100. Markova includes a photograph of herself in the altered Trefilova costume in *Markova Remembers* (Boston: Little, Brown, 1986), p. 22.

23 V. Duke, *Passport to Paris: An Autobiography* (Boston: Little, Brown, 1955), p. 121.

24 "Russian Ballet Novelties. Interview with M. Diaghileff. Stravinsky's Visit. Spanish Dancers and Their Art," in *The Observer*, June 5, 1921, p. 8.

25 "'Les Noces.' M. Diaghileff Replies to the Critics. A Wedding or a Funeral?" in *The Observer*, June 20, 1926, p. 11.

26 S. Diaghilev, "Principles of Art Criticism," trans. O. Stevens and ed. J. Acocella, in Garafola and van Norman Baer 1999, p. 90.

27 N. Nabokov, *Old Friends and New Music* (London: Hamish Hamilton, 1951), p. 66.

28 Ibid., p. 83.

29 *The Designs of Léon Bakst for "The Sleeping Princess,"* pref. A. Levinson (London: Benn Brothers, 1923), p. 1.

30 "Carnet de Serge de Diaghilev, 1922–1923," Pièce 133, Fonds Kochno, Bibliothèque de l'Opéra (Paris).

31 "Cahier de travail de Serge de Diaghilev avec indications de répertoire 1915–16," Pièce 124, Fonds Kochno. As all the references to casting, currency, and repertoire belong to the immediate postwar period, the dating of this workbook is obviously incorrect.

32 Lifar, *Serge Diaghilev*, 1976, pp. 230–33.

33 "How could I ever forget th[ose] rehearsals," he marveled to a French interviewer forty years later, "when the man at my side … was Ravel himself?" See L. Survage, "George Balanchine: trente-sept valses … pour Paris," in *Le Figaro*, June 20, 1965. Dossier d'artiste (Balanchine), Bibliothèque de l'Opéra, Paris.

34 René Léon, Letter to Serge Diaghilev, March 14, 1925, Palace Archives, Monaco.

35 René Léon, Letter to Serge Diaghilev, March 14, 1925, Palace Archives, Monaco.

36 Raoul Gunsbourg, Letter to René Léon, March 27, 1925; René Léon, Letter to Serge Diaghilev, March 30, 1925, Palace Archives, Monaco.

37 A. Haskell, *Balletomania: The Story of an Obsession* (London: Gollancz, 1934), pp. 76–77.

44

The Diaghilev Project

Zelfira Tregulova

Sergei Diaghilev's Ballets Russes: what were those famous Saisons Russes which shook the civilized world of the early twentieth century and forever remained a myth, a festive fairy tale which we long to apprehend and relive today?

The legend terminated in the death of its creator in Venice, of which the circumstances are so well known, thanks to the abundant testimony of those in attendance, including Serge Lifar. It was not by accident that Serge Lifar (who later became Diaghilev's biographer and wrote what in all likelihood became the best book on the history of the Ballets Russes), so meticulously collected everything in Venice back then—everything that could remind everyone who knew Diaghilev of those last, tragic days. Although Diaghilev was not an easy person and not amicable to all, it was clear that August 19, 1929, marked not only the death and demise of the impresario and ideologue of the Saisons, but also the finale of a miracle entitled Ballets Russes. That day also marked the conclusion to one of the few Russian artistic phenomena which the Western world recognized as unique and of universal significance to the cultural history of the twentieth century.

So we may well ask: How did this phenomenon come to be, what were the reasons which prompted a large and disparate ballet company, at times torn by squabble and intrigue of epic proportions, to come on stage, and why the capricious audiences of Paris, London, and Berlin erupted in storms of applause?

Diaghilev's biography is well-known, but certain milestones and episodes should be underscored so as to make his primary mission in life appear coherent and motivated. From his youth, Diaghilev had been drawn to music and even composed some himself, only to turn away from composition, if one is to believe his contemporaries, following negative reviews by Nikolai Rimsky-Korsakov. After gaining entry into the intellectual circles of St. Petersburg's gilded youth which later formed the core of the "Mir iskusstva" (World of Art) movement, Diaghilev became interested in painting and architecture and even contemplated creating his own museum. Then came his work for the *Mir iskusstva* magazine, the first exhibition of Russian and Finnish artists (1898) and the promotion of the best of Russian contemporary art abroad. His duties at the Imperial Theaters resulted in a disgraceful termination, but he transformed *The Yearbook of the Imperial Theaters* into a truly artistic periodical dedicated to opera and ballet.

Diaghilev's most important cause of the mid-1900s was his preparation for the exhibition of Russian historical portraits at the Tauride Palace in 1905, an enterprise which demonstrated an almost superhuman capacity for addressing complex issues, an unsurpassed taste, and an uncanny artistic intuition. His next undertaking came in the form of a Russian art exhibition at the Salon d'Automne in Paris in 1906. Never before had Paris—or, vicariously, Europe—seen works of Russian art in such quantities, because to the Paris of 1906, Russia, a country which was long believed to be the epigone of the West, now proved to be a superior and independent culture. It was for a reason that Pablo Picasso could be seen in those days in the halls showing works by the blind and insane Mikhail Vrubel.

What should be the next step in the conquest of the West by Russian art? It had to be something extreme, new, and unexpected. In his prior feats, Diaghilev merely collected and presented the best of Russian art, be it traditional or modern, but now he set out to create something fresh and unprecedented, and to conquer the world. In addition to the testimony of contemporaries illustrating Diaghilev's titanic

45

Rehearsal in the Hall of
the Ekaterininsky Theater,
St. Petersburg, March 1909.
Igor Stravinsky is second
from left, seated at the piano;
Michel Fokine is leaning
against the piano, Tamara
Karsavina is standing
in the center
Photograph by I. A.
Aleksandrov
Original print
SPSMTM (GIK 5448/8)

Léon Woizikovsky, Serge Lifar,
Lydia Sokolova and Sergei
Diaghilev at the Lido,
Venice, 1927
Original print, 24.7 × 19.1 cm
Archives NMNM
(2002 7 12 C 37 03 00 18)
Serge Lifar Collection

efforts to prepare for the first Saisons in Paris, there are a number of unique photographs which record rehearsals in St. Petersburg in 1909. True, Diaghilev himself is not in them, but we can understand the enthusiasm, the sense of a common cause, and the camaraderie permeating these images. Of course, in reality things were less than idyllic, but, even so, we are agape at the young Tamara Karsavina and the adolescent Vaslav Nijinsky.

Today, it is clear that modern Russian culture owes much to Diaghilev. It was in the first quarter of the twentieth century that Russian artistic potential reached heights unseen, graduating from a parochial and secondary status to the cutting edge of cultural discovery—and no one did more than Diaghilev to assure the international recognition of that achievement. Paris and Monte Carlo named streets after Diaghilev and they still lovingly preserve his archives, photographs, playbills, scraps of paper with notes, personal effects, and trinkets. This is part of Europe's history, a beautiful legend whose centennial is being celebrated in 2009. As for Russians today, the date acquires a radically different meaning: many of us

recall the two great Moscow patrons of the arts, Sergei Shchukin and Ivan Morozov, who, just as Diaghilev was introducing Russian art and Russian ballet to the Western stage, were importing the best of what Paris had to offer. Now that Russian museums possess exquisite works by the great French artists of the early twentieth century, we can truly appreciate the foresight and intuition of those two Russian collectors. But it is much more difficult to grasp what Diaghilev did for Russia—in view of the fact that he left the country in 1909, never to resettle in his native land, and died abroad twenty years later. Actually, in 1924, serious attempts were made to lure Diaghilev to the USSR, through the efforts of Vladimir Maiakovsky and Leonid Krasin, although the honest Krasin stated outright that he could guarantee entry, but not exit, while the naïve Maiakovsky even wrote a letter to Osip Brik (who, as we now know, was an NKVD agent), asking him to show Diaghilev the best of Moscow (see the Serge Lifar archives at the Nouveau Musée National de Monaco).

Appreciative of the artistic potential of contemporary Russia, Diaghilev created the phenomenon

of the Ballets Russes which, for the first time, combined great music, the images of leading Russian and then European and American painters, ground-breaking choreography (many of those who choreographed Diaghilev's ballets after Michel Fokine seem to have implemented his private ideas about dance) and superior dance skills. Here was a true *Gesamtkunstwerk*. Many, not least, Richard Wagner, attempted to recreate a united harmony of disparate arts into a single performance, a skill which had been lost since Classical and Mediaeval times. Evidently, Diaghilev succeeded, although the methods which he utilized for the purpose were far from being a mere archaeological reconstruction of a scenic action from antiquity.

What was presented at the Théâtre du Châtelet during the first seasons in Paris was astoundingly exotic: Diaghilev gave pride of place to the Russian classics such as *Boris Godunov* and *Ivan the Terrible* (*The Maid of Pskov*), to Mediaeval Russian history, to the imposing figure of Fedor Chaliapin, and to the Orient—the Orient of Polovtsian dances from *Prince Igor* and *Schéhérazade*. The Orientalism of the latter, designed by Léon Bakst, triggered a veritable explosion. It was an extravaganza which dazed the audience with its riot of colors, free-flowing choreography (by Fokine) and tempest of emotions. A fad for Oriental motifs overwhelmed everyone, including famous couturiers such as Paul Poiret and jewelers such as Louis Cartier. At the same time, Diaghilev put Classical French choreography into play—*Les Sylphides* and *Le Spectre de la Rose*—with their weightless and unearthly dancers, as well as Adolphe Adam's *Giselle*. What the audience saw in those performances was an astounding vision, ethereal and fantastic. But the Russian theme returned in 1911—in Igor Stravinsky's *Petrouchka* where Nijinsky played the lead role, a visionary role for a dancer who, in his crazed delirium of later years, would call himself "god's mad clown."

The Oriental arabesque was then replaced with Greek antiquity in *Narcisse* (1911) and *Daphnis et Chloé* (1912), both designed by Bakst, and then in *L'Après-midi d'un Faune* (1913) also featuring pastoral scenes by Bakst and the novel choreography of Nijinsky and Diaghilev himself. Unfortunately, even with Bakst's vigorous sketches, it is difficult to imagine how all of it looked on stage. According to contemporaries, the first night of *L'Après-midi d'un Faune* in Paris was a failure, with some of audience even leaving the hall, of-

The cortège of Sergei Diaghilev, Venice, August 21, 1929
Original print, 9.4 × 13.9 cm
Archives NMNM
(2002 7 12 C 37 04 00 41)
Serge Lifar Collection

The cortège of Sergei Diaghilev arriving at the cemetery of San Michele, Venice, August 21, 1929
Original print, 9.4 × 14 cm
Archives NMNM
(2002 7 12 C 37 04 00 37)
Serge Lifar Collection

The funeral of Sergei Diaghilev, Venice, August 21, 1929. In the center are Serge Lifar and Pavel Koribut-Kubitovitch (Diaghilev's cousin)
Original print, 12.6 × 17.6 cm
Archives NMNM
(2002 7 12 C 37 04 00 43)
Serge Lifar Collection

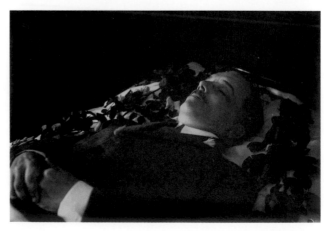

Sergei Diaghilev lying in state, August 21, 1929. He died in the Grand Hotel, Venice, on August 19
Original print, 12.9 × 17.9 cm
Archives NMNM
(2002 7 12 C 37 04 00 01)
Serge Lifar Collection

fended by the unconventional choreography based on sharp, stereotypical gestures, and, in particular, by the "indecency" of the faun's final motions perpetrated by Nijinsky. Still, the beautiful photographs by Baron Adolphe de Meyer do provide an insight into the world of this ballet—which became a milestone for the company and for Diaghilev himself, who was realizing that Fokine's choreography was out of date and no longer in line with his own aspirations.

How clairvoyant, how sensitive Diaghilev was to the new and imminent developments. Together with Nijinsky, he produced *Le Sacre du Printemps* by Igor Stravinsky, with sets and costumes—still traditional at the time—by Nicholas Roerich, and then *Jeux* (1913), featuring the music of Claude Debussy, Nijinsky's experimental choreography, and designs by Bakst, even though by that time Diaghilev undestood that the time for change had come—so for his next ballet, *Le Coq d'Or* (1914), he solicited the talent of Natalia Goncharova. The ballet still embodied the "Russian" theme, but the approach both to design and choreography was different and constituted the starting point for Diaghilev's "avant-garde" period, in the course of which he collaborated with Goncharova and Mikhail Larionov as designers and Bronislava Nijinska and Léonide Massine as choreographers.

In 1917, Diaghilev invited Picasso to design scenes for *Parade*; a few years later, the same Picasso produced sets and costumes for *Le Tricorne*. Thus started yet another—and the final—period in the history of the Saisons Russes, during which Spanish, French and other non-Russian artists and composers played a dominant role in Diaghilev's team. Nevertheless, in 1921 he did produce *The Sleeping Princess*—based on Peter Tchaikovsky's *Sleeping Beauty* and with sets and costumes by Bakst—as a tribute to the great tradition of Classical Russian ballet, although the production, the most expensive and glamorous to date, was a commercial failure. But Diaghilev moved ahead feverishly, planning his repertoire for the next seasons and mixing and matching older productions with radical innovations. His notebooks are full of remarks on various production ideas, interspersed with bills and never ending lists of things to do.

The Ballets Russes continued to exist in Europe well after Diaghilev's death, and, despite financial difficulties, it was a successful commercial venture. Several new companies split, Vera Nemtchinova founding her own company and Colonel Wassily de Basil directing the ballet troupe in Monte Carlo. They continued to benefit from Diaghilev's legacy, reviving older productions and renewing previous repertoires. Many of the dancers who worked with Diaghilev died many years later, but all long cherished the fond memories and personal effects which connected them to this remarkable individual and man of great distinction.

Reaction and Revolution:
Sergei Diaghilev's Formative Years

Sjeng Scheijen

What do we know about Sergei Diaghilev's intellectual background? What, if any, were his religious, philosophical, political, and moral beliefs? And if he had none, what was the reason for this lack? Diaghilev left an enormous amount of archival material and thousands of pages could be filled with lists of the hotels he stayed in, the restaurants he dined at (and even what he had to eat), and the contracts he signed. Little or nothing is known, however, as regards his deeper convictions.

Contemporaries write that he was not religious—being above all superstitious—and that he avoided political and ideological discussions. While this may well be true, it does not tell us much. If Diaghilev borrowed money from people of different political persuasions, he tended to keep his own views to himself. His public was also highly varied, ranging from progressive, left-wing Parisian bohemians to the community of right-wing Russian émigrés on the Côte d'Azur and the conservative British establishment. No one wishing to cater to such very different groups could manifest particularly pronounced political convictions.

It has also suited Diaghilev's historians to paint him as an apolitical aesthete. For their own ends, both left-wing Soviet historians and right-wing émigré writers have insisted on his lack of interest in all ideological discussion. While the latter have chosen to present Diaghilev as a typical figure of pre-revolutionary Russia (cf. Arnold Haskell and Walter Nouvel) or to relativize his intellectual status (cf. Alexandre Benois), more was at stake for Soviet historians. In the 1970s and 1980s, when authors cautiously began to publish work on him again after decades of oblivion, this was only possible through radical depoliticization. Ilia Zilbershtein could, therefore, do little other than claim that Diaghilev displayed "total indifference to philosophical, social and theoretical problems in general."[1]

But is this the same Diaghilev who toasted the revolution of 1905 with champagne and concluded a performance of the *Firebird* after the revolution of February 1917 by sending a revolutionary with the red flag onto the stage? The Diaghilev who learned Vladimir Maiakovsky's verses by heart and expressed violent anti-German sentiments in interviews with the *Daily Mail* after World War I? The truth is, of course, more complex and there is a great deal to say about Diaghilev's convictions. The foundations were laid during his formative years for a worldview that may have been non-political, but was certainly not indifferent.

The military family in which Diaghilev grew up is hard to interpret from an ideological standpoint. While his grandfather suffered from a form of religious mania, which was not, however, passed on to the children,[2] his father instead appears to have felt a certain aversion for any conviction manifested with too much ardor, be it religious, ideological, or political. As a soldier, he upheld unquestionably a certain form of social conservatism, but the family's political views were rather of a liberal nature. Not all of its members were equally moderate in their convictions. Diaghilev's aunt Anna Diaghileva (later Filosofova) was one of Russia's best-known feminists and greatly esteemed in left-wing liberal circles. Valerian Panaev, the father of his beloved stepmother Elena, was a prosperous industrialist and a known political activist. The author, among other things, of a book on the emancipation of the serfs published in London by Alexander Herzen in 1858, he was considered an authority on liberal reform of the State. He was a friend of the left-wing poet Nikolai Nekrasov (and made a speech at his funeral) and also of Herzen and Vissarion Belinsky.[3] A supporter of the latter, he firmly believed in the liberating and educational role of the arts and accordingly was an extraordinarily munificent patron. He had one of Russia's first private the-

Valentin Serov
Portrait of Sergei Diaghilev
1904
Oil on canvas, 97 × 83 cm
SRM (Zh-1922)

aters built on the Admiralty Embankment on the Neva in St. Petersburg, and it was there that Fedor Chaliapin made his first appearance in the city in 1895, with Diaghilev unquestionably present in the audience.

When the 23-year-old Sergei decided to become a patron of the arts ("I have everything necessary but the money"), he must have been thinking of this grandfather on his stepmother's side.[4]

Panaev's daughter Elena had a very strong influence on her stepson, to whom she transmitted the belief in the possibility of social salvation through the arts, above all literature, which she shared with her father. Philosophical and political issues were discussed in depth in the family circle and the children were encouraged to express their views. While it is difficult to reconstruct the level of these discussions, there is at least one document which sheds light on this aspect of the family life. Sergei read Ivan Goncharov's novel *Obryv* [The precipice] during a long stay on the family estate at Bikbarda and discussed the political issues described in it with the members present at the time. While the novel's weaknesses did not escape the young Diaghilev's notice, it appears to have prompted long reflection. It was above all the nihilist character Mark that attracted his attention:

> What an impression *The precipice* has
> made on me! Altogether an extraordinary
> work, at least if you disregard the three
> hundred pages that slow down the novel's
> development. … I'm afraid my opinion
> about Mark is none too certain. He is
> an intelligent person but a nihilist, and
> in my view you can't say that all nihilists
> are stupid. (I had a great row with aunt
> about this and uncle Bob now calls me a
> liberal and thinks I'm a nihilist.) … I'm
> not sure whether Mark was a swine not to
> marry Vera when he claimed he loved her.[5]

He wrote his mother three long letters on his discussions about the novel with his grandmother, uncle Bob and cousin Pavka. Although its psychological and affective themes seem to have interested more than the political ones, the exchange of letters conveys the impression of a typical family of the "intelligentsia," with Diaghilev's stepmother appearing clearly more left-wing than the others.

Sergei Diaghilev (far right) with his father, Pavel; stepmother, Elena Panaeva-Diaghileva; and half-brothers, Yurii and Valentin, 1880s
Original print, 23.6 × 17.7 cm
Archives NMNM
(2002 7 12 C 37 02 00 08)
Serge Lifar Collection

Diaghilev did not become involved in a lively exchange of political views until he moved to St. Petersburg to continue his studies. He spent much of the first year at the home of his paternal aunt Anna Filosofova and formed a close friendship (which later developed into a romantic relationship) with his cousin Dima Filosofov. The atmosphere in the Filosofov family was very different from that of the Diaghilevs in Perm. The house was a center of political activity and aunt Anna was known throughout Europe for her battles in favor of women's rights. The dreaded "third section" of the Tsar's secret police had a thick file on her and she was also sent into exile for a short period in the winter of 1879–80.[6] The discussions in her home were not only about Goncharov but also Sergei Nechaev, Mikhail Bakunin, and Karl Marx. Her closest friends were the activist Nadezhda Stasova and her husband the renowned critic and musicologist Vladimir Stasov, the father of both the "Peredvizhniki" and the "Moguchaia kuchka" ("The Mighty Five"). Anna Filosofova had far narrower and more radical ideas than grandfather Panaev, her understanding of art being dominated by sterile positivism and utilitarianism.

Filosofova's son Dima soon rebelled against her stubborn criticism. As he wrote later,

It is significant that Belinsky himself has never been of any interest for me. I have never read him. It is the eternal conflict between the generations. My mother's veneration for the 1860s and constant harking back to Belinsky, Chernyshevsky, Pisarev and so on aroused an instinctive dislike in me. Also involved in this to some extent were Tolstoi with his individualism and Dostoevsky with his mystical nationalism, later joined by enthusiasm for the French Symbolists and Decadentists. In short, what was to be expressed with such force a little later, in the years of *Mir iskusstva*, was formed precisely during our years at university.[7]

Diaghilev had to define his own position in this heated dispute between his aunt and cousin when he went to live with the Filosofovs in St. Petersburg. The idealized, provincial, amateur, impassioned experience of art that filled the evenings in Perm and on the estate at Bikbarda had to give way to Anna Filosofova's barren utilitarianism and Dima's radical aestheticism. The two cousins and lovers soon joined forces against the mother of one and aunt of the other. Diaghilev wrote to his stepmother that Anna Filosofova considered him "silly, frivolous and superficial," but does not appear to have attached too much importance to this criticism.[8] It was under Dima's influence that his opposition developed to the utilitarian aesthetic of earlier generations and in the domestic discussions with his aunt and her friends that the foundations were laid for the great battles later fought against Vladimir Stasov, Viktor Burenin and Ilia Repin. Philosophical differences of opinion were not ignored but always discussed openly. When Diaghilev decided to study at the conservatory in the mid-1890s (a plan that in any case fell through), he again had to face his aunt's criticism: "She reproaches me because I'm going to the conservatory. She is as dissatisfied with this as she is with Dima's decision to pursue a scientific career and remain at the university. She says it's selfish and that we don't need people to write symphonies or get carried away about abstract theories but to work for humanity."[9]

All these differences of opinion seem to have had no repercussions on the good relations within the family. Diaghilev continued to be a guest at Bogdanovskoe, the Filosofov estate, and to write both his aunt and his stepmother long letters during his travels.[10]

The young students seem to have regarded opposition to Anna's views above all as a challenge to hone their own, and sometimes she found the constant clashes with her son and nephew painful. She talks in her autobiographical notes about how disheartened she was over the young men's attitudes but also says that she later felt greater understanding for them:

> Russian decadentism was born in our home at Bogdanovskoe, given that the main initiators were my son Dmitrii and my nephew Sergei Diaghilev. *Mir iskusstva* was born in our home. As a woman of the 1860s, I found it so insulting that I could scarcely conceal my indignation. They laughed at me. Everyone will understand the painful moments I experienced over the birth of decadentism in my house. Like every new movement, it was then full of extravagance and exaggeration. Nevertheless, once the relationship lost its bitterness, I began to take an interest in their vision of life and must admit in all honesty that I found it fascinating … . If Sergei had never done anything more than *Mir iskusstva*, he would deserve eternal glory for that alone.[11]

In the late 1890s, however, the two sides were still at daggers drawn. While Diaghilev was setting off to conquer the Russian world of art, the leading figures of the previous generation were preparing their defenses. Stasov explained that he had "refrained for so long" from attacking Diaghilev "because he is the

The dining-room in the home of the Diaghilev family, Perm, c. 1880
Original print, 17.8 × 23.9 cm
Archives NMNM
(2002 7 12 C 37 02 00 10)
Serge Lifar Collection

Valentin Serov
*Portrait of the Composer
Nikolai Rimsky-Korsakov*, 1898
Oil on canvas, 94 × 111 cm
STG (1526)

nephew of a lady whom I hold dear and worship to an extraordinary degree … the splendid and enchanting Anna Filosofova."[12] The lady in question tried in turn to persuade Stasov to leave her nephew alone because he was just "a little boy lost in his dreams."[13]

Stasov did not allow himself to be deterred by Filosofova's entreaties and embarked upon a campaign of furious attacks against Diaghilev which obviously were intended to reduce him to silence, bringing the entire weight of his reputation and contacts with the press to bear. No newspaper or periodical was prepared to print Diaghilev's response, but he soon had his own magazine as a platform to make his views heard. Among other things, Diaghilev invited Stasov to write articles for *Mir iskusstva*, a proposal which Vladimir Vasilievich found intolerably impertinent.[14]

Dima Filosofov was right to state that with *Mir iskusstva* they had transformed the generational conflict with their parents into a public debate on the future of Russian art. And *Mir iskusstva* emerged victori-

ous, prompting a great revival of the arts in Russia with its promotion of poetry and inspiration, the relationship between art and the transcendental and its focusing of attention on form, craft, tradition, exoticism, and renewal. Nothing illustrates this victory better than the fact that Elena Diaghileva and Anna Filosofova both went over to *Mir iskusstva* and were always present at the philosophical-religious soirées organized by Dima together with Dmitrii Merezhkovsky and his wife Zinaida Gippius (regular contributors to the magazine). That particular brand of spiritual rebirth at the expense of the utilitarianism of the 1860s was the perhaps not entirely hoped-for result of Diaghilev's efforts. He was in fact barred from those meetings because his presence was unwelcome to the couple for primarily personal reasons. Diaghilev unquestionably had little feeling for the philosophical-religious diatribes to which his closest friends and relatives attached such importance. It must have been an at least unpleasant and perhaps even painful experience to see the fight against the materi-

Mikhail Larionov
Serge Diaghilev
Blue and black ink on paper
40.9 × 26.8 cm
NMNM (1974.14)
Serge Lifar Collection,
gift of Simone Del Duca

alism and radical utilitarianism of the 1860s end up in the Theosophical swamp of Merezhkovsky and Gippius.

As for many other Russians, the year 1905 was a formative watershed for Diaghilev, who greeted the spontaneous revolts which broke out against the autocratic system all over the country with great enthusiasm. When the news arrived that the great reform of the State designed to transform Russia into a parliamentary monarchy had been approved, he hurried to the Filosofovs with champagne. As he wrote to Alexandre Benois at the time, "in any case, two solutions are possible now. You can either take to the streets and subject yourself to every possible madness of the moment (which is naturally more than justified) or you can sit in your study and wait, but thus remain cut off from life. The first solution is not practicable for me. I only like the streets in operas or small Italian towns. As regards the study, that's for bookworms, which I am not."[15]

Deep though his aversion was for direct political action, Diaghilev did not remain wholly detached. When Zinovii Grzhebin, the editor of the satirical magazine *Zhupel*, was arrested for his attacks on the government, it was pressure from Diaghilev which led to his release. He also had talks in that period with Maxim Gorky and Igor Grabar about founding a new left-wing art magazine, which was never to see the light of day. While Diaghilev was certainly more moderate than Grzhebin and Gorky, it is clear where his political sympathies lay.[16]

All this goes to show that Diaghilev—the "incorrigible sensualist," as he described himself[17]—was by no means superficial and oblivious to political reality, as he is not infrequently presented. He was a moderate liberal forced to overcome his anti-political views in a highly politicized and radicalized environment where the arts were in danger of succumbing to the pressure of political forces. Underlying all this was a deep-seated aversion for the unilateral nature of monolithic systems and the conviction that plurality, tolerance, and the pragmatic acceptance of social divergence were the very basis of modern civilization, which found its highest expression in the beauty of art.

[1] I. Zilbershtein and V. Samkov (eds.), *Sergei Diagilev i russkoe iskusstvo*, 2 Vols. (Moscow: Izobrazitelnoe iskusstvo, 1982), Vol. I, p. 16.
[2] The celebrated publicist Ariadna Tirkova has provided a detailed description of the grandfather's status and condition. She claims, for example, that he suffered from a "mental disease." See A. Tirkova (ed.), *Sbornik pamiati A. P. Filosofovoi* (Petrograd: Golike and Vilborg, 1915), p. 7.
[3] On Valerian Panaev (1824–1899, not to be confused with his cousin, Ivan Panaev) see, for example, E. Diagileva, *Semeinaia zapis o Diagilevykh* (St. Petersburg and Perm: Bulanin, 1998), p. 259.
[4] This well-known quotation is from a letter from Diaghilev to his step-mother dated October 1895. The original is in IRLI (Institute of Russian Literature, Moscow). Call no. f. 102, no. 88, ll. 1–2.

[5] Letter from Sergei Diaghilev to Elena Diaghileva [1890]. For other letters see IRLI. Call. no. f. 102, ed. khr. 79, ll. 85, 93–94.
[6] See Tirkova 1915, p. 333.
[7] Dima Filosofov's notes are quoted by Aleksandr Laskin in his book, *Dolgoe Puteshestvie s Diagilevym* (Ekaterinburg: U-Faktoriia, 2003), pp. 111–12.
[8] Letter from Diaghilev to Elena Diaghileva dated September 8, 1891, in IRLI. Call. no. f. 102, ed. khr. 82, l. 211.
[9] Letter from Sergei Diaghilev to Elena Diaghileva dated August 28, 1894, in IRLI. Call no. f. 102, ed. khr. 87, ll. 443–44.
[10] In a letter to his step-mother, for example, Diaghilev refers to a letter to his aunt in which he describes a meeting with Emile Zola; see IRLI. Call. no. f. 102, ed. khr. 87, l. 21 (430) ob – 22 (431).
[11] From notes by Anna Filosofova quoted by Tirkova 1915, p. 390.

[12] Letter from Vladimir Stasov to Elena Polenova dated May 31 (June 12) 1898, Frankfurt. Quoted in Zilbershtein and Samkov 1982, Vol. I, pp. 156–57.
[13] Ibid., Stasov is quoting Filosofova.
[14] Ibid.
[15] Letter from Sergei Diaghilev to Alexandre Benois dated October 16, 1905. Quoted in Zilbershtein and Samkov 1982, Vol. II, p. 95.
[16] See Mstislav Dobuzhinsky's letter to Igor Grabar of January 27, 1905. Quoted in Zilbershtein and Samkov 1982, Vol. II, p. 176. Also see Dobuzhinsky's letter to Ivan Bilibin of January 28, 1906. Quoted in G. Chugunov (ed.), *M. V. Dobuzhinsky. Pisma* (St. Petersburg: Bulanin, 2001), p. 73.
[17] S. Diaghilev, "V chas itogov," in *Vesy*, no. 4, Moscow, 1905. Quoted in Zilbershtein and Samkov 1982, Vol. I, pp. 193–94.

Silver Strands, Silver Age: Sergei Diaghilev and the Modernist Aesthetic

John E. Bowlt

The cultural renaissance of early-twentieth-century Russia affected many facets of life, particularly the literary, visual and performing arts as well as science and technology. Poets and painters were quick to recognize this apogee, referring to their time as a "Silver Age" after the Golden Age of seventy years before illumined by the resplendent poetry of Alexander Pushkin and Mikhail Lermontov.[1] The aesthetic and philosophical generator of Russia's new artistic flowering was Symbolism and its repertoire of ideas—the rejection of the world of appearances, the occult dimension, the synthesis of the arts, the aspiration towards purer artistic forms, the undermining of social and moral standards and the engagement with the subjective world—left an indelible impression upon the artists and musicians, writers and thinkers of that generation, not least, Sergei Diaghilev and his colleagues within the group known as the "Mir iskusstva" (World of Art).

Alien to both the Imperial Academy and nineteenth-century didactic Realism, the World of Art owed its special vision, administrative efficiency and intellectual success mainly to the talents of Diaghilev, who, by late 1890s, had become a close friend of Léon Bakst, Alexandre Benois, Konstantin Somov and other young artists, writers and musicians in St. Petersburg. In November 1898, he began to publish the journal of the group, i.e. *Mir iskusstva* (until 1904), the next year he initiated a sequence of national and international art exhibitions (until 1906) also under the name "World of Art" and then, with diplomatic brilliance, began to promote Russian art, literature, music, and dance in Europe and America.[2] True, Diaghilev was neither a painter, nor a dancer, but he was a talented singer, an acute critic and a tireless organizer. Indeed, it was thanks to his energy and vision that *Mir iskusstva* enjoyed the financial patron-age of the railroad tycoon, Savva Mamontov (the owner of the art colony Abramtsevo) and Princess Mariia Tenisheva (owner of textile manufactories and of the art colony Talashkino) and that the World of Art exhibitions scored such a remarkable success. Perhaps there is a fateful coincidence between Diaghilev's close alliance with the Silver Age and his silver forelock which he tended with such deliberation and contrivance, suggesting narcissistic analogies with Oscar Wilde with his green carnation or Viacheslav Ivanov with his perpetual cigarette.

To a considerable degree, the World of Art group, molded and guided by Diaghilev, may be viewed not only as Russia's response to the concurrent secessions of Western Europe, but also as the ideological and aesthetic laboratory of Diaghilev's Ballets Russes. As a matter of fact, the international reputation of many members of the World of Art, especially Bakst and Benois, rests on their stage designs for Diaghilev's most monumental venture, which, with its commitment to the integration of the arts, to archaic and exotic improvisation and to the exploration of new codes of choreographic, musical and visual application, was, to a large extent, the embodiment of many of the principles elaborated by the World of Art.

The *miriskusniki* never published a common declaration of faith, but their concentration on artistic technique, their fascination with antiquity and the antique and their evocation of the subjective landscape indicated a willing acceptance of "art for art's sake" and, more immediately, of the graceful order peculiar to the fading beauty of their native city of St. Petersburg. As Diaghilev wrote in the lead article "Complicated Questions. Our Apparent Decline" of 1898, his generation sought "only the personal and believes only in its own cause. This is one of our great qualities, and whoever wishes to know us—may he cease thinking that, like Narcissus, we love only ourselves. We are greater, broader than anyone else."[3] In one respect, Diaghilev's homosexual attraction to the "architecture of the male physique"[4] and his enticing, if often pragmatic, dealings with both friends and foes were ever expressive of his forceful, even despotic, individuality: "Firstly, I'm a great charlatan," he wrote to his stepmother, "albeit a brilliant one; secondly, I'm a great *charmeur*; thirdly, a great lout; fourthly, someone with a great amount of logic and very few principles."[5]

A citizen of the world, at home in St. Petersburg, Paris, Venice, and London and in touch with the social, literary, and artistic celebrities of his age, Diaghilev still stressed the need for a stronger nationalism in Russian culture, one which would eclipse the alleged stylistic indifference of the nineteenth century—which is why he focused special attention on the Neo-Russian artists such as Aleksandr Golovin, Konstantin Korovin, Nicholas Roerich, and Viktor Vasnetsov, some of whom later worked for the Ballets Russes. These Neo-National painters, central to the evolution of Russia's decorative revival, fostered their folkloric styles at the art colonies of Abramtsevo and Talashkino, which, in turn, served as veritable sources for the development of the *style moderne* (Russia's counterpart to Art Nouveau) and to the subsequent, more famous designs of Léon Bakst and Alexandre Benois for the Ballets Russes.

The World of Art tolerated an eclectic mélange of canons and styles, collocating John Ruskin and Dmitrii Merezhkovsky, Maurice Denis and Friedrich Nietzsche, Hokusai and Aubrey Beardsley, Edward Burne-Jones and Andrei Belyi, Puvis de Chavannes and Oscar Wilde. In fact, according to Dmitrii Filosofov, Diaghilev's cousin and a littérateur of high standing, the journal addressed "everything"—"Gainsborough and Beardsley, Levitsky and Briullov, Velázquez and Manet, sixteenth-century German woodcuts and Goya's prints, steel engravings and lithographs of the 1830s, Orlovsky's sketches and those of Daumier."[6]

Of course, this focus on the eighteenth and early nineteenth centuries was only one fragment in the historical mosaic of the World of Art activities, a principal aspiration being, for example, to establish a new artistic canon through the assessment and assimila-

Léon Bakst
Portrait of Walter Nouvel, 1895
Watercolor and gouache
on board, 56.8 × 45 cm
SRM (R-13488)

tion of the antique, in other words, only by looking backwards could culture move forwards.

In his essays in *Mir iskusstva*, Diaghilev identified the zenith of culture with "Egypt, Greece, and the Middle Ages" and the heroes of that culture with "Giotto, Shakespeare and Bach."[7] Similarly, Benois and Somov were charmed by the era of Versailles, Bakst was drawn to Egypt, Greece and the Orient,[8] Golovin engaged with the traditions of Spain, while Mstislav Dobuzhinsky and Evgenii Lancéray yielded to the charms of eighteenth- and nineteenth-century St. Petersburg. In any case, their antiquarian passion was not limited to the appreciation of accepted legacies such as the cultures of Classical Greece or Louis XIV. A strong concern with popular myth and the primitive condition also attracted artists such as Roerich and Vrubel whose art was often regarded as the incarnation of a vital force lacking at the twilight of Imperial Russia.

Two of Diaghilev's early public successes—his elegant *catalogue raisonné* of Dmitrii Levitsky's portraits[9] and his organization of the "Historical and Artistic Exhibition of Russian Portraits" at the Tauride Palace in St. Petersburg in 1905 (at the moment of the First Revolution)—are clear reflections of what was both a proud effort to promote Russian painting and a clear recognition that the pomp and circumstance of the Imperial and aristocratic portrait now belonged to the past. Diaghilev expressed this sentiment in his speech after the vernissage of the exhibition—to the effect that "We are witnesses to a great historical moment of reckoning and ending in the name of a new, unknown culture."[10] Indeed, awareness of Russia's mercurial political temperament inspired other attempts to rescue Russia's cultural heritage, such the specialist journals *Khudozhestvennye sokrovishcha Rossii* (Art treasures of Russia, St. Petersburg, 1901–07) and *Starye gody* (Bygone years, St. Petersburg, 1907–16), which the World of Art members supported. Benois announced: "The forms which … have grown naturally from the Russian soil are closer to the Russian heart. However, to cease being a European now … would be odd, even absurd. That is why, alongside works of our own national art, we will not fear to present all things foreign and European."[11]

However, Diaghilev is remembered not as the champion of the aristocratic portrait or of the sometimes trite and superficial Neo-Russian style, but as the champion of the new dance, so it is reasonable to ask whence derived this interest and how it was nur-

tured within the Silver Age. After all, the Ballets Russes offered their audiences not only new choreography and new design, but also new and often highly experimental music: suffice it to recall that Claude Debussy and Igor Stravinsky, Maurice Ravel and Sergei Prokofiev, Jules Massenet and Nikolai Cherepnin and Erik Satie and Nicolas Nabokov were among the many modern composers whom Diaghilev commissioned for his Paris and Monaco productions and that, as a result, many people were first introduced to modern music precisely via the Ballets Russes.

The spirit of music commanded a special place in the Symbolist milieu. In 1901, for example, Alfred Nurok and Walter Nouvel, both members of the World of Art, initiated the Evenings of Contemporary Music in St. Petersburg which sponsored regular performances of works by modern Russian and European composers until 1911; and *Mir iskusstva* published regular critiques of concerts and recitals. The great Russian (and Polish) instrumentalists of the first decades of the twentieth century—many of whom were promoted by Diaghilev, such as Mischa Elman, Jascha Heifetz, Wanda Landowska, Sergei Rachmaninoff, Sergei Prokofiev, Alexander Skriabin and

Alexandre Benois
Italian Comedy. The Billet Doux, 1905
Watercolor, gouache, pen, Indian ink on paper on board
49.5 × 67.4 cm
STG (9188)

Igor Stravinsky—owed a great deal to this fertile environment. Diaghilev himself even entertained his colleagues singing Schubert and Wagner in fine baritone voice and playing piano duets, and he dreamed fondly of embarking upon a musical career, taking lessons in musical theory at the St. Petersburg Conservatoire and even composing an opera entitled *Boris Godunov*.

In opera, Diaghilev held very strong opinions, paying homage to a vogue of his time by praising Wagner and the operatic drama and publishing appreciations of *Tristan und Isolde*, *Die Walkyrie*, and *Die Götterdämmerung*[12] and a translation of Nietzsche's statements on Wagner at Bayreuth in *Mir iskusstva*.[13] "I'm fed up with Beethoven," wrote Benois in 1896, "what is he in comparison with Bach!! Or Wagner!!!"[14] Diaghilev ensured that opera was well represented at his *Cinq concerts historiques russes* for the Salon d'Automne in Paris in 1907 and his presentation of *Boris Godunov* with Fedor Chaliapin in Paris the following year is legendary.

On the other hand, neither Diaghilev, nor Benois waxed enthusiastic over the ballet during their tenure in the World of Art and their opinion of the Imperial ballet, for example, was less than respectful. Still, it would be misleading to conclude that in the late nineteenth and early twentieth centuries the Imperial theaters were bereft of momentum. After all, most of Diaghilev's key dancers received their training within the Imperial system and a number of his stars and productions for the Saisons Russes came directly from the Imperial stage. *Le Pavillon d'Armide* for instance, was first produced by Michel Fokine at the Maryinsky in 1907, while *Egyptian Nights*, produced there the following year, became *Cléopâtre* in Paris in 1909. Furthermore, Enrico Cecchetti, who tutored many of Diaghilev's dancers, was ballet-master at the Maryinsky and ballet teacher at the Theater Institute in St. Petersburg from 1892–1902.

Be that as it may, the *miriskusniki* saw the ballet as only one synthetic discipline, observing that architecture, fashion and particularly book design could also be promising fields of artistic experimentation. As an artistic synthesis, therefore, the book, with its covers, illustrations, and internal decorations attracted the talents of Bakst, Benois, Bilibin, Dobuzhinsky, Golovin and Roerich. Limited de luxe editions of books of poetry, albums and folios were

Alexandre Benois
Bathing of the Marquise, 1906
Gouache, tempera and graphite pencil on board
51.5 × 48 cm
STG (1597)

Konstantin Somov
Harlequin and a Lady, 1912
Watercolor and gouache on paper, 62 × 48 cm
STG (5322)

Léon Bakst, 1916
Photograph by E. O. Hoppé
Hand-colored gravure
CALA (2204-B-11)

printed as collectors' items, often evoking a nostalgia for the exploits of Russia's Imperial past such as Nikolai Kutepov's grandiose *Tsarskaia i imperatorskaia okhota na Rusi* (The Tsarist and Imperial hunt in Russia, St. Petersburg, 1902) with illustrations by Bakst, Benois, Valentin Serov and others. Books treating of taboo subjects such as erotica and demonism, corporal punishment and psychic phenomena multiplied during this time, Somov's titillating illustrations to *Le Livre de la Marquise* being among the most celebrated.

The accomplishments of the World of Art group exerted a profound and permanent influence on the development of Russian culture of the Silver Age, not least, the Ballets Russes. But born at the twilight of the Imperial order, the Russian Silver Age coincided with major social and political dislocations signaled by the Russo–Japanese War, the First Revolution, the Great War and the October Revolution. Viewed in this fateful context, the Ballets Russes, charged with bright imagery and strong resonance, served as a rich ornament to the final course of the Russian Silver Age.

[1] See S. Makovsky, *Na parnase Serebrianogo veka* (Munich: ZOPE, 1962). For a detailed discussion of the term "Silver Age" see O. Ronen, *The Fallacy of the Silver Age in Twentieth Century Russian Literature* (Amsterdam: Harwood, 1997).

[2] The primary sources on the "World of Art" group are V. Petrov, *"Mir iskusstva"* (Moscow: Izobrazitelnoe iskusstvo, 1975); J. Kennedy, *The "Mir iskusstva" Group and Russian Art, 1898–1912* (New York: Garland, 1977); N. Lapshina, *"Mir iskusstva"* (Moscow: Iskusstvo, 1977); J. E. Bowlt, *The Silver Age. Russian Art of the Early Twentieth Century and the "World of Art" Group* (Newtonville: ORP, 1979); V. Petrov and A. Kamensky, *The World of Art Movement* (Leningrad: Aurora, 1991); E. Petrova et al., *Mir iskusstva* (St. Petersburg: Palace Editions, 1998); and G. Guroff et al., *Mir iskusstva. Russia's Age of Elegance*, catalogue of the exhibition circulated by the Foundation for International Arts and Education, Bethesda, 2005–06.

[3] S. Diaghilev, "Slozhnye voprosy. Nash mnimyi upadok," in *Mir iskusstva*, no. 1, St. Petersburg, 1898, p. 2.

[4] Serge Lifar attributed these words to Diaghilev. See S. Lifar, *Serge Diaghilev* (London: Putnam, 1940), p. 180.

[5] S. Diaghilev, Letter to Elena Panaeva-Diaghileva (October 1895). Quoted in Lapshina 1977, p. 23.

[6] D. Filosofov, "Tozhe tendentsiia," in *Zolotoe runo*, no. 1, Moscow, 1908, p. 73.

[7] S. Diaghilev, "Osnovy khudozhestvennoi otsenki," in *Mir iskusstva*, no. 3–4, 1899, pp. 51, 57.

[8] For useful information on the connections between the Modernist stage and the Orient in Russia see S. Serova, *Teatralnaia kultura Serebrianogo veka v Rossii i khudozhestvennye traditsii vostoka* (Moscow: Iv-Ran, 1999). On Russia's Egyptomania see L. Panova, *Russkii Egipet* (Moscow: Vodolei, 2006), two volumes.

[9] S. Diaghilev and V. Gorlenko, *Russkaia zhivopis v XVIII veke: Tom 1-yi. D. G. Levitsky, 1735–1822* (St. Petersburg: Evdokimov, 1902).

[10] S. Diaghilev, "V chas itogov," in *Vesy*, no. 4, 1905, pp. 45–46. Diaghilev delivered his speech at a dinner held in his honor at the Metropol Hotel, Moscow.

[11] A. Benois, unsigned preface to *Khudozhestvennye sokrovishcha Rossii*, no. 1, St. Petersburg, 1901, p. 11.

[12] See D[iaghilev], "K postanovke, Tristan i Izolde," in *Mir iskusstva*, 1899, Vol. 1, Art Chronicle, pp. 135–37; A. Benois, "Postanovka Valkirii," ibid., 1900, Vol. 4, Literary Section, pp. 241–43; S. Diaghilev, "Gibel bogov," ibid., 1903, no. 4, pp. 35–38.

[13] F. Nitche [Nietzsche], "R. Vagner v Bairete," ibid., 1900, Vol. 3, Literary Chronicle, pp. 59–63, 99–102.

[14] Letter from Alexandre Benois to Walter Nouvel dated late November 1896, in RGALI (Russian State Archive of Literature and Art, Moscow). Call no. f. 938, op. 1, ed. khr. 46, l. 45.

Sergei Diaghilev and His Company

Vadim Gaevsky

Sergei Diaghilev's Ballets Russes had its opening night in Paris on May 19, 1909, at the Théâtre du Châtelet, restored for the purpose, a date of the utmost importance to the calendar of ballet. It was then that the history of new ballet in the twentieth century actually began and it was also a key moment in Diaghilev's life—his true birthday as a great organizer and leader, unprecedented impresario and romantic, avant-garde theater director and visionary.

However, neither on that spring day, nor in the coming summer days of 1909, and not even in the following summer of 1910, did the permanent troupe of Diaghilev's Ballets Russes come to exist yet. Such an idea would hardly have occurred to anyone. Back then, there were no private ballet schools, and all graduates of the Imperial ballet school on Theater Street (now called "Architect Rossi Street") in St. Petersburg were automatically employed by the Imperial Maryinsky Theater, where they would labor until retirement. Yet, Diaghilev contemplated the impossible, using his tremendous success of the two previous "seasons" in Paris as his sole argument—and, as always happened, he combined an insane idea with perfect common sense. No-one could resist his offers. Thus, if Vaslav Nijinsky, "the first classical dancer" of the new troupe, and Adolph Bolm, its "first character dancer," were to sever their ties with the Maryinsky, opting for higher pay from Diaghilev instead of a guaranteed stipend, neither Tamara Karsavina, the "first classical dancer" (and the first beauty, too), nor Michel Fokine, the "chief ballet-master," were about to leave the Maryinka— and their contracts with Diaghilev took account of their own interests. In this way, through a combination of grandiose gesture and common sense, persuasion and carrot-dangling, Diaghilev won one of his chief victories against inflexible rules and capricious fate, and moved to organize a private ballet company

in possession of its own troupe, repertoire, and artistic aspirations. Following in the steps of the Moscow Art Theater, he founded an independent ballet center, an autonomy about which Diaghilev rarely spoke, but which was as important as the search for innovation that he was touting on every street corner. What was truly amazing about the Diaghilev saga—which lasted, with a brief intermission at the onset of World War I, just a tad short of twenty years—was that he never failed to put theory into practice. All of the ballets he produced radiated artistic originality and his self-imposed obligation to tread his own path was discharged in full. Despite a chronic shortage of funds—and, as a consequence, the necessity to adapt to the tastes of donors, patrons, business partners, and show promoters—he did manage to preserve the artistic independence of his company. He made some concessions too, of course.

Diaghilev's original idea—to position ballet as the bearer of a theatrical and artistic avant-garde—was very much like Diaghilev himself, fascinating and insolent. His intentions would appear particularly bold, paradoxical even, to the public in Paris, where classical ballet had long fallen on hard times. The legendary era of ballerina Maria Taglioni and painter Edgar Degas, a legend in his own, albeit slightly different, right, had been long gone. The most famous ballet productions of the nineteenth century, *Les Sylphides* and *Giselle*, disappeared from repertoires for years to come. The Paris Opéra offered ballets with such unappetizing names as *The Busy Bees* and *Two Doves*, and the educated public stayed away from it altogether. On the other hand, the immense and carefully renovated Théâtre du Châtelet was an immediate hit with the most demanding audience. It was there that one could enjoy the most innovative, most modern theater, it was the place to come see the so-called "new" ballet,

Valentin Serov
Portrait of Ida Rubinstein
1910
Oil, graphite, gouache and
charcoal on canvas
147 × 233 cm
SRM (Zh-1915)

listen to new music, and view new set designs. Playbills for the "Saisons Russes" advertised obligatory integration of those three art forms into a harmonious and equal whole and with mutual interaction and justification. The ballet stage would provide a venue for a synthesis of arts—what Wagner had intended to achieve through opera. In other words, Diaghilev was creating the formula for a new kind of ballet, one which would become universal much later, in the mid-twentieth century.

However, Sergei Diaghilev started his conquest of Paris not with Russian ballet, but rather with a Russian opera that he produced in 1908, a year before the start of the regular "Saisons Russes." That opera, *Boris Godunov* by Modest Mussorgsky, was directed by Aleksandr Sanin, a former director with Moscow Art Theater, and Fedor Chaliapin played the lead. For a number of subsequent years, up until the beginning of World War I, ballet performances were intermingled with opera, and the presence of Chaliapin bestowed upon Diaghilev's tours not only dazzling brilliance, but also a particular sense of meaningfulness and drama. It would be fair to say that there were two men of genius—one of the opera and one of the ballet, Chaliapin and Nijinsky—on the threshold of Diaghilev's "World of Art" kingdom which astounded Paris and, subsequently, other European and American capitals. Both of them, the monumental singer and the miniature dancer, jointly defined the duality of Diaghilev's undertakings: his single company combined elements of the large-scale, ostentatious style (fast disappearing) and the more intimate style (still in embryo), the epic theater and the lyrical one. The contrast was stark indeed: Chaliapin's powerful basso was pulling one way, the silent flying *sautés* by Nijinsky, the other. Chaliapin as Boris Godunov evoked the historical past, the trying events of the seventeenth century, and, first and foremost, the so-called "psychological times"— Boris's own past as the actual murderer of the tsarevich Dmitrii. It was about the moral ordeals and unbearable pangs of consciousness that the great Chaliapin was singing in his signature operatic testimony.

The great Nijinsky, on the other hand, danced not the pangs of consciousness, but those of love (as in *Petrouchka*) and servility, whether coming from man, art, or dance. In his own, amazing way, with his incomparable *sautés*, Nijinsky was striving towards the future—the future of art, the future of man (as be-

came clear from his diaries, Nijinsky was deeply concerned with such matters). He longed for his own future too—that of the eternal youth which he seemed to be and whom Diaghilev always wanted him to be while on stage. One needs to imagine that beautiful contrast—the man singing and the boy dancing—in order to fully appreciate the two directions which Diaghilev simultaneously followed in his productions: the heroic and tragic spirit of classical Russian opera and the lyrical, often vernal character of Russian ballet—danced in the spirit of revival and of a sacred springtime. It is not fortuitous that one of the last pre-World War I ballets which Diaghilev showed in Paris was named *Le Sacre du Printemps*, even if that particular ballet was not a success. Moreover, it provoked a scandal of grandiose proportions, which, to an extent—only to some extent—was incited by its hot-tempered, fearless avant-garde director.

But that was not all, of course. What stood out in Diaghilev's character was his artistic plasticity, the ability to react in timely and appropriate fashion to abrupt changes in public and cultural life. In that re-

Alexandre Jacovleff
Portrait of Anna Pavlova, 1924
Oil on canvas, 190 × 121.5 cm
STG (Zh-1080)

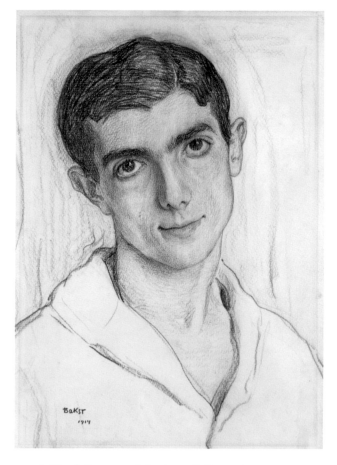

Léon Bakst
Portrait of Léonide Massine
1914
Pencil on paper, 33.6 × 23.5 cm
MKMAM, gift of Robert
L. B. Tobin (TL 1998.89)

Natalia Goncharova
Portrait of Olga Spessivtseva
1932
Indian ink and pen on
parchment, 27 × 20.2 cm
STG (R-8668)

spect, Diaghilev was of the twentieth century, a true son of uncertain, trying times. Such were the personal qualities which he passed on to his unusually flexible company which would owe its long existence—from 1909 through 1929—to an unfailing ability to move with the times. Times were dramatic and disparate.

One may note a distinct watershed for Diaghilev in that restless decades: before and after the Great War. World War I provided a natural, defining moment, raising the question of the viability and even moral justification of a ballet company. Initially, however, that question was non-existent for Diaghilev. For him, as for his entire entourage, art needed no moral justification whatsoever, and, after all, it had been on the strength of this premise that the movement—and its magazine—known as the "World of Art" came to be. The first "Saisons Russes" built upon the same foundation, and both the ballet troupe and the World of Art movement exerted an important liberating influence on Russian public awareness. The World of Art painters made an important contribution to the success of Diaghilev's ballets, and their leader, Alexandre Benois, became a de-facto ideologue of the company and one of the authors of famous *Petrouchka*.

Nevertheless, the Great War interrupted Diaghilev's union with the old World of Art members and their emphasis on the refined, aesthetic, oneiric *style moderne* went out of vogue overnight. Thanks to his organic ties to his native land, Diaghilev first noticed Russian folklorists, such as Mikhail Larionov and Natalia Goncharova, and then the Constructivists of Russian and European fame: Naum Gabo, Anton Pevsner, and Georgii Yakulov. His main emphasis, however, was on collaboration with painters of the Ecole de Paris.

Diaghilev was now turning to a different kind of artist. Generally speaking, one may make a distinction between the pre- and post-War generations, but another comparison may prove more meaningful: a generation that greeted the twentieth century at the very beginning of their professional careers, full of fervent hope and of the most optimistic expectations—and yet another age group had survived the World War as adolescents and then embarked upon their new lives in peacetime, fully aware of the insolvency of lofty ideals and of the gravity of the humanitarian disaster which they had lived through. The first believed in the miracles which the new century was about to bring—and Russian Symbolist poetry, the most powerful trend of the so-called Silver Age, was full of such miraculous expectations; the second, if they believed in anything at all, tended to have faith only in themselves—in their own energy and entrepreneurship, in their own success and good fortune. They looked forward to no miracles and expected none. These are the two psychological and aesthetic generations of Diaghilev's artists, close in time, but so different in a human sense. Anna Pavlova, Tamara Karsavina and Vaslav Nijinsky, to name just three of the most legendary and most luminous stars, represented the Silver Age as artistic and bodily incarnations of the sublime poetic spirit with which that era was permeated and the exalted beauty it worshipped. In a way, they became focal points of that worship, a conjecture that, incidentally, may be proven by the multitude of painted and drawn portraits of Pavlova, Karsavina and Nijinsky which have preserved the incomparable features of their faces—beautiful, refined, inspired. Coincidentally, the more progressive Russian portrait painters left no images of ballerina Mathilde Kschessinska, a beautiful woman who perhaps belonged more to imperial courtiers than to poetic circles. There are photographs of her, but no portraits, and, surely, this is not fortuitous.

Undoubtedly, Michel Fokine, ballet-master for Diaghilev and a leading dancer to boot, was yet another representative of the Silver Age, just like his artists. It was Fokine who had immortalized, choreographically, the Silver Age with his early oeuvre, *Chopiniana* (which became *Les Sylphides* in Diaghilev's rendition; and this is the name under which this ballet has been staged in theaters world over). Young Fokine's ability to create his amazing compositions in the shortest time possible bordered on the miraculous, and most of them would take just a few intense, inspired rehearsals—*The Swan* (later renamed *The Dying Swan*), for example, required only a few minutes, just as long as was needed for the music by Saint-Saëns. More importantly, the very choreographic fabric of Fokine's early pieces created for, and in collaboration with, his artists, proved to be a true artistic miracle. In this regard, one should note the above-mentioned *Swan*, the lead part of which Anna Pavlova danced for over twenty years, and *Le Spectre de la Rose* with principal roles danced by Karsavina and Nijinsky. Fokine, Pavlova, Karsavina, and Nijinsky eliminated all notion of effort from their dance, every kind of muscle work. There was only the fantasy of flight, only the pure flame of inspiration, only the glow of fabulous delight and inner beauty.

To unify those metaphorical characteristics under a single critical (or historical) rubric—it was a myth, and both of Diaghilev's ballet-masters, Fokine and Nijinsky (who replaced Fokine), built their compositions upon myth, whether of antiquity, Slavic, Persian or European. All their major characters were mythological: warriors in *Polovtsian Dances*, the Firebird in *L'Oiseau de Feu*, Schéhérazade in *Schéhérazade*, the Sylphides in *Chopiniana*, Petrouchka in *Petrouchka*, the Faun in *L'Après-midi d'un Faune*, the Chosen One in *Le Sacre du Printemps*. Nijinsky as an artist himself presented a certain mythological substance of classical ballet on stage; he entered the legend as a mythical dancer, or, rather, as a dancer of myth. The same may be said of Pavlova as The Swan and Pavlova as the Classical ballerina.

Parade, directed by Léonide Massine in 1917 to the sarcastic music of Erik Satie and against the background of Cubist sets by Pablo Picasso, signified a new trend for Diaghilev's company, for it attempted to demythologize all components of ballet, such as plot, locus, and actors' masks (*Parade* depicted the life of a traveling circus) and replace them with a different phenomenon—the foibles of fashion. The everyday fashions of Paris, Pan-European stylistic fads (Cubism, Futurism), the global vogue for free (to some extent) dance. But the real reason for this innovation lay somewhere else: Massine (and later, Serge Lifar) brought a whiff of the twentieth century into Diaghilev's company, the survival psychology attitudes of those spared by the Great War, those who had drawn a lucky card. In his productions of 1917 (*Les Femmes de Bonne Humeur*) and 1919 (*La Boutique Fantasque* and *Le Tricorne*), as well as in his solo dances for those ballets, Massine expressed the new perception of life, not as tragedy, but as a new passion for reality—a true reality, not the fantastic or phantasmal kind. He was especially good at Spanish and Italian dances as well as the Paris can-can that had come back into vogue.

Massine was a dancer from Moscow. He had started his career at the Bolshoi Theater where the perspicacious Diaghilev had noticed this handsome young man performing in the corps de ballet. Massine had no ties to the strictly academic St. Petersburg tradition, so remote from everyday life. The new lead classical dancers whom he introduced to Diaghilev, first and foremost, the two talented Poles, Stanislas Idzikowski and Léon Woizikovsky, both of whom had been professionally educated in Warsaw, were bearers of the same vital spirit, shared the same interest in character dancing, and, furthermore, manifested a supreme and passionate sense of competitiveness. As for Lifar, this capacity was enhanced by the athletic nature of his body. Diaghilev's new prime donne, Vera Nemtchinova, Félia Doubrowska and Alice Nikitina, presented typical examples of the Classical ballerina, elegant and artistic in Diaghilev's sense. Moreover, they had yet another quality in common: a pragmatic view of life, something which was characteristic of the post-War 1920s, but which Diaghilev's prime donne of the early years lacked entirely. Here were new, modern style ballerinas. But the main quality, typical of both male and female new dancers, was emotional reserve, even a certain coldness, or, to put it in a different way, an emotional closedness, so dissimilar to what Nijinsky had projected as Petrouchka, Bolm as the Chief Warrior, Pavlova as Ta-Hor, and Karsavina as the Firebird. If the legendary stars had lived their roles to the full, creating astoundingly vigorous, though fabulous, characters, the new artistes now displayed what would be lat-

er called "estrangement," namely, a certain distance between the performer and his or her character. Total impersonation was neither required, nor welcome.

In 1924, Diaghilev signed up the most progressive and most refined and sensitive of his last ballet-masters, i.e. the former St. Petersburgian Georgii (later, George) Balanchine, who four years later, in 1928, directed *Apollon Musagète* by Igor Stravinsky, in which he manifested a new aesthetic system. Here, in the portraits of his muses and the structure of his compositions, was the aesthetics of estrangement. Indeed, the cool muses of Balanchine (Alexandra Danilova, Lubov Tchernicheva, and Félia Doubrowska) were hardly reminiscent of Nijinsky's timid nymphs (*L'Après-midi d'un Faune*) or Fokine's sad and tremulous Sylphides, while their dance en pointe failed to disguise their Classical training. In brief, the character of the main hero had changed. The Petersburgian dreamers, as represented by Nijinsky, Pavlova, and Karsavina, were replaced by dynamic Europeans personified by Lifar and, on the female side, by Bronislava Nijinska in her Parisian ballets, *Les Biches*, and *Le Train Bleu*.

Diaghilev did things in a coherent, logical way. Having conceived of *Les Biches* and *Le Train Bleu*, he turned to the most modern artistic material: a stylish high society resort. With *Apollon Musagète*, Diaghilev demonstrated that he had no intention of parting with the mythological past; only the treatment of myth changed, becoming more lucid, and in some ways, more prosaic. As a result, the final seasons of Diaghilev's Ballets Russes were marked by two productions which added permanent wealth to the ballet theater. These productions are still alive today, although on different stages, i.e., *Apollon Musagète*, known simply as *Apollon*, and *Le Fils Prodigue*, directed by Balanchine to Sergei Prokofiev's music for the 1929 season. Inspired by Diaghilev himself, *Le Fils Prodigue* became an epilogue to his twenty-year-old saga.

What was Diaghilev thinking about, when he suggested that Prokofiev and Balanchine create a ballet after an evangelical parable? Was it an act of repentance—or blasphemy? Did Diaghilev think of the native land which he had left or the fellow travelers whom he had dropped along the way? Was he concerned with the fortunes of Classical ballet and of his own? This is something we will never know. But what we do know is that by the end of the 1929 season Diaghilev was gravely ill (although he would not admit it to himself) and was losing interest in the ballet. He developed a new pastime—collecting rare Russian books scattered throughout the second-hand bookstores of Europe. But then, perhaps Diaghilev was not deviating all that much, since, in creating his unique productions throughout those twenty turbulent seasons, he had also been cultivating the precious and the rare. It had been a religion of innovation, but perhaps by the end of his life he had just stopped believing. In his early years, not only had he been able to recognize apparent yet unappreciated genius, as was the case with Stravinsky, but what was more important, he possessed a gift for identifying potential genius, as in the case of Massine and Balanchine. However, now Diaghilev started betting on debutants with little future and no particular talent, and that is what happened with the young composer Vladimir Dukelsky (Vernon Duke). But what was more important, he was mortally tired—weary of the constant fight for everything: money, repertoire, recognition, fortune, weary of the need to strive for achievement. His death on August 19, 1929, was mysterious and obscure. He was fully aware of his severe diabetes, yet followed no advice from doctors. Who knows? Perhaps his secret wish was for deliverance.

Alexandre Benois and Léon Bakst: Their Visual Sources

Elena Fedosova

The phenomenal success of the Saisons Russes derived from the efforts of all participants. For the first time in the history of the Russian theater and on an equal footing, the ballet-master, painter, composer, librettist, and actor contributed to a truly synthetic performance.

It was vitally important, therefore, that the visual appearance of the spectacle be defined by a common, collective conception, not just by the original talents of its painters, such as Alexandre Benois, Léon Bakst, Aleksandr Golovin, and others. Everyone contributed.

This essay treats of the concrete historical sources used by the designers of the first seasons of the Ballets Russes and is based on the Michel Fokine collection now at the State Museum of Theater and Music in St. Petersburg and on personal comments by the painters themselves. Among the artifacts in the Fokine collection, which numbers over one thousand pieces, there are drawings, prints, photographs, and personal effects which belonged to Fokine, the primary ballet-master of the Saisons Russes. Here is what Benois wrote about Fokine: "He is one of the very first choreographers who had a serious, equal interest not only in his own field of specialization, but also in other forms of art as well: painting, sculpture, music."[1] Preparing for a new production, Fokine would give studious attention to the culture, customs, and ethnographic artifacts of the environment into which he was planning to place his characters. He drew upon sculptures, paintings, prints, and miniatures to assemble the movement sequences for his recitals. A close look at the Fokine collection illustrates just how concrete and fruitful his recommendations to the painters were.

Even the first joint project of Fokine and Benois, i.e. Nikolai Cherepnin's ballet *Le Pavillon*

d'Armide staged at the Maryinsky Theater, St. Petersburg, in 1907 (Benois created the libretto, Fokine the choreography), illustrates their mutual knowledge of eighteenth-century French culture. Fokine, for example, was inspired by the art of the great French ballet-master Jean-Georges Noverre (1727–1810). As for Benois, working on the scenes for *Le Pavillon d'Armide* gave him great satisfction: as a painter, Benois came of age during his sojourn in France in 1896–99; passionate about the era of Louis IV, he was an expert in eighteenth-century French painting and social history. "I wanted this ballet [*Le Pavillon d'Armide*] to possess the radiance, magnificence, and festivity of the ballets of old … Also, I wanted it to reflect my admiration for the baroque and rococo periods," he explained in his memoirs.

In actual fact, Benois' costume sketches for the characters of the fairy castle of Armide are elegant stylizations of eighteenth-century ballet costumes—so-called "Graecian" costumes of the French type. For example, Benois looked to drawings by the French stage designer Louis-René Boquet (1717–1814), who worked on costumes for performances at the Royal Court and whose designs were actually used to make costumes for a production of the opera, *Armide*, in 1761. Boquet also collaborated with Noverre to produce a series of theatrical costumes to go with Noverre's treatise *Letters on the Dance*. Benois studied Boquet's drawings and Noverre's text in the library of the Academy of Arts in St. Petersburg. Benois even signed his own costume sketch for Armide's Slave (played by Nijinsky): "Benois d'après Boquet."

It would make an interesting and telling exercise to compare Boquet's drawings to Benois' costume sketches, even if, for all their apparent similarity, the sketches by Benois are not mere museum copies, but remarkable stylizations done by a twentieth-century

Léon Bakst
Portrait of Alexandre Benois
1898
Watercolor and pastel
on paper, 64.5 × 100.3 cm
SRM (R-26999)

Louis-René Boquet
Costume designs for the ballet
Rinaldo und Armide composed
by Jean-Joseph Rodolphe
(1730–1812) and produced at
the Court Theater of Stuttgart
in 1762, with choreography
by Jean-Georges Noverre
Watercolor, Indian ink and
pen on paper, 24.5 × 15.3 cm
SPSMTM (GIK 5639/20)
and 24.3 × 15 cm
SPSMTM (GIK 5639/6)

artist. While preserving the general look of the costumes, Benois leaves out small, fractional details; essentially, he turns the ballet costume, intended to be observed at close range, into a theatrical costume. A tender irony informing technical fluency is what characterizes his style. Here is Benois's dream of a palatial festival of days gone by, for, on a whim, he combines eighteenth-century costumes with details from Oriental fairy tales. The magnificent pink tunics of Armide are combined with a turquoise turban.

The pinnacle of the Russian seasons, the ballet *Petrouchka*, is one of the most accomplished creations of an "indigenous" choreography in the twentieth century. The first night was in Paris on June 13, 1911, at the Théâtre du Châtelet. Three authors had collaborated to produce the ballet: the composer Igor Stravinsky, the painter Benois, and the ballet-master Fokine, the plot being written jointly by Benois and Stravinsky. For both *Petrouchka* became one of the most important events in their creative lives, and for Benois, *Petrouchka*, his finest piece of work for the theater,

also represented the total embodiment of his artistic views on synthetic spectacle. The rare balance of music, libretto, painted sets, and choreography astounded everyone who saw Stravinsky's, Fokine's and Benois's *Petrouchka*. Nijinsky, who danced the title role, became a true legend; Karsavina as the Ballerina was the incarnation of femininity and temptation. All the creators of that ballet immersed themselves in the world of Russian carnival, recreating the hustle and bustle of a grandiose folk fair.

For his costume and set designs, Benois relied upon works by St. Petersburg painters of the 1830s and 1840s and the margins of many of his sheets for *Petrouchka* contain comments such as "after Shchedrovsky" and "after Timm." Vasilii Timm was a painter of battle and genre scenes, but from 1851 through 1862, he served as the editor of a collection of lithographs called *Russkii khudozhestvennyi listok* (Russian artistic sheet), where he published both his own drawings and those of other painters, along with brief explanatory comments. Timm received acclaim for his genre illustrations, in which, realistically and often with a good dose of humor, he depicted the everyday lives of St. Petersburg's residents from different strata of the society. Ignatii Shchedrovsky (1815–1870) was a watercolorist and author of multiple lithographs from Russian life. Benois also wrote in his memoirs that "all of *Petrouchka* was as if it came out of a single painting by Makovsky." Benois had in mind a picture by the popular St. Petersburg painter, Konstantin Makovsky (1839–1913), called *Butter Week on Admiralty Square in St. Petersburg.*

From the entire series of Benois's sketches for *Petrouchka*, it is the set for Scene 1, "The Maslenitsa [Butter Week] Festival," which, probably, is the most popular. In a compositional sense, the drawing *Maslenitsa Festivities on Isaac's Square in 1858*, which Timm also published at Miunster's Lithographic Press, is the closest precedent to Benois's sketch. On the right of the lithograph, Petrouchka, clad in a white robe and a coxcomb, is performing on a wooden stage. The entire symmetrical composition of Benois's design is remarkably reminiscent of Timm's drawing.

It should be noted that in 1827–72 popular festivals in St. Petersburg took place on Admiralty Square.

The wooden amusement park would stretch for over half a kilometer from Palace Square to Isaac's Square, which is to say that we should not be too worried by the discrepancies in the titles of Makovsky's painting and Timm's drawing. They are both portrayals of the same festival, but from different standpoints. In the background of Makovsky's painting, we can see Palace Square with a view of the Winter Palace, while the drawing by Timm shows the cupola of St. Isaac's Cathedral in the background. It is interesting to note that the specific architectural background of St. Petersburg is missing altogether in the Benois design. His is a theatrical set, not a genre scene from the everyday life of nineteenth-century St. Petersburg.

Although it is possible to trace the historical sources of the costume designs for the main characters in *Petrouchka* (Petrouchka himself, the Ballerina, and the Blackamoor), it is not especially reasonable or profitable to do so: Benois put so much artistry into his costume designs, so many intimate recollections of his childhood that they stand out as absolutely independent characters. However, his sketches for the secondary characters—the coachmen, servants, nannies, policemen, etc.—were copied in minute detail from drawings by Timm, i.e. from Timm's folio, called *Russkie kostiumy* (Russian costumes), which was produced by the Lemercier Lithographic Press in 1843. Yet there is a substantial difference between the drawings of Benois and those of Timm: Timm's characters are static, while Benois depicts his protagonists in motion, assigning a strong individual personality to each. The detailed academic drawing of Timm is replaced with a freer line—and the colors differ too. Rather than just register visual images of men and women in city streets, each sketch by Benois elicits respect and sentimental affection for his characters.

Bakst began to work as a stage designer more or less at the same time as Benois. In 1909, *Cléopâtre*, with sets and costumes by Bakst, premiered at the Théâtre du Châtelet in Paris—the prehistory of which deserves special attention. In 1908, Fokine had used his own script to direct *Nuits d'Egypte*, a ballet with music by Anton Arensky at the Maryinsky Theater. Artist-in-residence Orest Allegri painted the sets and the costumes were produced from sketches by Mikhail Zandin. Fokine recalled that he did not like Zandin's costumes and had to pick and choose alternatives from the so-called "theatrical collection." Even "Egypt-

Anonymous
The Hunt, late nineteenth century
Persian miniature from Michel Fokine's collection
Watercolor, gouache and gold leaf on paper, 36.8 × 24 cm
SPSMTM (GIK 7324/313 OR 13601)

ian" collars from *Aida* came back into service. Six albums with reproductions of architectural details preserved among the Fokine archive illustrate the extent to which he knew the culture and art of Ancient Egypt. He studied the images meticulously and then pasted the ones he needed into his albums, according to the exigencies of this or that plot. It is likely that, in the course of his work on *Cléopâtre,* Fokine showed these images to Bakst, and, in any case, Fokine's own costume for the role of Amoun in *Nuits d'Egypte* is very similar to that of Cleopatra herself, produced after a design by Bakst.

Upon Diaghilev's insistence, different music—"of the highest quality," to use his own characterization—was selected for the first Saisons Russes in Paris, music by Russian composers Nikolai Cherepnin, Aleksandr Glazunov, Mikhail Glinka, Modest Mussorgsky, Sergei Taneev, and Nikolai Rimsky-Korsakov. Fokine wrote: "It is quite remarkable how we managed to find compositions which were a perfect match for the rhythm, character, and sometimes even the measure of what was being replaced."[2] Essentially, Fokine did not change any dances except for the "Bacchanalia" to Glazunov's music and the "Finale" to Mussorgsky's which were rearranged. In other words, Bakst was painting for a production ready to go and, undoubtedly, tried to accommodate Fokine's wishes, so here there was little of the equal partnership which would characterize subsequent ventures. It is not accidental that one of Bakst's set designs for *Cléopâtre* comes very close, in composition and style, to Allegri's own scenes which we can recognize from photographs commissioned by the Imperial Theatres.

Fokine and Bakst's next joint project was *Carnaval,* a ballet based on music by Robert Schumann. Fokine directed *Carnaval* for a charity ball held by the writers and artists of the *Satyricon* magazine at the Pavlova Hall in St. Petersburg on February 20, 1910. In May of that year Diaghilev showed the same ballet in Berlin and in February, 1911 the Imperial Theater Directorate also included *Carnaval* in its repertoire. It is notable that the St. Petersburg State Museum of Theater and Music received all of Bakst's costume designs for *Carnaval* as part of the Fokine collection, i.e., Fokine actually owned Bakst's designs. The strong reflection of the style of the time period in question (mid-nineteenth century German Romanticism) places Bakst's *Carnaval* costumes among his best theatrical

work. In his notes to these stage costumes, Bakst referred to different issues of the ladies' fashion magazine *Der Bazar* published in Berlin—and, indeed, it would be of particular interest to compare Bakst's female costume designs with fashion trends of the 1830–40s: ribboned bonnets and bodice sleeves date to the 1830s; skirts with multiple flounces are of the late 1840s; from 1840 onwards, the lower part of the skirt would be decorated with a wide flounce; starting in 1842, two or three flounces would be used—which Bakst did in his sketch for Estrella; while, in line with the fashion trends of 1845 through the early 1860s, Bakst's skirt for Chiarina featured six flounces. Comparison with fashion magazines illustrates how, by freely combining the more graphic elements of everyday dresses, Bakst created multiple poetical variations of the stage costume so as to showcase the characters of the ballet.

1910 also saw the premiere of *Schéhérazade,* featuring music from the symphonic poem by Rimsky-Korsakov. Fokine was ballet-master and scriptwriter; Bakst painted the sets, although he, too, participated in the scriptwriting process. For the ballet, both ballet-master and artist used Iranian miniatures as a visual reference. Fokine maintained a long-standing interest in the culture of the East, perceiving it as fantastic and fabulous, and his collection includes fifteen nineteenth-century Turkish and Iranian miniatures.[3] These are genre compositions illustrating works by Ferdowsi and scenes from *Layla and Majnun*, which, in all likelihood, Fokine bought during his trip to the Caucasus in 1900. The most artistically valuable of them is the sheet from a manuscript on Fat'h Ali Shah Qajar (Inventory no. 7324/313). Fat'h Ali Shah, the ruler of Iran from 1797 through 1834, is portrayed as a horseman surrounded by his troops. Interestingly enough, the headgear of Shahriar in *Schéhérazade* mimics the crown of Fat'h Ali Shah in the miniature from Fokine's collection.

There is no doubt that in their work on *Schéhérazade*, both ballet-master and painter drew substantially upon historical sources. But, of course, the Orient of Fokine's ballet had nothing in common with the ethnographically correct dances of the people of the East, despite his assertion that he had imported "authentic" Arab, Persian and Indian moves into his choreography. Bakst's sets and costumes (and Valentin Serov's drop curtain) reflect only a few details of the Iranian miniatures, but he did borrow the most important element, color, for the prominent blue, green and red of the miniatures defined the gamut of colors in the ballet's sets and costumes. On the other hand, the pronounced gold of the ancient miniatures was missing.

Fokine's collection contains the drawing of a female dancer from antiquity carrying Bakst's (undated) inscription: "To Mikhail Mikhailovich Fokine from his devotee, L. Bakst." The long scarf, billowing behind the dancer, is arresting, indeed. No doubt, the drawing also pays tribute to the painter's ingrained passion for the culture and art of Ancient Greece. Together, Bakst and Fokine created two ballets concerned with antiquity, i.e. Cherepnin's *Narcisse* (1911) and Maurice Ravel's *Daphnis et Chloé* (1912). The St. Petersburg State Museum of Theater and Music acquired Bakst's costume sketches for *Narcisse* as part of Fokine's collection.

Narcisse was first shown in Monte Carlo on April 26, 1911. It was not Fokine's most successful choreographic miniature and its stage life was rather short, but even so, Bakst's costume designs for *Narcisse* have become classics in the history of European theatrical painting. Of course, it would make little sense to seek Ancient Greek parallels here, for this is the artist's free-flowing interpretation and his personal vision of antiquity spiced with the flavor of the East.

Art critic Sergei Makovsky called the World of Art painters "retrospective dreamers,"[4] and we may add that Fokine, in his balletic art, was yet another of those dreamers. However, as our comparison of Bakst's and Benois's work with the traditions of centuries past would indicate, all three creators were and remained of their own time. Their works were identified by artistic techniques typical of the *fin de siècle*, which they enriched with their own unique, deeply individual styles.

[1] Here and elsewhere the quotations are from N. Aleksandrova (ed.), *A. N. Benois, Moi vospominaniia* (Moscow: Nauka, 1990).
[2] Here and elsewhere the quotations are from M. Fokin, *Protiv techeniia* (Leningrad and Moscow: Iskusstvo, 1962).
[3] I would like to thank Anatolii Ivanov, chief of the Department of the East at the State Hermitage Museum, for his help with the attribution of the miniatures.
[4] S. Makovsky, *Stranitsy khudozhestvennoi kritiki* (St. Petersburg: Pantheon, 1909), Vol. 2, p. 115.

Dance, Memory!
Tracing Ethnography in Nicholas Roerich

Nicoletta Misler

One important aspect of Sergei Diaghilev's Ballets Russes which may not have received due attention concerns the ethnographic sources upon which Russian artists drew in such abundannce and with such "Post-Modern" freedom so as to create a new and exotic figurative art. The various sources tapped by the senior members of the *Mir iskusstva* (World of Art) group—including Russian folk decoration, the nomads of the steppes, the Middle and the Far East, and Apollonian and Dionysian Greece—are readily identifiable. What may be less evident is the fact that some of these artists, in particular Léon Bakst, Alexandre Benois, Ivan Bilibin, and Nicholas Roerich, often studied the same sources in a determined effort to restore strength and vitality to their "contemporary" world.

From Roerich to Natalia Goncharova, the older and younger generations of Diaghilev's artists differed markedly in their relationship to ethnography and the primitive world, and it was here that the impresario displayed his extraordinary ability to incorporate their different approaches into a single enterprise. The focus of this essay is on one of the models of ethnographic assimilation, namely, the importance of the sources regarding shamanic cultures and their survival—masked in proto-Slavic dress—in the sets and costumes for the Roerich-Stravinsky *Le Sacre du Printemps*. In accordance with Diaghilev's utopian ideal of a Russian renaissance,[1] Roerich focused on the pre-Slavic peoples, the Slavic and non-Slavic ancestors of northern Russia, the Varangians (who were the first to rule over the Slavic tribes), and the still unsullied life of the peasant. All this was seen as a single, autochthonous spiritual world detached from the Classical European tradition, but still encompassing the rituals of the Siberian and Altaic shamans and those of pagan Russia, subsequently reinterpreted in Christian Russia. The integrity of the popular conscious-

ness of pre-Petrine Russia and the authenticity of popular folklore, deriving from these sources, not only acted as a powerful source of inspiration, but also served ideologically to connect the Russian renaissance with its indigenous roots.

The *succès de scandale* caused by the first performance of *Le Sacre du Printemps* in Paris in 1913, described as "a rock full of holes from which unknown beasts emerge,"[2] was due not only to the bewilderment of the Parisian public, "brutally thrust into the presence of an especially unusual form of art"[3] (meaning the baffling barbarity of primitive sources), but also to the collisions between three different approaches to the primitive world within one and the same ballet. Roerich, for example, brought a passion for ethnographic sources which, however, he linked closely with scholarly research and appreciation. Comparatively indifferent to historical and scientific truth, Igor Stravinsky contributed and conveyed a vaguer, but more modern "inner resonance" of the primitive world,[4] while Vaslav Nijinsky offered the "ecstatic" and physiological identification of the artist with the "animal" reality of the primitive as his own reality.

A further clash is to be found between the actual sets and costumes which Roerich designed for *Le Sacre du Printemps*, in that while the former made obvious references to ancient pre-religious rituals rooted in archaeology, the latter were based on forms of Russian folk dress still extant in 1913. Roerich studied these costumes, particularly those in the collection of Princess Maria Tenisheva at her Museum of Russian Antiquities in Smolensk,[5] and discussed them with Stravinsky while both were hard at work on the libretto during their stay at Talashkino in the summer of 1911.[6] Evidence is provided by Roerich's use of peasant smocks and bast shoes (*lapti*), the embroidered motifs copied with meticulous precision in the draw-

Page from the journal *Comoedia illustré*, Paris, June 5, 1913, showing Roerich's second version for the Sacrifice of the Virgin in *Le Sacre du Printemps*

Right
Nicholas Roerich
• 1–2, 6. Vignettes for the journal *Vesy*, no. 8, Moscow, 1905, pp. 16, 4 , 5
• 3–4. Examples of shaman objects reproduced in Aleksandr Spitsyn, *Shamanskie izobrazheniia* (St. Petersburg: Skorokhodov, 1900), p. 67
• 5. Illustration from Ivan Tolstoi and Nikodim Kondakov, *Russkie drevnosti v pamiatnikakh iskusstva* (St. Petersburg, 1890), Vol. III, Table XXV

ings for the costumes and in the contrast of red and white so characteristic of the long pieces of embroidered cloth used to decorate household icons.

The decorative motifs of the garments were then radically stylized in the actual costumes, some of which contrast the gamut of bright reds and oranges with the green and blue backgrounds of the scenery for *Kissing the Earth*.[7] This sort of divergence between costume and décor confirms Roerich's intention to conflate and stratify sources, superimposing historical and prehistoric eras[8] so as to demonstrate a supra-historical spiritual continuity of the Slavic world. In his article entitled "Art and Archaeology," Roerich (who by 1918 had collected and catalogued no fewer than 3500 archaeological items) explained his attitude towards the relationship of the two entities, between spiritual and scientific truth: "Exact copies of archaeological objects are right for museums, but not for art [because a relationship of] this kind with the object also ruins it as a historical creation, turning it into something incredibly boring for the public."[9] Despite this, Roerich advocated a close connection between historical painting and archaeological research, as demonstrated by the sets he produced from 1909 to 1913, which, with a common denominator of ethnographic motifs, form a single group. At the same time, however, this ap-

parent integration is countered by the fact that the same motifs reappear in more or less camouflaged form in works with very different themes—from *Prince Igor*, *Snegourotchka*, and *Peer Gynt* to *Le Sacre du Printemps*.

Anticipating the "fashion"[10] for digging up artifacts from the ancient civilizations of the Russian Empire, Roerich began excavating (illegally) at an early age on his father's estate at Izvara in northern Russia with the help of his young servant, and produced his first two studies of *kurgan* burial mounds in 1893. Roerich's enthusiasm was such that the year before he had already been made an official member of the excavation team led by the celebrated archaeologist Lev Ivanovsky, an acquaintance of his father's, so as to work on ancient *kurgany* in the Volosovsk district. At age 19, he even began to undertake independent excavations for the Russian Archaeological Society.

During 1900–10 Roerich elaborated a number of key images based on his archaeological studies and offered them as reconstructions of age-old rituals still surviving throughout the Russian Empire, specifically those linked to the tradition of shamanism as filtered through the early religious practices of the pro-

Feliks Kon
Vintage photograph of a sacred shaman site in the basin of the River Enisei, North East Mongolia, showing the universal stone and the celestial tree, 1903
Ethnographic Museum, St. Petersburg (1134-1137)

Nicholas Roerich
Kissing the Earth, 1913
Tempera on paper on wood
53 × 82 cm
Astrakhan State Picture Gallery (AKG-Zh-319)
Note: The painting evokes the sacrificial scene in *Le Sacre du Printemps*

to-Slavic peoples. It was in ecstatic ritual and especially in the rites associated with hunting, an activity which he himself practiced,[11] that Roerich, unconsciously, searched for the *Pathosformeln*[12] of the Russian renaissance initiated by the World of Art. His desire was to present the power of images as the survival of memory.

The landscape of the six sets for *Le Sacre du Printemps* (the first three for *The Great Sacrifice* produced in 1910 and the second three for *Kissing the Earth* in 1912) features the elements of nature with which only chosen individuals such as wizards, shamans, seers or simply wise men can communicate; while the locus itself seems to be at a hiatus, in a state of expectation. Implicit in the various temperas and watercolors for *Kissing the Earth* is the special relationship of the shaman with the spirits of nature as manifested in the signs of the clouds or the waters, in the profiles of the hills and in the shapes of the trees and sacred stones. The menacing, personified cloud which occupies almost the entire scene in the first variant of *The Great Sacrifice* recalls the 1909 picture entitled *Battle in the Heavens*[13] and foreshadows the arrival of the one who—as in the painting—will interpret its omens. The intermediaries manifest themselves in the assembly of the shamans dressed in elk hides in the second variant of *The Great Sacrifice*, which was to have constituted the set for Act II of the Paris production, but was then deferred for financial reasons.[14]

Roerich reduced other natural elements in the set for Act I: the pine and, above all, the oak (the sacred tree par excellence) standing on the hill in the first and second variants of the set for *Kissing the Earth* (as symbolic representations of the celestial tree connecting the worlds above and below ground) were replaced with the great boulder in the third variant symbolizing the universal stone. Both tree and stone or stones, sometimes together, can be seen in photographs taken by travelers of the period.[15] In accordance with the animism characteristic of pre-religious forms of faith, shamanism holds that spirits "can be embodied on earth in natural objects or artifacts [...] but forests, rivers, mountains, lakes, and the earth also possess their own spirits in the form of spirit-lords."[16] Roerich associated these *Pathosformeln* not only with archaeology, but also with faith or rather religiosity in the primitive sense: "We do not know.

They know. The stones know. And even the trees know. And they remember. They remember who gave the mountains and rivers their names. [...] Knowing and remembering. Remembering and knowing. This means having faith."[17]

The scenic "territory" of *Le Sacre du Printemps* is strewn not only with the celestial and terrestrial "memory signs" of the shamanic cosmos—knolls with stones alluding to *kurgany*, magical stones, storm clouds for divination—but also with the "actual" presence of intermediaries between the different worlds: shamans (in the second and third variants of *The Great Sacrifice*) or sages and wizards, as he prefers to call them (cf. his 1905 painting entitled *Wizards*[18] where the personages are disguised in bear- and wolfskin, another significant animal in the shamanic world).[19]

Shamans, wizards, spells, and divinations are recurrent images in Roerich's paintings of those years, featuring characters in the costumes of the Siberian peoples, to which the artist paid tribute with an entire "Siberian" frieze at the "Contemporary Art" exhibition in St. Petersburg in 1903. Further confirmation of his interest in the costumes of these peoples is provided by the stylized graphic decorations which he used as tail-pieces for the magazine *Vesy* in 1905. In particular, those representing scenes of bear or reindeer hunts in a kind of circular embrace seem to be informed by the rich atlas of "shamanic images" compiled by the famous archaeologist Aleksandr Spitsyn, with whom the young Roerich had been in contact during his last years at high school in St. Petersburg. Spitsyn asserted that the artifacts found in the northwestern part of European Russia and in Siberia were clearly religious in character and were to be considered objects of shamanic worship, because shamanism was the religion of the peoples of those regions: "Shamanism still presents itself to us as a great riddle."[20] The stylized representation of the bird of prey with outspread wings instead recalls a typical accessory of the shamanic costume,[21] similar to those represented in Nikodim Kondakov's collection called *Russkie drevnosti* [Russian antiquities], which was well known to the World of Art artists and writers.[22]

Roerich's "Slavicization" of *Le Sacre du Printemps* corresponded to a tendency identifiable with many artists who supported both the World of Art aesthetic and the Neo-Russian style. Confirmation is provided by a statement made by Sergei Ernst, one of the most

Chuk (ritualistic object used by the Evenki for bear hunting) Reproduced from Georgii Vasilevich, "O kulte medvedia u Evenkov," in L. Potapov and S. Ivanov (eds.), *Religioznye predstavleniia i obriady narodov Sibirii v XIX – nachale XX veka* (Leningrad: Nauka, 1971), p. 166

penetrating critics of the Russian Silver Age: describing the Nationalist tendencies of the Neo-Russian style as "so artificial, devoid of living spirit, and even hostile to the authentic relics of past ages," Ernst claimed that the young artist "wanted to divine the traces of the unknowable and the mysterious in the chalice of Russian antiquities and endeavored to make the visions of the ancients to rise again from oblivion."[23]

In an attempt to grant these formula-images a national, historical location, Roerich immersed them in a proto-Slavic context. This is what justifies the fact that the third variant of *Kissing the Earth* was again presented in identical form as a set with the title *The Valley of Yarilo*[24] for the opera *Snegourotchka* staged at the Reineke Theater in St. Petersburg in 1912.

The libretto of *Le Sacre du Printemps* describes choreutic ceremonies which Roerich attributes to the early Slavs, but, in fact, they are the reincarnation of far more ancient rituals. In this connection, Roerich asserts that the ancient "sages" who witnessed the sacrifice of the Chosen One "throw bear skins round their shoulders and, in recognition of the fact that the bear is considered the ancestor of man, they deliver the victim to Yarilo, god of the sun."[25] A group of shamans in elk skins appear in Roerich's second variant of *The Great Sacrifice* of 1910, which also includes two hunters with bows and arrows (underscoring the connection with hunting rituals), while a sketch for costumes for the production of *Le Sacre du Printemps* at the New York Metropolitan Opera in 1930[26] shows three figures dancing in bear skins. Among the Siberian peoples, the killing of the bear was followed by long and complex celebratory rituals (which were well known at the beginning of the twentieth century having been de-

scribed by the traveler and ethnographer Konstantin Rychkov in 1906–08) and ended with the head of the slain bear being hoisted on to long pointed poles of young pine as a propitiatory rite. This practice was especially widespread among the Evenki peoples: the shaman would organize a gathering called a *kamlanie* in honor of the dead bear and would sometimes wear its skin.[27] A work entitled *Paganism* painted by Roerich in the 1910s or 1920s shows a shamanic *kamlanie* with bear skins around a wooden statue representing a goddess of fertility.[28] Roerich constructs his *Pathosformeln* syncretically by placing the unmistakable image of long poles topped with animal skulls and banners around the sacred stone of *Kissing the Earth*.

The sacred enclosure of the *kurgan* containing the idols, fenced off with stout poles and bearing animal skulls, appears in the painting *Idols* of 1901,[29] one of Roerich's first "historical fantasies" based on his archaeological excavations and concluding his countless variations on the theme of idols from the 1890s onwards. True, the same theme makes a phantasmal appearance in the sets for *The Polovtsian Dances* of 1909. But while the long poles in the different variants of the yurt encampment look like banners of the Tartar army, closer scrutiny reveals similarities with those adorned with fabric and used to mark places of sacrifice in the steppes of Central Asia, as seen in the drawings and photographs made by travelers at the turn of the century.[30] The object assumes a precise shape in the painting *Signs* (1913).[31]

It is, however, the libretto for *Le Sacre du Printemps* which focuses on the "initiatory" theme of the rebirth of life after death, a subject which Roerich identified and explored from the very outset of his archaeological excavations. It was while digging up the ancient soil of the *kurgany* and bringing artifacts to light that he made this intensely emotional observation: "The first ancient object extracted from the earth aroused an almost overwhelming sense of pleasure [...]. What mystery! What wonders! And boundless life in death itself!"[32]

[1] S. Diaghilev, "V chas itogov," in *Vesy*, no. 4, Moscow, 1905, pp. 45–46.

[2] J. Rivière, *La nouvelle Revue Française*, November 1913. Quoted in M. Kahane, *Les Ballets russes à l'Opéra. 1909–1929* (Paris: Hazan and Bibliothèque nationale de France, 1992), p. 83.

[3] L. Schneider, *Comoedia*, May 31. Quoted in ibid.

[4] For an analysis of Stravinsky's ethnographic musical sources see R. Taruskin, *Stravinsky and the Russian Tradition* (Berkeley and Los Angeles: University of California Press, 1996), especially the section "The Great Fusion: Le Sacre du Printemps" on pp. 849–966.

[5] An exhibition of the Smolensk collection was held in Paris in 1907. See [M. Tenichév], *Objets d'art Russes anciens faisant partie des collections de la Princesse Marie Tenichév exposés aux Museé des Arts Décoratifs du 10 mai au 10 octobre 1907* (Paris, 1907).

[6] E. Yakovleva, *Teatralno-dekoratsionnoe iskusstvo N. K. Rerikha* (Samara: AGNI, 1996), p. 52. Much of the information used in this essay is drawn from Yakovleva's book which is of fundamental importance to the study of Roerich as a set designer.

[7] These are the main colors of the third variant, which was used in the décor for the 1912 Paris performance. It is now in the Astrakhan State Picture Gallery. See Yakovleva 1996, pp. 55 and 133.

[8] A. Rostislavov, *N. Rerikh* (Petrograd: Butkovskaia, undated).

[9] N. Roerich, "Iskusstvo i arkheologiia," in *Iskusstvo i khudozhestvennaia promyshlennost*, no. 3, St. Petersburg, December 1898, pp. 185–94. This is the transcription of Roerich's inaugural lecture for a course on the "use of artistic technique in archaeology" held at the St. Petersburg Institute of Archaeology. The text is reprinted in *Nikolai Rerikh v russkoi periodike*, no. 1, St. Petersburg, 2004, pp. 75–84. This quotation is on p. 186.

[10] The fashion also involved avant-garde artists such as the Burliuk brothers who carried out excavations on the estate of Chernianka which their father managed. See G. Kraiski (ed.), *B. Livsič: L'arciere dall'occhio e mezzo* (Bari: Laterza, 1968).

[11] Or rather what Roerich called "historical" hunting, i.e. with bow and arrows. See A. Kornilova and A. Ekk, "N. K. Roerich v Izvare," in M. Kuzmina (ed.), *N. K. Roerich. Zhizn i tvorchestvo* (Moscow: Izobrazitelnoe iskusstvo, 1978), pp. 118–22. The relationship between hunting and the history of the natural sciences was a subject which Roerich addressed in his first publications in the magazines *Priroda i okhota* and *Russkiy okhotnik*. See V. Kniazeva, *Nikolai Rerikh. Letopis zhizni i tvorchestva* (St. Petersburg: SOTIS, 1994).

[12] From the definition which Aby Warburg gave to the image of the nymph in Italian Renaissance painting. See P.-A. Michaud, *Aby Warburg et l'image en mouvement* (Paris: Macula, 1998).

[13] The painting *Battle in the Heavens* (1912) is in the collection of the State Russian Museum, St. Petersburg.

[14] This sketch was reproduced as the set for Act II in M. Casalonga, "Nijinsky et Le Sacre du Printemps," in *Comoedia illustré*, Paris, June 5, 1913.

[15] See for example the photograph of 1903 from the collection of the ethnographer Feliks Kon (now in the Russian Museum of Ethnography, St. Petersburg) published in V. Gorbacheva (ed.), *Na grani mirov. Iz sobraniia Rossiiskogo Etnograficheskogo muzeia, Sankt Peterburg* (Moscow: Khudozhnik i kniga, 2006), p. 42.

[16] U. Marazzi (ed.), *Testi dello sciamanesimo* (Turin: SEI, 1984), p. 19.

[17] N. Rerich, "Sviashchennye znamena" [1915], in V. Sidorov (ed.), *Nikolai Rerikh. Pismena, Stikhi* (Moscow: Sovremennik, 1977), p. 25.

[18] See the reproduction in Yakovleva 1996, p. 11.

[19] A youthful Roerich can be recognized in a 1912 photograph showing the hunting trophy of a wolf skin in the background. See D. Popov (ed.), *Derzhava Rerikha* (Moscow: Izobrazitelnoe iskusstvo, 1994). The photograph is between pp. 48–49.

[20] A. Spitsyn, *Shamanskie izobrazheniia* (St. Petersburg: Tipografiia Skorokhodova, 1900), p. 1.

[21] See the tailpieces on pp. 4 and 17 of *Vesy*, no. 8, 1905.

[22] See the bronze artifacts from the Urals illustrated in I. Tolstoi and N. Kondakov, *Russkie drevnosti v pamiatnikakh iskusstva* (St. Petersburg: Benke, 1890), Vol. III, pl. XXV.

[23] S. Ernst, *N. K. Rerich* (Petrograd: Izdanie Obshchestva Sv. Evgenii, 1918), p. 43.

[24] Location unknown, formerly in the collection of Princess Maria Tenisheva. The work is reproduced as no. 145 in Yakovleva 1996, p. 142.

[25] Letter from Nicholas Roerich to Sergei Diaghilev, early 1913. Quoted in I. Zilbershtein and V. Samkov (eds.), *Sergei Diaghilev i russkoe iskusstvo. Stati, otkrytye pisma, interviu. Perepiska. Sovremenniki o Diagileve* (Moscow: Izobrazitelnoe iskusstvo, 1982), Vol. 2, p. 120.

[26] Now in the Roerich Museum, New York. Reproduced as no. 421 in Yakovleva 1996, p. 245.

[27] The shamans (dressed in reindeer skins) of the Amur and the Transbaikal, in particular, used this type of *kamlanie*, which was connected with the ancient mysteries of the hunt. See G. Vasilevich, "O kulte medvedia u Evenkov," in G. Vasilevich et al., *Religioznye predstavleniia i obriady narodov Sibiri v XIX – nachale XX veka* (Leningrad: Nauka, 1971), pp. 150–69.

[28] See illustration no. 12, on p. 180 in E. Matochkin and V. Melnikov, "Idoly v proizvedeniiakh N. K.Rerikha," in N. Spirina and V. Lantsev (eds.), *Rerikhovskie chteniia* (Novosibirsk: Sibirskoe Rerichovskoe obshchestvo, 2000), pp. 165–84.

[29] On the subject of "idols" in Roerich's work and their variants and provenances see Matochkin and Melnikov 2000.

[30] For example, in the variants to be found in the State Russian Museum, St. Petersburg, and in the Glinka Museum of Music, Moscow, both of which are reproduced as nos. 23 and 25 in Yakovleva 1996, pp. 115 and 116.

[31] *Signs*, 1913 (formerly in the collection of Elena Roerich). See Ernst 1918, p. 124.

[32] N. Rerikh, "Na kurgane. V Vodskoi piatine (Spb. gub.)," in N. Rerikh, *Sobranie sochinenii* (Moscow: Sytin, 1914), Vol. 1, p. 14.

The Ballets Russes: Mikhail Larionov and Natalia Goncharova

Evgenia Iliukhina

Eli Eganbiuri (pseudonym of the poet Ilia Zdanevich) once wrote, "One event which has really astounded the public in Paris and London these past years has been, without doubt, the Ballets Russes … The [company] owes its success and glory not only to the fact that it was the first to demonstrate the high caliber of the Russian ballet school in Europe … [But] the Ballets Russes was also the first to bring new painting to the stage and to create a new stage design. The Russian painters Goncharova and Larionov, pioneers of the cause, who made their debut at the Paris Opéra in 1914, have gone on to apply the latest innovations in painting to the theater and have won the battle hands down."[1]

Indeed, the resounding triumph of the dance cantata *Le Coq d'Or* with sets by Natalia Goncharova served as a watershed between the two historical stages of the Diaghilev company. For Diaghilev, *Le Coq d'Or* testified to the validity of the new course of action and prompted an inevitable estrangement from Alexandre Benois and Léon Bakst, friends of younger years. However, in 1913 the Ballets Russes had reached a moment of crisis, for Vaslav Nijinsky had left the company after the public failure of his *Sacre du Printemps*, and, although to some extent, Michel Fokine's kind of choreography was, for Diaghilev, also passé, the impresario had no choice but to woo him back. Diaghilev, then, was ready, willing, and able to accept bright new artistic ideas—which he found in an exhibition of Goncharova's work in Moscow in 1913.[2] He noted Goncharova's interpretations of the *lubok* (a traditional, handcolored print) and recommended that Fokine pay special attention to them.

Two distinct hands or artistic styles can be identified with the corpus of designs for *Le Coq d'Or* now in the State Tretyakov Gallery in Moscow. Rejecting Benois's call to follow the canons of the *lubok* as practised under Peter the Great,[3] Goncharova turned for in-

spiration to a more familiar source—her own paintings. Executed with powerful, broad strokes, in bright colors, and with no particular regard for the rules of stage design, Goncharova's sets for *Le Coq d'Or* do, indeed, appear to have evolved from the imagery of her painting: the sunflowers and apple-trees of her still-lives turn into the fantastic blooming trees of Dodon's Tsardom, her floral ornaments now grace the theatrical wings, while the figures in the costume designs are reminiscent of characters from her cycle of peasant paintings. Paper cutouts pasted on to a new sheet of cardboard, these personages seem literally to have been "extracted" from the studio canvas so as to act out their role—only to return to the more familiar milieu of their landscapes and other compositions. Dodon's warrior sons, therefore, remind us of the painting *Archangel Gabriel* (1909–10, State Tretyakov Gallery, hereafter STG), while the Astrologer paraphrases the *Prophet* (1911, STG).

However, Goncharova was still faced with the problem of the characters of the Tsardom of Queen Shemakhan, for here was a world of fanciful, magical images lacking precedent in the studio paintings—which is where Larionov came in, as one may judge from preliminary drawings also in the Tretyakov. His were the Shaitans, the housekeepers, the female serfs, and dancers who hopped on by, barely touching the sheet of paper as they left their picturesque footprints of vermilion. Larionov's costumes spelled motion—dance was already on his mind. But it was difficult for Goncharova to use Larionov's ideas, because her almost maniacal honesty would not let her call them her own and, ultimately, she invented her own versions of "Eastern costumes"—which, unwittingly, echoed the East of the World of Art painters, especially, Bakst and Ivan Bilibin.

The sets and most of the costumes for *Le Coq d'Or* were produced at the workshops of the Bolshoi

Mikhail Larionov
Portrait of Natalia Goncharova
1915
Gouache, tempera and collage
on board, 99 × 85 cm
STG (ArchGr-2451)

Theater. The large-scale format, of which Goncharova the studio painter had long dreamed, became a reality. In his review of Goncharova's 1913 exhibition, Benois made a very telling remark: "Wherein lie the reasons why Goncharova's remarkable decorative gift of style has remained hitherto unemployed? … Where are the theaters which should be commissioning her to paint their temples?"[4] The Paris Opéra became just such a theater and it was here that Goncharova enjoyed a supreme triumph which changed her from being an "obscure lady artist from Moscow to a famous theatrical painter."[5] This first professional theatrical experience defined the fate of both Goncharova and Larionov. Inspired, Diaghilev decided to renew the collaboration and invited them (Goncharova refused to be parted from Larionov) to Switzerland so as to design scenes for *Liturgy*. It was as if Diaghilev still desired to "adapt" Goncharova's studio paintings to the theater and, in some sense, *Liturgy* was very reminiscent of her designs for the ecclesiastical compositions shown at the 1913 exhibition.

The libretto of the new ballet *Liturgy* was based on scenes from the life of Christ. For a visual source, Goncharova turned to the Russian iconostasis, although her goal was not to stylize, but rather to render specific features and peculiarities of Mediaeval art—something of its highly conventional iconography, its canonicity, and monumentality. She explored new materials and turned costumes into rigid structures with slits for arm and leg positions, restricting the movements deliberately and making the actors look like puppets.

However, it was soon apparent that to produce such a ballet would be very difficult and Diaghilev tasked Goncharova to make set and costume sketches for a new ballet, *Les Noces*. Goncharova spent almost seven years working on this project before the premiere finally took place June 13, 1923. Actually, Stravinsky had begun to compose his music for this ballet—depicting a village wedding—as early as 1914, when, as Goncharova recalled, right after the premiere of *Le Coq d'Or*, he suggested she should design sets and costumes "in the manner of *Le Coq d'Or*"[6] for his new ballet. Upon Diaghilev's request, Stravinsky made several visits to Ouchy so as to acquaint his colleagues with the completed parts of *Les Noces*, Larionov and Goncharova also being present at those auditions. Remembering Stravinsky's offer, Goncharova made sketches reminiscent of those for *Le Coq d'Or*; only the locus

Mikhail Larionov
The Shaitan and the Servant
of Shemakhan in *Le Coq d'Or*
1914
Gouache and graphite pencil
on paper, 48.5 × 31.8 cm
STG (R-4505)

changed—an *izba* (hut) replaced the tsar's palace and a table appeared, the essential attribute of any wedding. The costumes, too, were somewhat different, because Goncharova wanted to "create a theatrical version of a peasant Sunday dress,"[7] and although that first version was still too close to *Le Coq d'Or*, the "similarity of theme—a peasant holiday—led me astray."[8] So it is not surprising that these designs, many of which found their way into different museums and private collections, have been misidentified as sketches for *Le Coq d'Or*, even though, upon closer scrutiny, one can see that the designs for *Les Noces* and *Le Coq d'Or* do differ. Goncharova's initial experience of theater had not been in vain for now the set designs clearly reflected the structure of theatrical space, while the costume designs acquired a distinctly frontal quality with pronounced detail and ornamental flourish.

Les Noces was *Liturgy* revisited. Not all the music had been composed yet (the short version of the score would be completed only in 1917), the libretto was missing, and Goncharova had yet to design the recital based on the musical fragments and on her own perception of what village weddings looked like. Her al-

Natalia Goncharova
Costume design for one
of the Wise Men in the ballet
Liturgy, 1915
Gouache, collage and graphite
pencil on board, 60 × 47.5 cm
STG (R-4474)

bums of that time, full of pencil outlines of sets and costumes, allow us to pursue her avenue of enquiry and trace the sources upon which she was drawing. Reminiscing upon *Les Noces*, she described her train of thought: one day, she pondered, a wedding might evoke the seasons or the states of nature, on another occasion—social issues. Having no text while working on *Les Noces*, Goncharova used the same reference material Stravinsky was working with, the collection of ritual songs assembled by Petr Kireevsky,[9] images of which she presented in her curtain and set designs. In fact, all the ornamental details which seem to be mere decorations are semantically justified: the horse-drawn carriage is the groom's wedding cortège on its way to fetch the bride; the pigeons under the roof are symbolic of the "bride, a pure dove."

But in appealing to folkloric sources, Goncharova treated them not as a departure-point for mere stylization but, in one sense, elaborated the initial sacral meaning of those pagan ornaments. Thus, the curtain featuring images of deer and weaving women is an allusion to a pagan deer goddess—the patroness of families, in deference to whom married women wore a *kika* or "horned" headdress. Bronislava Nijinska disapproved of that particular folk design, because she

thought it impossible to dance in such cumbersome, albeit beautiful, outfits. Goncharova had a long way to go and many choices to test, and she found the ultimate, radically different solution only in 1923, shortly before the premiere. By then, a new era had dawned—of Constructivist sets and of simple costumes suitable to the theme of labor and the factory floor.

Paradoxically, the idea of a Russian festival found resonance in Diaghilev's endeavors to produce "Spanish ballets" during his sojourn in San Sebastián in 1916. Deeply impressed with Spanish dances, he came up with the idea of a soirée which would combine Spanish and Russian folk motifs. At some point, the concept even embraced a double show contrasting and comparing Spanish and Russian fairs. Goncharova, hard at work on *Les Noces*, tried to assess and understand what a village feast denoted in Spain and in Russia. Similarly, as Eganbiuri wrote, Goncharova's ballets *Espagne* and *Triana* "revealed two Spains ... the extremist *Espagne*, ultimately contorted in the artistic pathos of Rayism and Cubism, and the flexible, worldly, and broadly comprehensible *Triana*—which did not exist, but might very well have."[10] Spanish dances were the main theme of these plot-less ballets and therein Goncharova recognized the ideal solution to her own vision of ballet theater. Based upon numerous sketches of street dancers drawn from life, she designed costumes reminiscent of her work on *Liturgy* on the one hand, and full of the somber plasticity, formal severity, and clarity of the flamenco, on the other.

If Goncharova was disturbed, even irritated, by the need to be working on several projects at the same time, Larionov just loved the fast pace in Ouchy. Later on, in his characteristically telegraphic style, he recalled: "Immediately Diaghilev asked that Larionov grapple with a ballet to Rimsky-Korsakov's music from *Snegourotchka* ... A month later, Larionov had designed the sets and costumes and even invented a name for the new ballet—*Night Sun*."[11] The emphasis shifted from the lyrical story to the pagan ritual, i.e. to the holiday celebrating the end of winter and welcoming Yarilo the Sun. Larionov based his design concept on the disc of the sun, decorating the costumes with solar motifs and creating headwear in the form of round discs, and the main hero, played by Léonide Massine, even wore "suns" on his sleeves. Larionov also placed images of red solar discs along the borders of the ceiling which, in accordance with his con-

Mikhail Larionov
Curtain design for *Chout*, 1915
STG (The Department
of Manuscripts)

Natalia Goncharova
Curtain design (not realized)
for *Les Noces*, 1915–16
Graphite pencil on paper
26.1 × 34.1 cm
STG (P 71342)

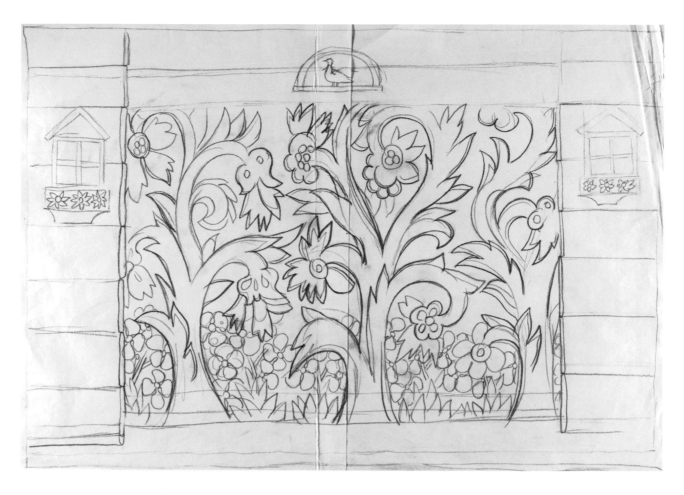

cept, were to rotate rapidly. He depicted all the figures in motion, as if to dictate the plasticity of the dance.

Even at that early stage, Larionov was infatuated with the subject of choreography. Of course, he realized that his spectacular, but cumbersome, costumes would hinder the dance movements which he was devising and, consequently, adjusted them to his choreography. Later on, Larionov elaborated his own artistic credo, defining the stage designer as a "painter who designs the costume and the background commensurate with motion and ties the motion to the costume and the costume to the background."[12]

What was now called *Soleil de Nuit* had its premiere in Geneva on December 20, 1915, and was an instant success. By then, however, Larionov had already moved on to his next project—the designs for Sergei Prokofiev's ballet *Chout*, which, in some sense, became the embodiment of the artist's theatrical and choreographic vision. The very idea of a buffoonery, of a merry, spectacular farce, derived from Larionov's Russian period, especially from the first exhibition of the Jack of Diamonds in 1910,[13] when the image of the playing card had been used as a symbol of swindler and thief. Reviewing *Chout*, one Parisian critic who was

unlikely to have known anything about Larionov's Russian exhibitions, compared the action on stage to the blurred shuffling of cards in the hands of a skilled cheater.[14] In any case, the buffoonery fooled around with the viewer, narrating not only the story of the Buffoon, but also the history of the making of *Chout* itself. Costumes were changed and substituted, the actors moved, built, and altered the sets, and everything morphed into the dance structure of the spectacle. Larionov took theatrical convention to the extreme, making no effort to conceal this from the audience. There was no illusion.

The work on *Chout* falls into two stages. Larionov had his designs ready six years before the opening night, so all he had to do in 1921 was to manufacture them. Goncharova, who stayed behind in Paris, supervised the procedure and from time to time would receive instructions from Larionov to "put finishing touches as she saw fit." At that time, Larionov, now in Monte Carlo, had lost all interest in set design and, very much in isolation, was fervently engaged with his new hobby—composing choreography. Serge Grigoriev recalled: "Finding no-one to direct the production [of *Chout*], Diaghilev … decided upon the young

Mikhail Larionov
*Sergei Diaghilev and Léonide
Massine at Table*, 1930–40s
Indian ink and pen on
watermarked cream paper
23.2 × 36.9 cm
STG (R-4677)

dancer Slavinsky. I pointed out that Slavinsky had
neither directing experience, nor training in choreography and would thus find it difficult to interpret
Prokofiev's music. To that, Diaghilev replied: 'You
know, Larionov, whom I have made Massine's mentor,
dreams of directing his own new ballet. But he is a
painter, he will not be able to go it alone. He needs a
dancer who could demonstrate the others the *pas* and
scenes which he has composed. Thus, I have decided
to put them together. Let them work in unison. I don't
know what will come of it. But since Prokofiev has
composed his music to the plot of an old fairy tale and
the ballet has to have a modernized folkloric sense
(and Larionov is an undisputed expert here), I think
that this will solve the problem. In any case'—he
chuckled— 'It would be an interesting experiment.'"[15]

In the end, Larionov had to compose practical-
ly all the choreography himself. He based his dance
routines on folkloric movements which he researched,
gradually accumulating visual references, such as the
drawn copies of bas-reliefs and miniatures depicting
buffoons dancing and photographs of peasant ritual
dances. Those were augmented with so-called "func-
tional movements—marches, swaying, sitting."[16] En-
deavoring to record his findings, Larionov devised his
own notation system using conventional, "fleshless"

dancing figures and special diagrams which illustrated the movements of the corps de ballet. These figures
would become independent characters in his studio
paintings, while ballet classes and rehearsal halls would
become a main topic in his pictorial repertoire.

The work on *Chout* lasted several years, and in
the interval between its initial design and actual production, Larionov had time to contemplate the sets and
costumes for yet another ballet, i.e. the *Contes Russes*
which continued the choreographic representation of
Russian folk themes. Exploring and interpreting the
Russian tales, Larionov moved back from their literary
transposition to the original sources in epics and legends.
The actual production, therefore, consisting of separate
ballet miniatures, was a veritable encyclopedia of pre-
Christian Slavic culture, showcasing the entire pantheon of pagan spirits: Leshii the wood goblin, Kikimora the female hobgoblin, Devils, the Bird-Maiden, the
evil witch Baba-Yaga, the Mermaid, etc., as well as a
broad range of Russian folkloric genres: the exordium,
the fairy-tale, the prelude, and the epic.

In *Contes Russes* motion plays the defining role.
In addition to the visual effect of the moving lines—
criss-crossing logs and diagonal trees—Larionov fills
the set with shifting components: the swinging cradle
of Kikimora; the fantastic flower bells in the bewitched

forest of Baba-Yaga, and her dancing hut performed by live actors; even the set comes alive, one piece breaking off to be danced by a dancer in the costume of the Goblin. This time Larionov remembered to "liberate" the dancers' bodies and most of the corps de ballet, performing circular chain dances and round dances, wore simple costumes, similar to their rehearsal clothes. Wherever the costumes contained a constructive element, they defined the entire dance. Such were Baba-Yaga's bony leg, the Goblin's heavy "platform-shoes," and the Tsarevna's dress with its skirt huge enough to hide her friends. However, the trade secret of the performance was the application of "Rayonist" makeup, because, years before, Larionov and his friends had walked around Moscow, their faces painted to shock the public.[17] Now he perfected his "face-painting," the make-up became a physiognomic mask, rendering the face absolutely unrecognizable and changing its form. Thus, the theatrical image triumphed over the actor's personality.

Larionov's vision of ballet and the roles of costume, set, and performer evolved rapidly during his work on *A Tale about a Fox* (1922) and its subsequent version *The Fox*, i.e. *Le Renard*, of 1929. The first scheme of the plot may be traced back to 1915–16 when Stravinsky started to compose the music. Draft sketches of the costume for the Cock, although offering a witty variation on knightly weaponry, were rather cumbersome and Larionov rejected them. But almost at the same time, he investigated a different, folkloric approach: the Cock now donned a peasant shirt, the Ram—a *kosovorotka* (a blouse with the collar but-

toned to the side). The costume for the Fox (a male role in both versions) was the most interesting: it had a hand-mounted muzzle mask and an accessory tail which the actor held in the other hand. Gradually, Larionov's style was gravitating towards minimalism, because in the 1922 production he had already discarded bright color, and now the sets and costumes had become almost totally monochrome. Only on Diaghilev's insistence did Larionov refrain from substituting the pictorial, hand-painted background with the black-and-white photograph of a winter forest.

For Larionov the 1922 production of *Le Renard* was a moment of compromise, which he overcame while working with Lifar on the second version for the 1929 season (the third and last time that Larionov served as ballet-master). Introducing stunt acrobats and other elements of the circus into the choreography and design (a platform with a rope and a trapeze intended for aerial gymnasts and tightrope walkers) allowed for a maximum of action: Larionov the choreographer triumphed over Larionov the painter. He discarded everything that stood in the way of dynamic action—including libretto, colored sets, and "expressive" costumes, and, in the final version, simply wrote the names of the characters on the actors' leotards. he preferred the "pure action" of the circus where the self-conscious actor-cum-dancer was replaced by the acrobat with his non-intellectual "animal" plasticity. But, alas, *Le Renard* premiered the year Diaghilev died. The demise of the celebrated impresario was not just a personal loss for Goncharova and Larionov, but it also halted their bold theatrical experiments.

[1] E. Eganbiuri, "Kubizm v teatre," undated typsescript in the Department of Manuscripts, STG. Call no. f. 180 (M. Larionov and N. Goncharova Fund).

[2] See the catalog of the "Exhibition of Paintings by Natalia Sergeevna Goncharova," Moscow, 1913. The exhibition opened in the Mikhailova Salon.

[3] Describing the production of *Le Coq d'Or* later on, Benois asserted that the idea of an opera-ballet "in the style of a Petrine *lubok*" had been his and that he had asked Diaghilev to invite Goncharova as designer. For her part, Goncharova denied that Benois had participated in the project as a consultant. She wrote to Benois: "In a conversation with me about *Le Coq d'Or*, S. P. Diaghilev told me that he wished to see the production in the spirit of popular pictures from the time of Peter the Great. But I rejected this particular proposal. I agreed to accept the commission only on the absolute condition that there be no meddling in my plan or in the character that I wanted to im-

part to this. Diaghilev signed a contract with me on these conditions." Draft of a letter from Goncharova to Benois in response to his article "Vospominaniia o balete," in *Russikie zapiski*, Paris, June 1934. Department of Manuscripts, STG. Call no. f. 180.

[4] A. Benois: "Iz dnevnika khudozhnika," in *Rech*, no. 21, St. Petersburg, October 21, 1913, p. 4.

[5] Department f Manuscripts, STG. Call no. f. 180.

[6] Ibid.

[7] Ibid.

[8] Ibid.

[9] See M. Speransky (ed.), *Pesni sobrannye P .V. Kireevskim* (Moscow: Society of Lovers of Russian Literature at Moscow University, 1911).

[10] Eganbiuri, "Kubizm v teatre."

[11] Department of Manuscripts, STG. Call no. f. 180.

[12] Ibid.

[13] The Jack of Diamonds society was founded by Larionov in Moscow in 1910. After the first

exhibition of December 1910 –January 1911, it organized other shows, although as early as the fall of 1911 the group split and Larionov left.

[14] Léandre Vaillat wrote: "As for the design, the curtain, décors and costumes impart the feeling of a game of cards, of a fan of cards furled and unfurled at a single snap in the hands of a professional card sharper: [there is] the impression of vitality, of diced and fragmented figures, red and green, yellow and blue, and of a desired naïveté. They are laughed at, applauded, and booed." Department of Manuscripts, STG. Call no. F. 180.

[15] S. Grigoriev in N. Gontcharova and T. Loguine, *Gontcharova et Larionov. Cinquante ans à Saint-Germain-des-Prés* (Paris: Klincksieck, 1971), pp. 110–11.

[16] Larionov describes his choreography for the ballet precisely in these terms. Department of Manuscripts, SGT. Call no. f. 180.

[17] Larionov's face-painting escapades occurred in 1913.

Sergei Diaghilev and the Russian Avant-Garde

Jean-Claude Marcadé

"Astonish me!" Was Igor Markevitch, Diaghilev's last love and discovery, right to interpret the impresario's celebrated challenge to Jean Cocteau as the "whim of someone jaded, a parvenu of the language of art"[1] or, as is more probable, does it not show an essential characteristic of the genius for discovery peculiar to the organizer of pioneering events, exhibitions, and concerts which marked the twentieth century as a whole? Diaghilev was a sounding board for the radical aesthetic explorations of his time and quite naturally called upon the most original European painters, thus making his productions the place for experimentation with all the "isms" of art. Fired from the very outset of the century with the ambition to bring about the artistic revival of his country, Russia, known throughout the entire world, Diaghilev certainly did not fail to draw upon illustrious representatives of Russian and Soviet "left-wing art," what has come to be called the "Russian avant-garde." Europeans and Americans were thus offered the opportunity to acquaint themselves with Primitivism, Fauvism, Cubo-Futurism, Rayism, Orphism and various forms of Constructivism.

The sets and costumes of Natalia Goncharova for the production of Nikolai Rimsky-Korsakov's opera and ballet *Le Coq d'Or* staged in Paris in May 1914 mark a radical break with the previous Art Nouveau and Symbolism-dominated aesthetic of the Ballets Russes. Goncharova introduced the glowing color of Russian Primitivism steeped in the art of folk prints (*lubki*) and icons and ornament appropriate to the environment of a predominantly peasant and archaic civilization, especially its brightly adorned fabrics. The most innovative Cubo-Futurist and Rayist principles recently displayed by the artist and her companion Mikhail Larionov in Moscow, St. Petersburg, and Paris were grafted onto this basic structure. Reds and golds glitter in a festive explosion previously unknown to the pictorial palette. As Marina Tsvetaeva wrote: "The time and place are right

to speak about Goncharova's role in ferrying painting that is not only Old Russian, but also Chinese, Mongolian, Tibetan, and Indian from the East to the West. And not only painting. Our era readily accepts what is most ancient and remote from the hands of a contemporary capable of renewing and bringing it closer."[2] *Le Coq d'Or* inaugurated the close involvement of Goncharova and Larionov with the Ballets Russes, which continued until Diaghilev's death in August 1929.

Goncharova produced a series of gouaches on essentially religious subjects reflecting the pure, stylized, Byzantine tradition for *Liturgy*, a ballet set to plainsong, which was rehearsed in 1915, but not staged.

Larionov conceived "moving sets and mechanical costumes based on evidently Futurist artistic formulas"[3] in 1916 for a ballet based on Maurice Ravel's *Histoires naturelles*, which was again never staged.

The Russian dances and scenes of the ballet *Le Soleil de Minuit* in 1915 enabled Larionov to triumph with the Neo-Primitivism which he had been pursuing since 1908 to disrupt the age-old foundations of academic art on Russian soil. Larionov created multicolored costumes (with dominant notes of yellow, red, and violet) for this "festival of the sun" and fantastic flowers to adorn the heads of the characters. As Waldemar George wrote, "verisimilitude is sacrificed to rhythm. The gestures are convulsive and the tonalities contrast. Huge suns are painted on the dancers' multi-colored blouses. All the ratios of scale are altered."[4]

It was again Old Russia which appeared in *Contes Russes*, with its synthesis of archaism and modernity and alternation of burlesque and magic, in 1917. The southerner Larionov gave free rein to his humor here in creating half-human and half-animal beings based on characters from Russian folklore (the wicked Kikimora, the valiant Bova-Korolevich and the sorceress Baba-Yaga) and Ukrainian tradition (the Christ-

Natalia Goncharova
Decorative Composition
late 1910s
Gouache and pencil on paper
49.2 × 30.8 cm
STG (R-4532)

mas game *koliada*). For the sets, the artist "painted aquatic plants, scarlet flowers drenched in mist and an *izba* bathed in the dim green light of the forest, where the terrifying stories took place."[5]

Diaghilev continued his plunge into the colorful glitter of the Slavic world by commissioning Sonia Delaunay in 1918 to design costumes for the ballet *Cléopâtre*, staged in 1909 with sets and costumes by Léon Bakst which were then lost in a fire in 1917. The sets were by Robert Delaunay. It was thus that Orphism materialized on the stage. It was also Sonia Delaunay's colored Ukrainian prism which found sparkling expression there with the interplay of solar circles and stripes. The artist tells how she saw the character Cleopatra "appear as a mummy gradually unwrapped of its bandages, each completely different from the others ... When they had all been stripped off, the spotlights illuminated the queen in a solar costume with discs covering her breasts and concentric circles of all colors studded with pearls radiating sumptuously around the navel of the world. These discs adorn a sarcophagus in the Louvre."[6]

In 1921, *Chout*, a Russian legend to music by Sergei Prokofiev with choreography, sets, and costumes by Larionov, was a failure. The set placed the window looking north, the door leading south, and the walls to the east and west all simultaneously on the same plane. The costumes were made of paper, waxed canvas, and cardboard. It was the triumph of Russian Cubo-Futurism on a basically Neo-Primitivist structure. Waldemar George, who saw this production, described it as follows: "*Chout* is a spectacle of astounding verve combining the spirit of innocence with the spirit of derision. Hypotheses of the mathematician, the sensitive geometrician and the juggler are juxtaposed there with the wild flights of a delirious poetic imagination."[7]

It was another representative of the Russian avant-garde, namely Léopold Survage (or Stürzwage) whom Diaghilev called upon for the sets and costumes of Igor Stravinsky's opera-bouffe *Mavra* in 1922. One of the pioneers of abstract art in Paris with his *Rythmes colorés* in 1913, the painter had then invented an original form derived from Cubism which he described as follows: "Various simple geometric forms inscribed within one another and linked by a common center constitute a centralized, organic whole for the eye capable of suggesting depth without digging into the flat surface addressed, without imitating the foreshortening of objects by means of ordinary perspective."[8]

Scene from *Parade*, 1917
Reproduced from B. Kochno, *Diaghilev and the Ballets Russes* (New York: Harper and Row, 1970), p. 125

In 1922 Larionov and Goncharova began stripping away their settings of Eastern glitter tinged with their Rayonist and Primitivist Cubo-Futurism. The emergence of a certain element of "Constructivism" can be detected in Larionov's sets and costumes for the ballet-bouffe *Le Renard* (actually a vixen rather than a male fox). Like Georgii Yakulov, Larionov could of course say that sets "constructed" on private Russian stages had existed since about 1910. Moreover, before the theatrical Constructivism systematized by Liubov Popova and Varvara Stepanova in 1922 at the Meyerkhold Theater, there had been sets built by Alexandra Exter, Yakulov and Aleksandr Vesnin at Tairov's Chamber Theater since 1916. In any case, there were two versions of *Le Renard*, in 1922 and 1929. While the first was more traditional, done in the style of the Ukrainian *vertep*, the second marked a step toward very summary differentiation of characters (names embroidered on their shirts) as in the Mediaeval or Elizabethan theater. Dancers and gymnasts move in the middle of trapezes, trestles and tilted planes. This is how Larionov described it:

The perch on which the rooster was perched in 1922 expanded in 1929 to become a platform supported by a post and anchored to the ground by four steel cables.

Mikhail Larionov
Soldier Smoking, 1910–11
Oil on canvas, 100 × 72.7 cm
STG (Zh-1546)

Mikhail Larionov
Self-Portrait, late 1910s
or early 1920s
Graphite pencil on paper
42.2 × 26.2 cm
STG (R-4678)

The four dancer-characters and the three acrobat-characters standing in for them in the same costumes took their places alternately on this platform, resembling those used by acrobats in the circus, which was connected to the stage by a ladder. The acrobats used ropes of hemp hanging from the flies to launch themselves onto the platform from the wings with *pas-de-géant* or ascend to the flies.[9]

According to Boris Kochno, Diaghilev asked Goncharova to base the cut of the costumes for Stravinsky's ballet *Les Noces* ("choreographic movements in four tableaux") of 1923 on the regulation working clothes worn by the dancers of the troupe at rehearsals. There is an echo here of the *prozodezhda*, the production outfit introduced by Popova and Stepanova at the Meyerkhold Theater in 1922 to eliminate local color. Goncharova was to give these a Russian accent, however, by lengthening the female dancers' tunics to form sarafans and using a Russian collar for the men's shirts. H. G. Wells described this ballet, which did not show peasants dressed up as peasants but simply clad in black and white, as a visual and auditory transcription of the Russian soul. Paul Dukas noted in a very fine article that the work "shatters all frameworks, wrongfoots all classifications and places itself deliberately from the very outset at a distance from all the known kinds of ballet … . In what Russian village has such a wedding ever been seen? Are we even still in Russia, in the Russia of prehistory, or in a still more distant world beyond earthly times and realities, in this obscure limbo where human specters symbolically celebrate their bleak nuptials?"[10]

From now on, the Ballets Russes were to present settings involving variations on Constructivist themes, from the "constructive realism" and kinetics of Naum Gabo and Antoine Pevsner to the romantic Constructivism of Yakulov and the Surrealist Constructivism of Pavel Tchelitchew.

In 1926, when they addressed the staging of Henry Sauguet's ballet *La Chatte*, Gabo and Pevsner were already established sculptors. The use of celluloid circles and rectangles created a completely unprecedented transparent texture. These shapes were brought onto the stage and set in motion by the dancers in step with the development of the action. This kinetic approach had already been adopted by Popova in Moscow for *The*

Magnanimous Cuckold. The stage and the curtain were covered in black waxed canvas. As Kochno recalls,

> The sets for *La Chatte* were not easy to build. Gabo and Pevsner had to execute the metal parts of this entirely constructed décor themselves, and their appearance in the peaceful Monegasque hotels and boarding houses where they stayed to work caused general panic and led the normal clientele to take flight. On seeing them walking through the corridors with blow-torches in strange protective masks that made them look like deep-sea divers and hearing the infernal noises reverberating in their rooms, hotel managers lost no time in kicking them out.[11]

Diaghilev did not limit himself to this foray into a purely artistic form of Constructivism and invited the Armenian painter Yakulov to make the sets and costumes for Prokofiev's ballet *Le Pas d'Acier*. This "industrial ballet" definitively took the place of the "dying swans" and was to encapsulate the conquests of Soviet Constructivism in the eyes of Europe. Yakulov's setting took into account his own work for Tairov (*Giroflé-Girofla*, 1922),

but also Popova's mechanical sets for *The Magnanimous Cuckold* and *Earth on End* at the Meyerkhold Theater (1922–23). Yakulov thus presented ladders, platforms, spinning wheels, transmission systems, hammers of all sizes whose noise blended in with the orchestra and light signals that swayed and flickered and burst into flame and color. Traces of the scenographic developments of *Le Pas d'Acier* can be detected in various later productions including Charlie Chaplin's *Modern Times* (1936) as well as ballets like *Nucléa* (sets by Alexander Calder, 1952) and *L'éloge de la folie* (sets by Jean Tinguely, 1967). Finally, a short time before his death, Diaghilev commissioned Tchelitchew to design the sets for Nicolas Nabokov's ballet *Ode*. Tchelitchew had worked in Kiev in 1918–19 in Exter's workshop and designed his first sets and costumes, which never went into production, for the director Konstantin Mardzhanov (Kote Mardzhanishvili). The painter then developed his theatrical experience in Berlin, where he was a friend of Ivan Puni (Jean Pougny) in 1922–23. It was in 1923 that Diaghilev saw his ballet *Bojarenhochzeit* with its Cubist-Expressionist setting.[12] Tchelitchew's work for *Ode* was highly original: draped in blue tulle, the stage was geometrically organized with a web of wires that created objects and the light of a magic lantern and films were projected onto it. The projection of film material on the theater stage was still very

Mikhail Larionov, *Sergei Diaghilev Listening to Sergei Prokofiev Playing the Piano*
early 1920s
Pencil on paper, 44.5 × 55 cm
STG (R-4679)
Note: Prokofiev is playing his music from *Chout*

new at the time, having been inaugurated by Francis Picabia for the Ballets Suédois production of Erik Satie's ballet *Relâche* in 1924.[13] The Ukrainian painter Anatol Petrytsky and the director Gnat Yura used the collage of a movie screen for a theatrical adaptation of Nikolai Gogol's story *Vii* at the Franko National Theater, Kharkiv, in 1925.[14] The French critic J.-P. Crespelle spoke in connection with Tchelitchew about the "reticulated style" of his painting, which also applies completely to his sets for *Ode*. The same critic observed that the Russian artist "belonged to the world of alchemists, astrologers and magicians" and that this "magic … endeavored to make palpable the mysteries and dramas of mankind with respect to the cosmos."[15] It was thus, above all through the work of painters from the Russian Empire or Soviet Union, that the Ballets Russes assimilated the very latest techniques of set design. Diaghilev went on listening to the "sounds of the times" until the end, as attested by the way he drew upon the innovative experiments of the Russian avant-garde.

[1] I. Markevitch, *Le testament d'Icare*, a selection of writings presented by Jean-Claude Marcadé (Paris: Bernard Grasset, 1984), p. 153.
[2] M. Tsvetaeva, *Nathalie Gontcharova, sa vie, son oeuvre* (Paris: Clémence Hiver, 1990), p. 132 (translated into French by V. Lossky).
[3] V. Breyer in *Les Ballets Russes de Serge de Diaghilev. 1909–1929*, exhibition catalogue (Strasbourg: A l'ancienne douane, 1969), p. 141.
[4] W. George, *Larionov* (Paris: Bibliothèque des Arts, 1966), p. 92.
[5] B. Kochno quoted in Breyer 1969, p. 148.
[6] S. Delaunay, *Nous irons jusqu'au soleil* (Paris: Robert Laffont, 1978), pp. 78–79.

[7] George 1966, p. 100.
[8] L. Survage, "Essai sur la synthèse plastique de l'espace et son rôle dans la peinture" [1920], in *Ecrits sur la peinture* (Paris: L'Archipel, 1992), p. 35.
[9] Larionov, quoted in George 1966, p. 102.
[10] P. Dukas, "*Noces* d'Igor Stravinsky" [June 1923], in *Chroniques musicales sur deux siècles, 1892–1932* (Paris: Stock, 1980), pp. 158, 159.
[11] B. Kochno, quoted here by P. Brullé in *Pevsner 31 dessins*, exhibition catalogue (Paris: Galerie Pierre Brullé, 1998).
[12] See D. Windham, "The Stage and Ballet Designs of Pavel Tchelitchew" [1944], in *Pavel Tchelitchew 1898–1957. A Collection of Fifty-four Theater Designs c. 1919–1923*, exhibition catalogue (London: The Alpine Club, 1976), pp. 4–6.
[13] Denis Bablet, "Le photomontage de l'image à la scène," in *Collage et montage au théâtre et dans les autres arts* (Lausanne: L'Age d'Homme, 1978), pp. 100–01.
[14] V. Marcadé, *Art d'Ukraine* (Lausanne: L'Age d'Homme, 1990), p. 246.
[15] J.-P. Crespelle, "Pavel Tchelitchew 1898–1957," in *Hommage à Tchelitchew*, exhibition catalogue (Paris: Galerie Lucie Weill, 1966).

The Diaghilev Legend

Alexander Schouvaloff

It was winter 1954. England had finally emerged from the war. The Coronation of Elizabeth II the year before had hopefully heralded a new Elizabethan age of optimism. I was twenty years old, knew little about ballet and nothing about the Ballets Russes or Sergei Diaghilev. All London was talking about "The Diaghilev Exhibition." My father and I went to see it together. He was a theater and film designer who had recently won an Oscar for color art direction—so he knew about design.

The exhibition was arranged and designed by Richard Buckle to commemorate the twenty-fifth anniversary of Diaghilev's death. It had come down from the Edinburgh International Festival trailing a fanfare of a huge popular success. I remember well walking through snow flurries to Forbes House, empty for years, a derelict building just off Hyde Park Corner, which Buckle had converted for his exhibition. The house had been completely transformed. We walked past two gigantic, snow-covered sculptured blackamoors at the entrance into a mesmerising setting. It was the first time that an exhibition was arranged so that visitors were forced to follow a specific route through a series of rooms differently decorated with luxurious flocked wallpapers and enormous chandeliers.

The exhibition started on the second floor where each room was devoted to particular productions of the Ballets Russes. I was astounded by the rooms full of designs by Alexandre Benois, Mstislav Dobuzhinsky, Nicholas Roerich followed by one of designs by Léon Bakst, through other rooms of designs by Natalia Goncharova, Mikhail Larionov, Pablo Picasso, Henri Matisse, Georges Braque, André Derain, Georges Rouault. The route then led down stairs to the first floor with galleries of portraits and caricatures of those who had been involved with the Ballets Russes. Finally, the vis-

itor was made to walk down a grand staircase to discover a setting of the Enchanted Castle of *The Sleeping Beauty* designed by Leonard Rosoman. "Huntsmen on horseback sleep in the forest outside, and, guarded by sleeping sentinels, the Princess sleeps on her bed waiting for an unknown Prince to wake her."[1] In this setting visitors could sit and listen to a program of ballet music and then be sprayed with Guerlain's "Mitsouko," Diaghilev's favorite scent.[2]

Buckle's exhibition changed the meaning of the word. Those who saw it, as I did, kept a lasting memory of it. My father and I were dazzled and I was proud when he told me that Diaghilev was a cousin of mine. We both came out wondering that although it was called "The Diaghilev Exhibition" we had not learned about Diaghilev the man, but about what he had achieved with the Ballets Russes. In the background, somewhere, was Diaghilev the man who had achieved all this. He controlled everything and insisted on perfection. Serge Lifar, inheriting Diaghilev's notebook for 1926–29, described from it how "we see him noting available dates for performances, probable outlays, the names of singers … likely to suit him for such and such parts, ideas for décors, the whereabouts of scores and piano parts, and even managing to keep an eye on doors needing to be painted, velvet for the boxes, small tables in the buffet, publicity, advertising—not to mention the infinity of props needed for each production…"[3] Diaghilev started his own legend. His taste was impeccable. His mastery of publicity and his manipulation of public relations were supreme. He was capable of arriving at the theater a few days or even a few hours before a performance, sensing something was wrong and ruthlessly making drastic changes which he did with *Jeux* (1913), *Romeo and Juliet* (1926) and *Ode* (1928). He was almost always right. He had that very rare gift of being a genius impresario.

The Diaghilev exhibition would have been much the poorer if Buckle had not been able to borrow the collection from the Wadsworth Atheneum, Hartford. In 1933 Lifar took a small company of dancers and a large collection of Ballets Russes set and costume designs and other works which he had inherited from Diaghilev on a tour of the United States, ill-fated because it was too soon for American audiences.[4] Lifar, broke, needed money to be able to return to France with his company. He managed to sell his collection to Chick Austin, the mercurial thirty-three-year-old director of the Wadsworth Atheneum for just $10,000. For this modest sum, thought to be excessive by the Trustees, the museum instantly acquired a magnificent collection of modern art.[5] No exhibition on the Ballets Russes can now be contemplated without borrowing from the Wadsworth Atheneum. Indeed, Lifar had to borrow back the entire collection for his exhibition at the Louvre in Paris in 1939 commemorating the tenth anniversary of Diaghilev's death. The exhibition was popular enough to be extended and only managed to be returned to the United States just in time before World War II broke out.

A hundred and forty thousand people saw Buckle's exhibition, and, most significantly, it affected a lot of exhibition and theater designers. But not everyone was pleased. Dobuzhinsky in a letter to Benois, both members of the exhibition's Committee of Honor, wrote "I think that even you would agree with me that the whole exhibition is not 'in the spirit of Diaghilev' and that there is a vulgarity about it which he would not have tolerated," to which Benois replied "judging from your opinion not only did I not miss anything by not visiting it but even gained by saving myself from extra fatigue and irritation."[6] These were lone voices in the tumult of approbation.

Buckle, who never saw the Ballets Russes, did more than anyone for the Diaghilev Legend. His "baptism" took place in December 1933 on Liverpool Street Station, London on his way home to Norfolk when he saw Romola Nijinsky's book *Nijinsky* on the bookstall. When he got home there was the same book waiting for him. He was hooked for life. He later realized that "much of what Romola Nijinsky had written in her husband's biography was exaggerated and untrue"[7] and so he tried to get at a more accurate truth. Certainly, Buckle's exhibition revived an interest in the Ballets Russes which had somewhat lapsed and reinvigorated the Diaghilev Legend. Buckle became the renowned expert on the subject and remained so to the end of his life. He made other exhibitions, was frequently consulted by historians and auction houses and wrote two key books. In 1971 he published the definitive biography of Vaslav Nijinsky. He followed this in 1979 with his magisterial and indispensable biography of Diaghilev.[8] It has its flaws. He did not know Russian and so could not read many of Diaghilev's letters, articles, and criticisms. It was written before the release of much important material in Russia,[9] and most drastically the publisher made him cut his text by 60,000 words.[10] Calling the last part "The Kochno Period" was a mistake as currying favor with Boris Kochno hoping, with flattery, to be given some objects for the Theatre Museum was a useless gesture.

There was a huge resurgence of interest in the Ballets Russes on July 17, 1968, at the Scala Theatre in London.[11] The first of the sequence of Sotheby's sales of Ballets Russes costumes and curtains, held in store in Paris, Montréal and London, took place in a great storm of publicity and public excitement because Nubar Gulbenkian refused to go on paying for storage. That interest has not flagged since. The prize lot was the front cloth for *Le Train Bleu*, enlarged in 1924 overnight from a gouache by Pablo Picasso to 10 × 11 meters by Alexandre Shervashidze. It was delivered, incorrectly and unfortunately, folded, not rolled as it should have been, to be hung in Alick Johnstone's studio for examination. Buckle, then the cataloguer for Sotheby's, couldn't bear the suspense and announced he would return after lunch to see it hanging. John Martin, the head scene painter, told me several years later that such a dense shower of distemper flakes fell to the floor when the cloth was hung on the paint-frame that whole areas had to be repainted to bring it back to life and that the dedication and signature, originally painted by Picasso himself, "Dédié à Diaghilew / Picasso" was completely overpainted there and then. Buckle, unaware, bought the cloth "for the nation" for £69,000 with funds provided by Lord Grade. It is the most valuable object in the collections of the Theatre Museum, London.

The most tragic dispersal of materials was that of the Diaghilev–Lifar Library by Sotheby's in 1975.[12] Collecting Russian books had become an obsession for Diaghilev during the last years of his life. I have seen his comments in Russian (and prices) written in scruffy notebooks where he is anxiously trying to trace copies of rare books that might be held by various dealers. Among the most important volumes he acquired were the earliest book printed in Moscow,[13] the first systematic Russian grammar published in Western Europe,[14] the first mathematical book printed in Russia in 1703 and many first editions of works by Dostoevsky, Gogol, Lermontov, Pushkin, Tolstoi, and others. Lifar had tried and failed to sell the collection privately as a whole. Peter Wilson, chairman of Sotheby's at the time, wanting to start sales in Monaco prevailed upon Lifar to agree to sell the Library at Monaco as their inaugural sale there. It was a four-day sale from November 28 to December 1, with 826 lots. The sale was a disaster.[15] Lifar was furious and told me he would "never ever have anything to do with Sotheby's again."

But he did. On May 9, 1984, Sotheby's sold the Lifar Collection which included the original Chinese Conjuror's costume in *Parade* designed by Picasso.[16] The design for the costume had become the symbol of the Ballets Russes on posters, programs, books. Just before the sale I got a message from Lifar to say that he would like the Theatre Museum to acquire the costume and would provide £10,000 towards the price. Lifar and I always spoke in Russian and perhaps because I am Russian and could speak the language aroused in him a certain nostalgic feeling of homesickness. The costume was knocked down to me for £26,000, the highest price ever for a costume then, so

thanks to Lifar, the Theatre Museum acquired it for £16,000. Lifar later told me that Léonide Massine, who had created the role, gave the costume to Léon Woizikovsky who danced the role in the revival of *Parade* in 1926. Woizikovksy had buried the costume in a wood in Poland during World War II to protect it. Miraculously, when he exhumed it after the war undamaged he "gave" it to Lifar.

Kochno was generous in conversation imparting information about the Ballets Russes as he and I also always spoke in Russian, but he never gave anything or threw anything away. In 1975, at the instigation of Michel Guy, French Minister of Culture, part of the Kochno collection was acquired for the Bibliothèque nationale. At the end of his life he lived like a huge spider in the middle of an intricate web of glittering and fascinating objects. He died in 1990 and Sotheby's sold the collection over two days in Monaco on October 11–12, 1991. The most surprised beneficiary was Kochno's delightfully modest nephew, Vladimir Augenblick. He and his wife had had no idea that a large fortune would transform their lives. Soon after the sale they left their rather dingy flat in a poor part of Paris and moved to the Riviera with their two poodles.

Lifar died in 1986. Before he died he gave a large collection of Ballets Russes and personal material to the City of Lausanne where he had been living with Lillan Ahlefeldt, his companion for many years. On December 6, 2002, Ahlefeldt sold the mostly archival remnants of his collection at Sotheby's, London. For the most part all the archival material from these various sales has ended up in public collections and will go on intriguing historians for years to come.

Diaghilev died on August 19, 1929, in Venice. Lifar and Kochno, and Misia Sert and Gabrielle Chanel were with him when he died. Lifar described the final journey to the Orthodox corner of San Michele cemetery: "After the service the procession, wonderful in its solemn, silent beauty, re-formed, led by the magnificent black and gold gondola, bearing the coffin, smothered in flowers, followed by that containing Pavel Georgievitch [Koribut-Kubitovich], Misia Sert, Coco Chanel, Kochno and myself, and a whole string of others, full of friends and mourners. Then, over the smooth ultramarine surface of the Adriatic, sparkling with golden sunshine, the body was wafted to the island of San Michele, and there borne on our arms to

Front cover of the catalog for the auction "Ballet Material and Manuscripts from the Serge Lifar Collection" held by Sotheby's London on May 9, 1984. The costume being modeled is after Pablo Picasso's design for the Chinese Conjuror in *Parade*, 1917. Léonide Massine danced the role.

the grave."[17] Lifar asked Picasso to design a monument but he declined pleading lack of inspiration. Perhaps the real reason was lack of sufficient fee or Picasso's fear of graves. In any event, the sculptor Paolo Rodocanachi designed a rather overpowering baroque monument, intended to bear the inscription "Венеция постоянная вдохновительница наших успокоении" (or "Venise inspiratrice éternelle de nos apaisements," "Venice, ever our inspiration and fulfilment"). In 1966 Lifar persuaded the authorities to rename the space behind the Opéra "Place Diaghilev." Sipping tea in the Plaza Athénée one afternoon in 1984 Serge Lifar told me that he had never missed a single year in visiting Diaghilev's grave on August 19. We have to take his word for it.

For twenty years the Ballets Russes performed in Europe and America but nearly all the ballets have been lost or forgotten, even the few revivals soon lose their authenticity and became indistinct shadows of the original.[18] Ballet is the most ephemeral of all the performing arts. Nijinsky's legendary leaps are not recorded; photographs show him only with his feet firmly on the ground. There is no film of the Ballets Russes, which is surprising, even though the setting for one of the ballets, *Pastorale* (1926), is the making of a film. Regrettably, Stravinsky's compositions—Diaghilev produced twelve over the years—are now mostly performed as concert pieces.[19] There is, however, a continued fascination with the Ballets Russes. It is puzzling. Artifacts and records remain to obsess scholars. In this centenary year the Diaghilev Legend is continued with vigor: there will be exhibitions, books, seminars, conferences, lectures all over the world.

Visit www.findagrave.com, click on "Famous Grave Search," enter Serge Diaghilev. You will find Nancy and forty-six others who have left "virtual flowers" for him on August 19, as well as on March 21, his birthday, every year since 2001 when the site started.

[1] R. Buckle, "Introduction" to *The Diaghilev Exhibition*, exhibition catalogue (Edinburgh Festival and London, Forbes House, 1954), p. 13.

[2] Although a witty idea, it never worked properly and had to be stopped within a few days.

[3] S. Lifar, *Serge Diaghilev* (London: Gollancz, 1945), p. 326.

[4] Designs for thirty-seven Ballets Russes productions between 1909–1929. For the full catalogue see A. Schouvaloff, *The Art of Ballets Russes: The Serge Lifar Collection of Theater Designs, Costumes, and Paintings at the Wadsworth Atheneum, Hartford, Connecticut* (New Haven and London: Yale University Press, 1997).

[5] Lifar later first tried to get more money and then even started a court case to get the collection back.

[6] I. Vydrin (ed.), *A. N. Benua i ego adresaty. Perepiska s M. V. Dobuzhinskim (1903–1957)* (St. Petersburg: Sad iskusstv, 2003), pp. 261–63.

[7] R. Buckle, *In the Wake of Diaghilev* (London and New York: Holt, Rinehart and Winston, 1982), p. 84.

[8] R. Buckle, *Diaghilev* (London: Weidenfeld and Nicolson, 1979).

[9] Especially the two volumes by Ilia Zilbershtein and Vadim Samkov *Sergei Diaghilev i russkoe iskusstvo* (Moscow: Izobrazitelnoe iskusstvo, 1982) which have not been translated into English. A French translation is to be published in 2009.

[10] Which in themselves would make a substantial book. The cut text is in the Theatre Museum, London.

[11] Now demolished.

[12] There was a persistent rumor that Lifar had no right to the ownership of the Library, but when, much later, I helped to catalogue the remnants of the Kochno Collection I came across documents showing that Lifar had indeed bought the collection as he had always maintained.

[13] In 1564 by Ivan Fedorov, *The Acts of the Apostles*.

[14] By the Clarendon Press, Oxford in 1696.

[15] I left a bid on a lot of three books one of which had a "Schouvaloff" interest, got the lot well under my bid, and later sold the other two books at Sotheby's, London, for much more.

[16] Lifar had lent the costume to the exhibition "Parade" at the Edinburgh Festival in 1979 organized by the Theatre Museum, London.

[17] Lifar 1945, pp. 525–26.

[18] For example, according to a dancer in The Royal Ballet who was rehearsed by Bronislava Nijinska, *Les Biches* and *Les Noces* are now grotesque distortions of the originals.

[19] Nine ballets, two operas and one oratorio: *L'Oiseau de Feu* (1910), *Petrouchka* (1911), *Le Sacre du Printemps* (1913), *Rossignol* (1914), *Feu d'Artifice* (1917), *Le Chant du Rossignol* (1920), *Pulcinella* (1920), *Le Renard* (1922 and 1929), *Mavra* (1922), *Les Noces* (1923), *Oedipus Rex* (1927) and *Apollon Musagète* (1928).

Ballets and Operas

Fedor Chaliapin as Tsar Boris
Photograph by Seidenberg
Studio, Paris
Original print, 29.7 × 23.8 cm
Private collection

Boris Godounov

Opera in three acts and seven scenes by Modest
Mussorgsky with libretto based on a play of the
same name by Alexander Pushkin and on
Nikolai Karamzin's *History of the Russian State*.
Produced at the Théâtre National de l'Opéra,
Paris as part of Sergei Diaghilev's *Cinq Concerts
Historiques Russes*, on May 19, 1908, with
designs supervised by Aleksandr Golovin;
Alexandre Benois and Valter Lokkenberg also
designed part of the décor, Ivan Bilibin some
of the costumes and properties.
Staged by Aleksandr Sanin.
Principal performers: Fedor Chaliapin as Tsar
Boris, Dmitrii Smirnov as the False Dmitrii,
Vladimir Kastorsky as Pimen.

Aleksandr Golovin
Portrait of Fedor Chaliapin in the Role of Boris Godunov, 1912
Gouache, tempera, pastel, size paint, chalk, gold paint and silver foil on canvas
211.5 × 139.5 cm
SRM (Zh-4345)

Aleksandr Golovin
Costume for Fedor Chaliapin
as Tsar Boris in Act I, 1911
The ensemble includes a long
shirt made of silk and beads
and a satin and velvet caftan
with brocade, ribbon with
metal thread, artificial pearls,
paste jewelry
SPSMTM (GIK 10246/1
MEM 1103/1 1318/53
NVM 1318/53)
Note: Chaliapin wore this
caftan for the 1911
production of *Boris Godunov*
at the Maryinsky Theater
in St. Petersburg

Aleksandr Golovin
Boots for Tsar Boris, 1911
Velvet, jewels and Venetian
pearls
SPSMTM (GIK 10246/2–3
MEM 1103/2–3)

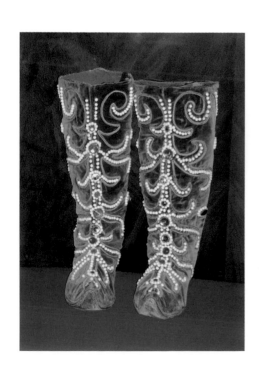

Aleksandr Golovin
Set design for the Coronation
(Scene 2 of the Prologue), 1908
Watercolor, pastel, whitening,
silver and bronze paint and
white and black chalk on
board, 71 × 86 cm
SBTM (KP 60439 GDD 1959)

Aleksandr Golovin
Set design for the Facetted
Chamber in the Kremlin, 1911
Watercolor, gouache, pastel
and bronze paint on paper
67.5 × 84 cm
The National Pushkin Museum,
St. Petersburg (KP–4993 R-811)
Note: Golovin produced this
reprise of his Paris 1908
set for the 1911 production
of *Boris Godunov* at the
Maryinsky Theater in
St. Petersburg

Salomé

Extract in one act ("Dance of the Seven Veils")
from the drama by Oscar Wilde based on
the Biblical story.
Staged at the Conservatoire of St. Petersburg
on December 20, 1908 with music by Aleksandr
Glazunov, choreography by Michel Fokine
and designs by Léon Bakst.
Performer: Ida Rubinstein.

Léon Bakst
Costume design for Ida
Rubinstein in the "Dance
of the Seven Veils," 1908
Watercolor, gouache, bronze
and silver paint and graphite
pencil on paper, 47 × 30.2 cm
STG (R-5444)

Anna Pavlova as Armide
and Vaslav Nijinsky
as Armide's Slave, 1907
Photograph by Karl Fisher
Original print
SPSMTM (GIK 16487/20)

Le Pavillon d'Armide

Ballet-pantomime in three scenes based on
Théophile Gautier's *Omphale*.
Staged at the Maryinsky Theater, St. Petersburg,
on November 25, 1907, with scenario by
Alexandre Benois, music by Nikolai Cherepnin,
choreography by Michel Fokine and designs by
Alexandre Benois. The ballet was then performed
by Sergei Diaghilev's Ballets Russes at the
Théâtre du Châtelet, Paris on May 19, 1909
with designs by Alexandre Benois.
Stage manager: Serge Grigoriev.
Principal performers: Vera Karalli and Anna
Pavlova as Armide, Mikhail Mordkin and Michel
Fokine as the Vicomte, Vaslav Nijinsky as
Armide's Slave, Tamara Karsavina as Armide's
Confidante.

Alexandre Benois
Set design: "The Tapestry"
1907
Gouache, graphite pencil and
ink on colored paper on board
59.3 × 68 cm
STG (5346)

Tamara Karsavina as Armide
and Adolph Bolm as the
Vicomte, 1912
Photograph by E. O. Hoppé
18.4 × 13.9 cm
CALA (01515-P-II)

Alexandre Benois
Costume for Armide's
Confidante, 1907
Silk, gauze, metal fabric,
tassels and fringe
SPSMTM (GIK 17796/15a, b
MEM 3427/a, b)

Alexandre Benois
Costume design for Anna
Pavlova as Armide, 1907
Watercolor, whitening,
graphite pencil, Indian ink,
pen and silver paint on gray
paper, 33.4 × 20.3 cm
STG (R-2828)

Alexandre Benois
Design for the backdrop
of Armide's Garden (Dream
Scene) in Scene 2, 1909
Watercolor, pencil, pen and
ink on paper, 22 × 28.5 cm
FAMSF. Theater and Dance
Collection, gift of Mrs. Adolph
B. Spreckels (T&D 1962.83)

Alexandre Benois
Set design for the palace
interior in Scenes 1 and 3
1909
Watercolor on paper
22.5 × 30 cm
CICF (KVP 682/107)

Georges Reinhard
Set model for Scene 2, after
a design by Alexandre Benois
Gouache on board
70 × 73 × 62 cm
Archives SBM (3008)

Alexandre Benois
Costume design for Rinaldo
1907
Watercolor, whitening, pencil,
silver paint and Indian ink
on paper, 37.8 × 26.1 cm
SPSMTM (GIK 7070/199
OR 9655)

Alexandre Benois
Costume design for
Armide's Slave, 1907
Watercolor, pencil, bronze
and silver paint on paper
35.6 × 27.6 cm
SPSMTM (GIK 12343
OR 18007)
Note: Vaslav Nijinsky danced
the part of the Slave in the
1907 production

Alexandre Benois
Costume for the Genius
of Hours, 1907
Silk and metal thread
Ravenscourt Galleries, London
(233 a, b, c)

Alexandre Benois
Costume for the Bugler, 1907
Feathers, canvas, brocade,
artificial pearls and metal
thread
SPSMTM (GIK 15629/1
MEM 1750)

Konstantin Korovin
Costume design for a
Polovtsian warrior, 1908
Graphite pencil, ink, tempera
and watercolor on paper
33.5 × 21 cm
WA (1933 490)
Note: This costume design was
used for the production of
Prince Igor at the Maryinsky
Theater, St. Petersburg on
September 24, 1909

Prince Igor

Opera in a prologue and four acts by Aleksandr
Borodin with a libretto by the composer after
a play by Vladimir Stasov completed by Nikolai
Rimsky-Korsakov and Aleksandr Glazunov.
Staged at the Maryinsky Theater, St. Petersburg,
on September 24, 1909, with choreography
by Michel Fokine and designs by Konstantin
Korovin.
Principal performers
• Singers: Pavel Andreev as Prince Igor, Elena
Nikolaeva as Princess Yaroslavna, Elizaveta
Petrenko as Konchakovna.
• Dancer: Adolph Bolm as the Chief Warrior.
Note: Diaghilev produced the same opera at the
Théâtre du Châtelet, Paris on May 19, 1909 with
designs by Nicholas Roerich.

Konstantin Korovin
Set design, 1909
Gouache on board
52.5 × 77 cm
NMNM (1974.13)
Serge Lifar Collection, gift
of Madame Simone Del Duca

The Polovtsian Dances

Ballet in one act extracted from *Prince Igor*, the
opera in a prologue and four acts by Aleksandr
Borodin with a libretto by the composer after
a play by Vladimir Stasov completed by Nikolai
Rimsky-Korsakov and Aleksandr Glazunov.
Produced on May 19, 1909 at the Théâtre du
Chatelet, Paris with choreography by Michel
Fokine and designs by Nicholas Roerich.
Staged by Aleksandr Sanin.
Stage manager: Serge Grigoriev.
Principal performers: Fedor Chaliapin, Sofia
Fedorova as the Polovtsian Maiden, Adolph Bolm
as the Polovtsian Chief Warrior.

© ARCHIVES SBM MONACO

Nicholas Roerich
Set design: "The Camp
of the Polovtsy," 1909
Pastel and tempera on board
43 × 60 cm
SRM (Zh 1983)

118

Michel Fokine as Amoun
in *Cléopâtre*
Photographic Studio of the
Imperial Theaters
Original print
SPSMTM (GIK 3783/16)

Léon Bakst
Costume design for Ida
Rubinstein as Cleopatra, 1909
Watercolor and pencil
on paper, 28 × 21 cm
CICF (KVP 682/56)

Cléopâtre

Choreographic drama in one act based on Anton
Arensky's *Egyptian Nights* with musical
additions by Nikolai Cherepnin, Aleksandr
Glazunov, Mikhail Glinka, Nikolai Rimsky-
Korsakov, and Sergei Taneev.
Staged at the Théâtre du Châtelet, Paris on June
2, 1909 with choreography by Michel Fokine
and designs by Léon Bakst.
Stage manager: Serge Grigoriev.
Principal performers: Ida Rubinstein as
Cleopatra, Anna Pavlova as Ta-Hor, Tamara
Karsavina as a Slave, Michel Fokine as Amoun,
Vaslav Nijinsky as a Slave.
Note: *Cléopâtre* was first produced by Michel
Fokine as *Nuits d'Egypte* at the Maryinsky
Theater, St. Petersburg in 1908.

Savelii Sorin
*Portrait of Tamara Karsavina
in the ballet "Les Sylphides"*
1910
Oil on canvas, 146 × 129 cm
SPSMTM (GIK 2351/1
OZh 362)

Valentin Serov
Poster advertising the
inauguration of the "Saison
Russe" at the Théâtre du
Châtelet, Paris in May–June
1909, with Anna Pavlova
as Sylphide
Print on paper, 231 × 177.7 cm
CICF (KVP 682/570)
Note: Reproduced from the
copy in the collection of the
Moscow State Library
(723–09), 257.4 × 199 cm

Les Sylphides

Romantic reverie in one act by Michel Fokine
based on music by Frédéric Chopin orchestrated
by Igor Stravinsky and with additional music
by Aleksandr Glazunov, Anatolii Liadov,
Nikolai Sokolov and Sergei Taneev.
Produced at the Théâtre du Châtelet, Paris
on June 2, 1909 with choreography by Michel
Fokine and designs by Alexandre Benois.
Stage manager: Serge Grigoriev.
Principal performers: Tamara Karsavina,
Anna Pavlova, Vaslav Nijinsky.

Tamara Karsavina as
Columbine, 1912
Photograph by E. O. Hoppé
Vintage silver gelatin print
25 × 21 cm
CALA (01515-T)

Carnaval

Ballet-pantomime in one act by Léon Bakst
and Michel Fokine based on music by Robert
Schumann, orchestrated by Nikolai Cherepnin,
Aleksandr Glazunov, Anatolii Liadov and Nikolai
Rimsky-Korsakov.
Produced at the Théâtre National de l'Opéra,
Paris on June 4, 1910 with designs by Léon
Bakst.
Stage manager: Serge Grigoriev.
Principal performers: Tamara Karsavina as
Columbine, Vaslav Nijinsky as Harlequin.

Léonide Massine as
Eusebius, 1918
Photograph by E. O. Hoppé
Vintage gelatin silver print
CALA (14630-B)

Adolph Bolm as Pierrot, 1910
Photograph by Jean de
Strzelecki
Original print
SPSMTM (GIK 6963/8)
Note: Bolm is pictured here in
the production of *Carnaval*
which Michel Fokine staged
at the Pavlova Hall,
St. Petersburg, in the spring
of 1910

Léon Bakst
Costume design for Estrella
1910
Watercolor and pencil
on paper, 31.8 × 24.9 cm
SPSMTM (GIK 7324/291
OR 8869)

Léon Bakst
Costume design for Florestan
1910
Watercolor and pencil on
paper on board, 27.8 × 21.2 cm
SPSMTM (GIK 7324/286
OR 8864)

Léon Bakst
Costume design for Pantalone
1910
Watercolor and pencil on
paper on board, 28 × 21.3 cm
SPSMTM (GIK 7324/287
OR 8865)

Léon Bakst
Costume design for Chiarina
1910
Watercolor and pencil on
paper on board, 27.8 × 21.2 cm
SPSMTM (GIK 7324/288
OR 8866)
Note: Bakst seems to have
drawn inspiration from the
colored illustrations published
in the *Gazette des Beaux-Arts*
and other nineteenth-century
fashion and high society
magazines

Léon Bakst
Costume for Harlequin worn
by Michel Fokine, 1910
Including a silk shirt and
bow tie held in place by
a broad band and printed
jersey trousers
SPSMTM (GIK 11718/a, b, c, d
MEM 1276/a, b, c, d)

Arthur Grunenberg
Michel Fokine as Harlequin
Drypoint etching with colored
ink and gold paint on laid
paper, 38.5 × 25 cm
NMNM (2002.3.6.3)

Mikhail Bobyshev
Portrait of Michel and Vera
Fokine in the ballet "Carnaval"
1916
Gouache and Indian ink
on paper, 97 × 64 cm
SPSMTM (GIK 17043
OP 22983)

131

Léon Bakst
Costume for a Male Servant
1910
Silk and satin
SPSMTM (GIK 17913/1a, b
MEM 3538/a, b)
Note: Original Persian
miniatures from Michel
Fokine's collection seem
to have inspired both Bakst's
and Serov's renderings
for *Schéhérazade*

Schéhérazade

Choreographic drama in one act with music by
Nikolai Rimsky-Korsakov, libretto by Léon Bakst
and Alexandre Benois and choreography
by Michel Fokine.
Produced at the Théâtre National de l'Opéra,
Paris on June 4, 1910 with designs by Léon
Bakst.
Stage manager: Serge Grigoriev.
Principal performers: Ida Rubinstein as Zobeida,
Aleksei Bulgakov as Shahriar, Vaslav Nijinsky
as the Favorite Slave.

Valentin Serov
Design for the drop curtain
1910–11
Gouache on board, 68 × 87 cm
STG (R-1159)

Vaslav Nijinsky as the Favorite
Slave, 1911
Photograph by Auguste Bert
Vintage gelatin silver print
CALA (02382-A)

Arthur Grunenberg
Vaslav Nijinsky as the
Wild Blackamoor and the
Dancing Moor
Drypoint etching with colored
ink and gold paint on laid
paper, 38.5 × 25 cm each
NMNM (2002.3.6.5 and
2002.3.6.7)

Léon Bakst
Costume design for an
Odalisque based on the ballet
Schéhérazade, 1911
Opaque watercolor, pencil,
ink and metallic paint
on paper mounted on board
44.9 × 30 cm
MKMAM, gift of Robert
L. B. Tobin (TL1999.2)

Michel Fokine as the Favorite
Slave and Vera Fokina as
Zobeida, 1914
Photograph by E. O. Hoppé
Vintage silver gelatin print
17.7 × 14.6 cm
CALA (02475-S)

Léon Bakst
Costume design for Shahriar
(Aleksei Bulgakov), 1910
Watercolor, gouache and
pencil on paper, 35.5 × 22 cm
Thyssen-Bornemisza
Collections (1974.35)

Georges Reinhard
Set model for the décor after
a design by Léon Bakst
Gouache on board
55 × 59.5 × 50.5 cm
Archives SBM (3004)

Tamara Karsavina as Zobeida
Photograph by E. O. Hoppé
Vintage silver gelatin print
SPSMTM (GIK 15237/4)

L'Oiseau de Feu

Produced at the Théâtre National de l'Opéra,
Paris on June 25, 1910, with choreography by
Michel Fokine, sets by Aleksandr Golovin and
costumes by Aleksandr Golovin and Léon Bakst.
Stage manager: Serge Grigoriev.
Principal performers: Tamara Karsavina as the
Fire-Bird, Vera Fokina as the Beautiful Tsarevna,
Michel Fokine as Ivan Tsarevich, Aleksei
Bulgakov as King Kashchei.

Aleksandr Golovin
Set design: "The Kingdom
of Kashchei," 1910
Gouache, bronze paint
and black pencil on paper
82.5 × 102 cm
STG (5624)

Aleksandr Golovin
Costume design for a Knight
1910
Pencil, watercolor, whitening
and bronze paint on paper
on board, 32.8 × 24.8 cm
SPSMTM (GIK 7324/273
OR 8959)

143

144

Aleksandr Golovin
Costumes design, 1910
Watercolor, pencil and
whitening on paper on board
31.9 × 23.3 cm
SPSMTM (GIK 7324/330
OR 3246)

Léon Bakst
Costume design for Bilibochka
1910s
Gouache and pencil on paper
on board, 48.8 × 33.2 cm
Private collection, Moscow

Romola Nijinsky's collage
of petals from Nijinsky's
original costume in *Le Spectre
de la Rose*, 1911 (dated 1957)
Patches of colored silks,
board and ink, 22.8 × 16.5 cm
Tamara and Kinga Nijinsky
Courtesy of Curatorial
Assistance, Inc, Los Angeles

Valentine Hugo Gross
*Tamara Karsavina and
Vaslav Nijinsky in "Le Spectre
de la Rose,"* 1912
Encaustic on wood, 54 × 44 cm
NMNM (1990.4.1)
Note: This rendering of
Karsavina and Nijinsky is
allied to the so-called "action"
drawings which Gross made
of the Ballets Russes between
1909 and 1913

Le Spectre de la Rose

Choreographic tableau adapted by Jean-Louis
Vaudoyer after the story by Théophile Gautier
with music by Carl Maria von Weber.
Produced at the Théâtre de Monte-Carlo
on April 19, 1911, and at the Théâtre du Châtelet,
Paris on June 6, 1911 with choreography
by Michel Fokine and designs by Léon Bakst.
Stage manager: Serge Grigoriev.
Principal performers: Tamara Karsavina
as the Young Girl, Vaslav Nijinsky as the Specter
of the Rose.

Valentine Gross

Jean Cocteau
Tamara Karsavina as the
Young Girl in *Le Spectre
de la Rose*, 1911
Lithographic poster, 93 × 60 cm
Archives SBM (1444)
Note: In the Moscow
exhibition, item SPSMTM
(GIK 4129/1), 201 × 132 cm
will be displayed

Jean Cocteau
Vaslav Nijinsky in the title role
of *Le Spectre de la Rose*, 1911
Lithographic poster, 93 × 60 cm
Archives SBM (1443)
Note: In the Moscow
exhibition, item SPSMTM
(GIK 4130/1), 201 × 132 cm
will be displayed

Léon Bakst
Design for stage props, 1911
Watercolor, gouache, gold
paint and pencil on paper
Annotated in ink
55.3 × 38.1 cm
TML (S.1004-1984)

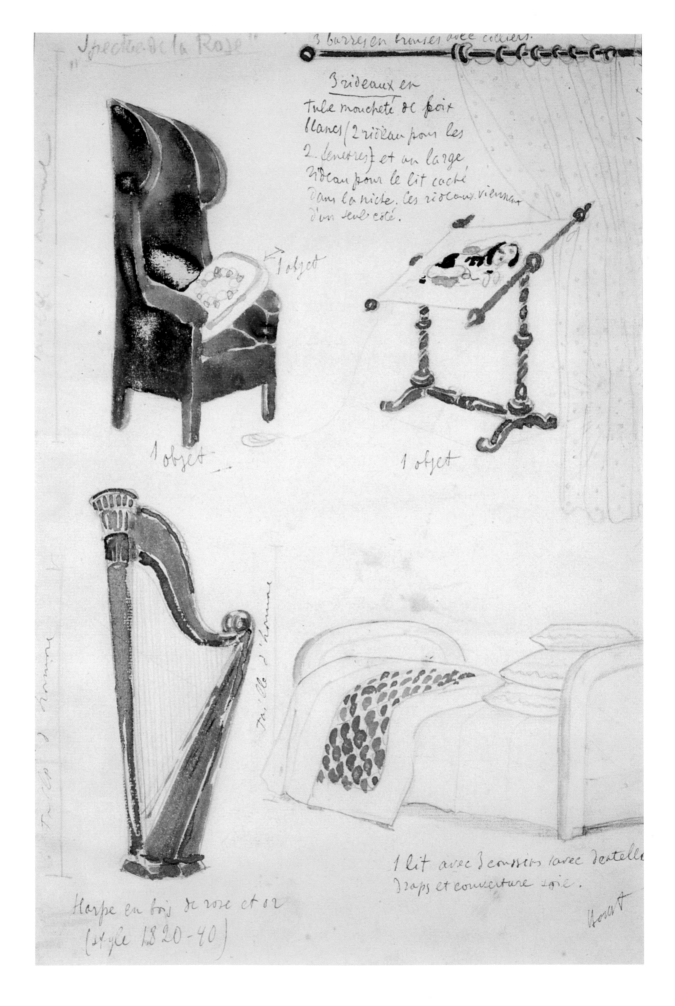

The set of *Le Spectre de
la Rose*, 1910s, after a design
by Léon Bakst
Original photograph
BNF, Opéra, Paris

Vaslav Nijinsky as the Specter
1911
Photograph by E. O. Hoppé
Vintage silver gelatin print
19 × 12.7 cm
CALA (02382-A)

Vaslav Nijinsky as the Specter
1911
Photograph by E. O. Hoppé
Hand-colored gravure
29.2 × 23.4 cm
CALA (02382-C)

Bronislava Nijinska as the
Young Girl and Vaslav Nijinsky
as the Specter, 1911
Photograph by E. O. Hoppé
Hand-colored gravure
30.4 × 22.8 cm
CALA (02382-L-I)

153

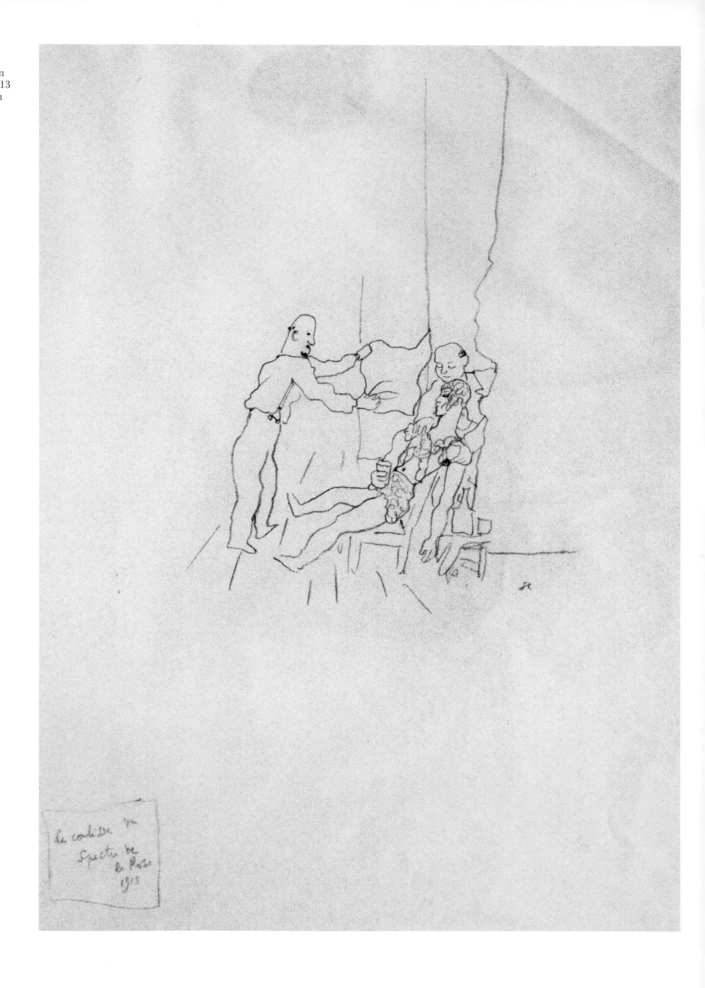

Ludwig Kainer
Sheet from the album of
fourteen lithographs *Ballet
Russe* (Leipzig: Wolff, 1913,
no. 44) depicting Vaslav
Nijinsky as the Specter
and Tamara Karsavina as
the Young Girl in *Le Spectre
de la Rose*
Hand-colored lithograph,
watercolor, gouache on paper
49.8 × 36.2 cm
SBTM (KP 315576/9
G III 871)

Narcisse

Mythological ballet-poem in one act by Léon
Bakst with music by Nikolai Cherepnin.
Produced at the Théâtre de Monte-Carlo on
April 26, 1911 and at the Théâtre du Châtelet,
Paris on June 6, 1911 with choreography
by Michel Fokine and designs by Léon Bakst.
Stage manager: Serge Grigoriev.
Principal performers: Tamara Karsavina as
Echo, Vaslav Nijinsky as Narcisse, Bronislava
Nijinska as a Bacchante, Vera Fokina as a
Young Béotienne.

Léon Bakst
Costume design for a Béotien
1911
Watercolor, pencil and
whitening on paper
40 × 27.5 cm
SPSMTM (GIK 7324/326
OR 8876)

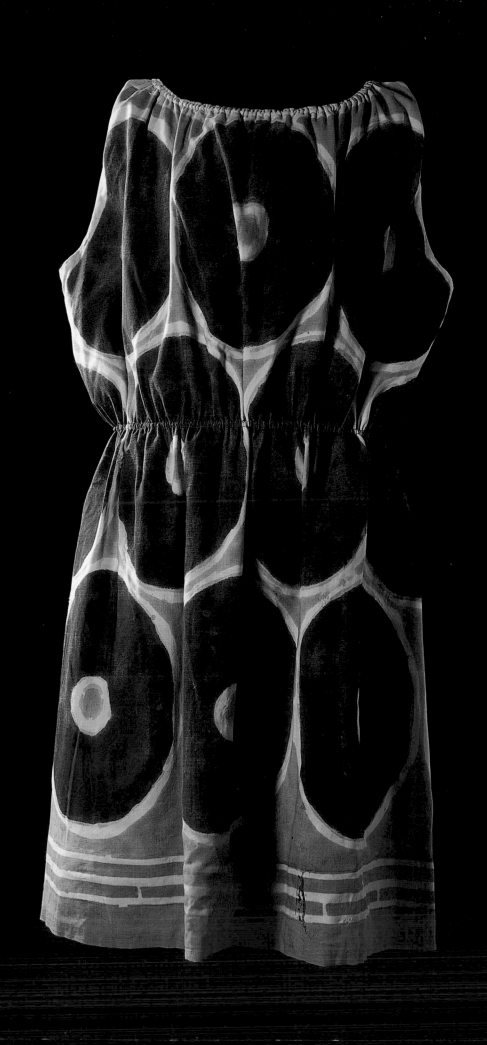

Léon Bakst
Costume for a Béotien
c. 1911
Canvas and painted cotton
NMNM (2006.27.1)

Léon Bakst
Costume design for a Béotien
1911
Watercolor and pencil
on paper, 27.3 × 39.9 cm
SPSMTM (GIK 7324/328
OR 8878)

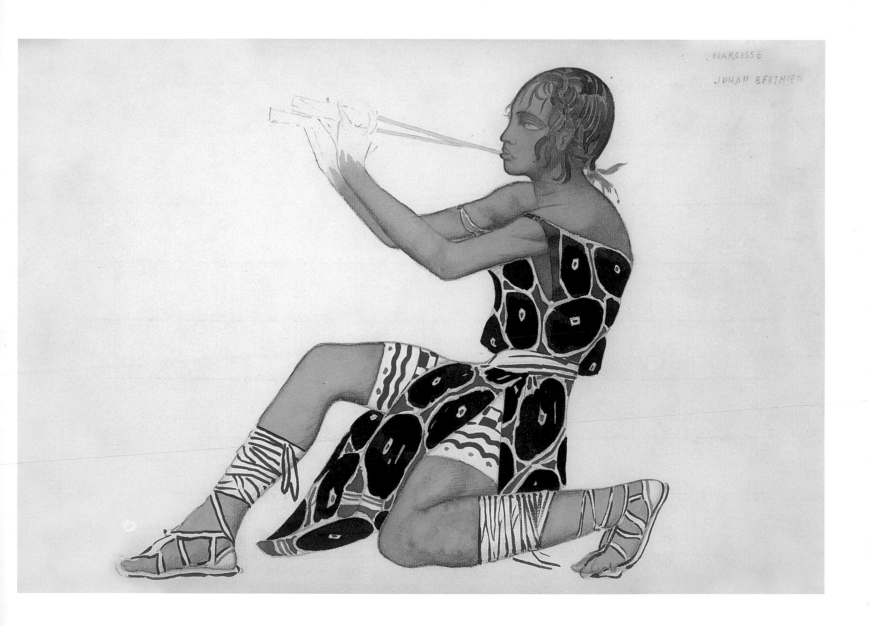

159

Léon Bakst
Costume design for
a Bacchante, 1911
Gouache, silver paint and
pencil on paper, 67.5 × 48 cm
Centre Georges Pompidou,
Paris (AM 2561 D)

Léon Bakst
Costumes design for Bronislava
Nijinska and Vera Fokina
as Two Béotiennes, 1911
Watercolor, pencil and silver
paint on paper, 40 × 27.5 cm
SPSMTM (GIK 7324/327
OR 8877)

Sadko (Scene 6)

Extract from the opera-ballet *Sadko* by
Nikolai Rimsky-Korsakov with libretto by Nikolai
Rimsky-Korsakov and Vladimir Belsky.
The Scene 6 (the Underwater Kingdom) was
produced at the Théâtre du Châtelet, Paris on
June 6, 1911 with choreography by Michel Fokine
and designs by Boris Anisfeld. Restaged in 1916
with a new choreography by Adolph Bolm
and designs by Natalia Goncharova.
Stage manager: Serge Grigoriev.
Principal performers: Lubov Tchernicheva,
Vera Nemtchinova and Léon Woizikovsky.

Boris Anisfeld
Costume design for the
Riverlet, 1911
Watercolor, whitening, silver
paint and pencil on paper
on board, 46.2 × 20.7 cm
SBTM (KP 122846 GKD 2010)

Boris Anisfeld
Costume design for the Golden
Fish, 1911
Watercolor, pencil, whitening
and bronze paint on paper
on board, 45.9 × 26.5 cm
SPSMTM (GIK 7070/237
OR 9510)

Boris Anisfeld
Costume design for a Rusalka
1911
Watercolor, whitening
and bronze paint on paper
on board, 46.8 × 28.5 cm
SPSMTM (GIK 7324/270
OR 9513)

Boris Anisfeld
Costume design for Princess
Volkhova, 1911
Watercolor, pencil, whitening,
silver and bronze paint on
paper on board, 46 × 28.8 cm
SPSMTM (GIK 7070/238
OR 9511)

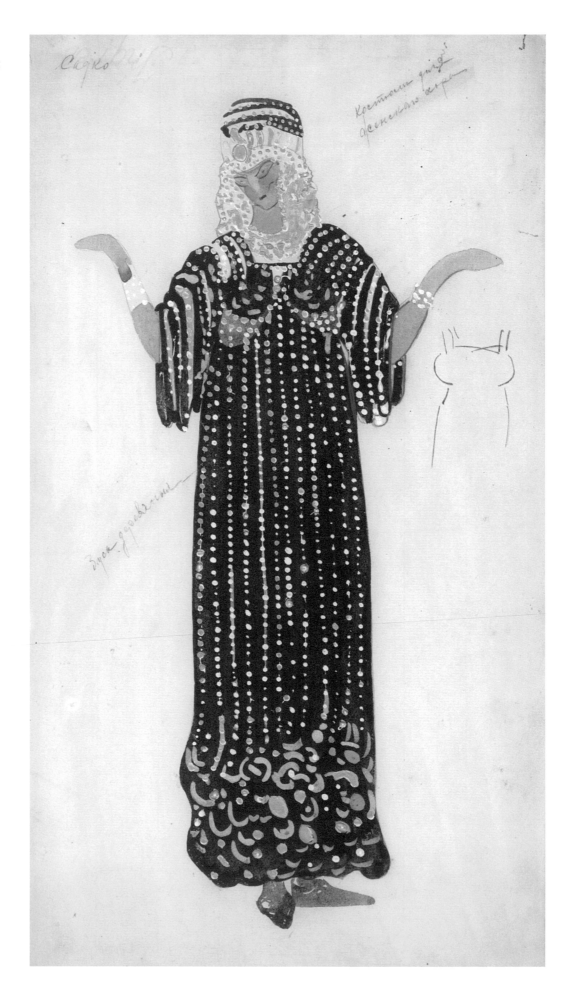

Petrouchka

Burlesque in four acts by Alexandre Benois and
Igor Stravinsky with music by Igor Stravinsky.
Staged at the Théâtre du Châtelet, Paris on June
13, 1911 with choreography by Michel Fokine
and designs by Alexandre Benois, assisted
by Boris Anisfeld.
Stage manager: Serge Grigoriev.
Principal performers: Tamara Karsavina
as the Ballerina, Vaslav Nijinsky as Petrouchka,
Aleksandr Orlov as the Magician, Enrico
Cecchetti as the Charlatan.

Valentine Hugo Gross
*Vaslav Nijinsky in the ballet
"Petrouchka,"* 1912
Encaustic on wood
45.5 × 55 cm
NMNM (2006.7.1)
Note: This rendering of
Karsavina and Nijinsky is
allied to the so-called "action"
drawings which Gross made
of the Ballets Russes between
1909 and 1913

Alexandre Benois
Costume design for
the Coachman, 1921
Watercolor, Indian ink
and pencil on paper
42.8 × 26 cm
MBT (KP 706)

Alexandre Benois
Design for Petrouchka's Room
1921
Gouache, watercolor, Indian
ink and bronze paint on paper
48 × 62 cm
MBT (KP 510)

Alexandre Benois
Design for the Blackamoor's
Room, 1921
Gouache, watercolor and
pencil on paper, 48 × 62 cm
MBT (KP 506)

Georges Reinhard
Model showing the
Fairground, 1910s, after a
design by Alexandre Benois
Gouache on board
56 × 63 × 50 cm
Archives SBM (3009)

Alexandre Benois
Costume design for a
Merchant's Wife, 1911
Watercolor, Indian ink
and pencil on paper
31.4 × 23.6 cm
NMNM (1974.11)
Serge Lifar Collection,
gift of Simone Del Duca

Alexandre Benois
Costume design for
the Second Merchant, 1911
Double-face design
Watercolor, Indian ink
and pencil on paper
31.4 × 23.6 cm
NMNM (1974.12)
Serge Lifar Collection,
gift of Simone Del Duca

Alexandre Benois
Costume design for
Petrouchka, 1943
Watercolor, pencil and ink
on paper, 25 × 16.5 cm
Archives SBM (530-17)

Alexandre Benois
Costume design for the
Magician, 1943
Watercolor, pencil and ink
on paper, 25 × 16.5 cm
Archives SBM (533-17)

Alexandre Benois
Costume design for the
Ballerina, 1943
Watercolor, pencil and ink
on paper, 25 × 16.5 cm
Archives SBM (531-17)

Alexandre Benois
Costume design for the
Blackamoor, 1943
Watercolor, pencil and ink
on paper, 25 × 16.5 cm
Archives SBM (532-17)

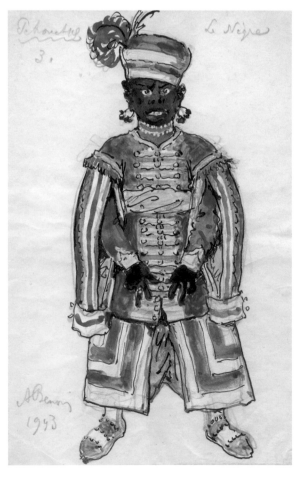

Alexandre Benois
Headdress for Nicolas Zverev
as the Blackamoor, 1920
Green velvet embroidered
with braid and furnished
with feathers
On permanent loan to SBM
at the NMNM (D.2002.7037)

Alexandre Benois
Costume for the Ballerina, 1920
Velvet, silk, cotton fabric
and fur
SPSMTM (GIK 17049/3a, b, c
MEM 3271/a, b, c)

Alexandre Benois
Costume design for the
Mummer-Devil, 1921
Watercolor, Indian ink
and pencil on paper
34.2 × 22.2 cm
MBT (KP 705)

Léon Bakst
Costume design for Vaslav
Nijinsky as Iskandar, 1922
Watercolor on paper
67.8 × 48.9 cm
The Metropolitan Museum
of Art, New York, gift of Sir
Joseph Duveen 1922 (64.97.1)

La Péri

One-act ballet based on a Persian fairy-tale
with music by Paul Dukas.
Rehearsed by Sergei Diaghilev's Ballets Russes
in Paris in 1911 with costumes by Léon Bakst,
but not produced.
Principal performers: Nathalie Trouhanova
as the Péri, Vaslav Nijinsky as Iskandar.

1912

Georges Reinhard
Set model after a design
by Léon Bakst
Gouache on board
55 × 59.5 × 50.5 cm
Archives SBM (3004)

Le Dieu Bleu

Hindu legend in one act by Jean Cocteau and
Federigo de Madrazo with music by Reynaldo
Hahn.
Produced at the Théâtre du Châtelet, Paris
on May 13, 1912 with choreography
by Michel Fokine and designs by Léon Bakst.
Stage manager: Serge Grigoriev.
Principal performers: Tamara Karsavina as the
Young Girl, Vaslav Nijinsky as the Blue God.

Léon Bakst
Set design, 1912
Oil on canvas, 150 × 211 cm
Private collection, Moscow
On permanent loan to the
Dansmuseet, Stockholm

Léon Bakst
Costume design for a Temple
Dancer, 1922
Based on a 1912 original
Watercolor, gouache, gold
paint, charcoal, metallic paint
and pencil on paper on board
64.8 × 47 cm
MKMAM, gift of Robert
L. B. Tobin (TL1998.49)

Léon Bakst
Costume design for a Monster
1911
Watercolor, gouache and pencil
on paper, 27.5 × 31.5 cm
Collection of Ekaterina and
Vladimir Semenikhin

Léon Bakst
Costume design for a Pilgrim
1911
Watercolor, gouache,
silver paint and pencil on
paper, 28.2 × 22.8 cm
Thyssen-Bornemisza
Collections (1981.60)

Vaslav Nijinsky in profile,
kneeling
Photograph by Baron Adolphe
de Meyer
Photomechanical proof
Collotype, paper
18.2 × 14.8 cm
Folio (Plate XXIII) from the
album *Le Prélude à l'après-
midi d'un faune* (Paris:
Paul Iribe, 1914)
Musée d'Orsay, Paris, gift
of Michel de Bry (PHO 1988
13 13)

L'Après-midi d'un Faune

Choreographic tableau in one act by Vaslav
Nijinsky based on *Le Prelude à l'après-midi d'un
faune* by Claude Debussy after the poem
by Stéphane Mallarmé.
Produced at the Théâtre du Châtelet, Paris on
May 29, 1912 with designs by Léon Bakst.
Stage manager: Serge Grigoriev.
Principal performers: Vaslav Nijinsky as the
Faun, Lydia Nelidova as the Nymph.

Léon Bakst
Vaslav Nijinsky as the Faun
1913
Gouache on paper with gold
and silver highlighting
67.7 × 48 cm
Private collection, Paris

Vaslav Nijinsky and Bronislava
Nijinska
Photograph by Baron Adolphe
de Meyer
Photomechanical proof
Collotype, paper, 12.1 × 18.4 cm
Folio (Plate IV) from the album
*Le Prélude à l'après-midi d'un
faune* (Paris: Paul Iribe, 1914)
Musée d'Orsay, Paris,
gift of Michel de Bry
(PHO 1988 13 4)

Mikhail Larionov
Vaslav Nijinsky rehearsing
"L'Après-midi d'un Faune,"
late 1920s–1930s
Indian ink, pen, whitening
and black pencil on paper
32.4 × 40.5 cm
STG (R-5888)

Vaslav Nijinsky in profile with
a pipe in his mouth, his right
leg bended, 1912
Photograph by Baron Adolphe
de Meyer
Photomechanical proof
Collotype, paper
19.2 × 29.4 cm
Folio (Plate XXVIII) from the
album *Le Prélude à l'après-
midi d'un faune* (Paris:
Paul Iribe, 1914)
Musée d'Orsay, Paris, gift
of Michel de Bry (PHO 1988
13 28)

Vaslav Nijinsky, supine, his
face towards the sun, 1912
Photograph by Baron Adolphe
de Meyer
Photomechanical proof
Collotype, paper, 16 × 22.7 cm
Folio (Plate XXX) from the
album *Le Prélude à l'après-
midi d'un faune* (Paris:
Paul Iribe, 1914)
Musée d'Orsay, Paris, gift
of Michel de Bry (PHO 1988
13 30)

Vaslav Nijinsky holding
a bunch of grapes, 1912
Photograph by Baron Adolphe
de Meyer
Photomechanical proof
Collotype, paper
20.9 × 15.8 cm
Folio (Plate XXI) from the
album *Le Prélude à l'après-
midi d'un faune* (Paris:
Paul Iribe, 1914)
Musée d'Orsay, Paris, gift
of Michel de Bry (PHO 1988
13 21)

Georges Reinhard
Set model for Act II after
a design by Léon Bakst
Gouache on board
52 × 56 × 50 cm
Archives SBM (3005)

Daphnis et Chloé

Choreographic symphony in three acts
by Michel Fokine after a pastoral by Longus,
with music by Maurice Ravel.
Produced at the Théâtre du Châtelet, Paris
on June 8, 1912 with choreography by Michel
Fokine and designs by Léon Bakst.
Stage manager: Serge Grigoriev.
Principal performers: Tamara Karsavina as
Chloé, Vaslav Nijinsky as Daphnis, Adolph Bolm
as Darkon.

Léon Bakst
Costume design for Tamara
Karsavina as Chloé, 1912
Graphite pencil, tempera
and watercolor on paper
28.2 × 44.7 cm
WA (1933/392)

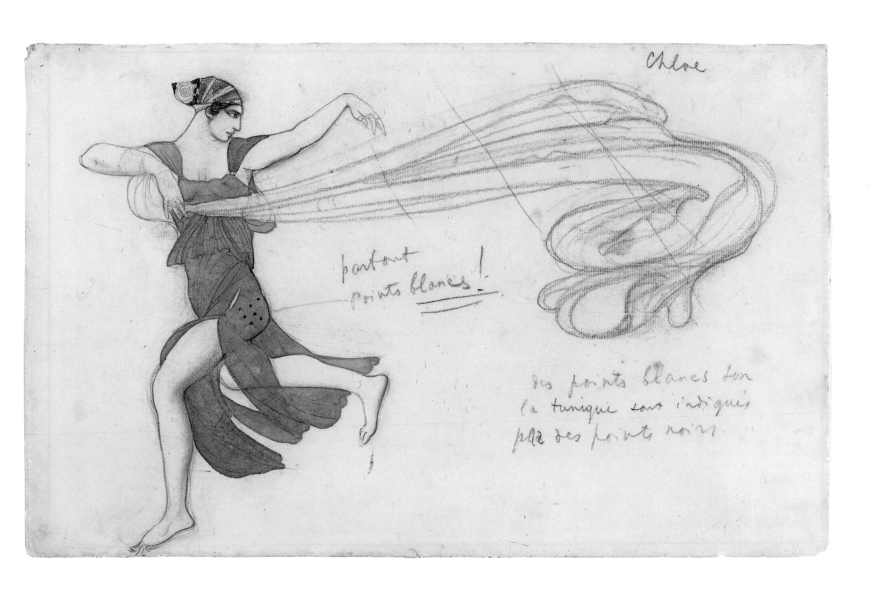

Léon Bakst
Décor for Acts I and II, 1912
Watercolor, gouache and
pencil on paper with gold
and silver highlighting
80 × 106 cm
Musée des Arts décoratifs,
Paris (21.770)

Georges Reinhard
Model for Act I after a design
by Léon Bakst
Gouache and board
52 × 56 × 50 cm
Archives SBM (3006)

Léon Bakst
Costume for a Brigand:
tunic and belt, 1912
Etamine of painted wool
and cotton fabric
NMNM (2006.27.2)

Léon Bakst
Costume for a Brigand: tunic,
culottes and belt, 1912
Etamine of painted wool
and cotton fabric
NMNM (2006.27.3)

Léon Bakst
Costume for a Brigand: toga,
trousers and belt, 1912
Painted wool
SPSMTM (KVP 559/1-3)

Ludmila Schollar, Vaslav
Nijinsky and Tamara
Karsavina
Photograph by Charles Gerschel
Bibliothèque nationale
de France, Paris

Jeux

Poème dansé with music by Claude Debussy.
Produced at the Théâtre des Champs-Elysées,
Paris on May 15, 1913 with choreography
by Vaslav Nijinsky and designs by Léon Bakst.
Stage manager: Serge Grigoriev.
Principal performers: Vaslav Nijinsky as
the Young Man, Tamara Karsavina and Ludmila
Schollar as the Young Girls.

Léon Bakst
Set design, 1913
Pastel and graphite pencil
on paper mounted on canvas
73.3 × 104.1 cm
MKMAM, gift of The Tobin
Endowment (TL1998.53)

Le Sacre du Printemps

Ballet in two acts with music by Igor Stravinsky
and libretto by Nicholas Roerich and Igor
Stravinsky.
Produced at the Théâtre des Champs-Elysées,
Paris on May 29, 1913 with choreography by
Vaslav Nijinsky and designs by Nicholas Roerich.
Restaged in 1920 with a new choreography
by Léonide Massine and with Lydia Sokolova
as the Sacrificial Virgin.
Stage manager: Serge Grigoriev.
Principal performer: Marie Piltz as the Sacrificial
Virgin.

Nicholas Roerich
Kissing the Earth, set design
for Scene 1 of *Le Sacre du
Printemps*, 1912
Tempera, gouache and Indian
ink on board, 62 × 94 cm
SRM (Zh-1979)

Nicholas Roerich
Costume design for a Young
Man in Act I, 1913
Pencil, gouache, bronze
and silver paint, Indian ink
and ink on paper on board
24 × 15 cm
SBTM (KP 123209 GKD 1992)

Nicholas Roerich
Costume design for a Maiden
in Act I, 1913
Pencil, gouache, silver
and bronze paint on gray
paper on board, 24.1 × 15.1 cm
SBTM (KP 123208 GKD 1996)

Nicholas Roerich
Costume for a Maiden in Scene 1 (with black pattern at waist), 1913
Long-sleeved, straight robe of off-white wool colored bright scarlet with "underskirt" and orange underarm gussets. There is an elaborate predominantly brown-red, orange, mauve and pale yellow pattern around the neck, shoulders and cuffs. On the chest are five nodular circles with a pomme-cross in pale yellow on a brown-red ground. Around the "hem" is an elaborate, multi-colored band of oranges, reds, yellow and turquoise geomantic shapes and on the hem of the "underskirt" a simpler decoration of lines and spots
TML (S.676.1980)

Nicholas Roerich
Costume for a Maiden in Scene 1, 1913
Very long robe of off-white wool, with long sleeves and orange underarm gussets. Attached is an underskirt of bright scarlet fine wool. The robe is completely over painted with elaborate multi-colored (yellow, green, orange, blue, red) geometric patterns. Narrow looped leather belt set with stamped metal studs and a metal stylized amulet of a "horse" with three hanging bars and lozenges
TML (S.680.1980)

Sergei Sudeikin
Costume for Herod, 1913
Felt, glass, metal, metallic
thread tassels, sequin
and brass stud trim
LACMA (M.68.51.5)

La Tragédie de Salomé

Ballet in one act with music by Florent Schmitt
after a poem by Robert d'Humières.
Produced at the Théâtre des Champs-Elysées,
Paris on June 12, 1913 with choreography by
Boris Romanov and designs by Sergei Sudeikin.
Stage manager: Serge Grigoriev.
Principal performer: Tamara Karsavina
as Salomé.

Sergei Sudeikin
Design for the drop curtain
1913
Oil on canvas, 101 × 117 cm
SPSMTM (GIK 16344
OZh 641)

Léonide Massine as Joseph
Reproduced from the cover
of *Comoedia illustré*, Paris,
June 1914

La Légende de Joseph

Ballet in one act with music by Richard Strauss
based on a text by Harry von Kessler and Hugo
von Hofmannsthal.
Produced at the Théâtre de l'Opéra, Paris
on May 14, 1914 with choreography by Michel
Fokine, set by José-Maria Sert and costumes
by Léon Bakst.
Stage manager: Serge Grigoriev.
Principal performers: Léonide Massine as Joseph,
Maria Kouznetsoff [Kuznetsova] as Potiphar's
Wife, Aleksei Bulgakov as Potiphar.

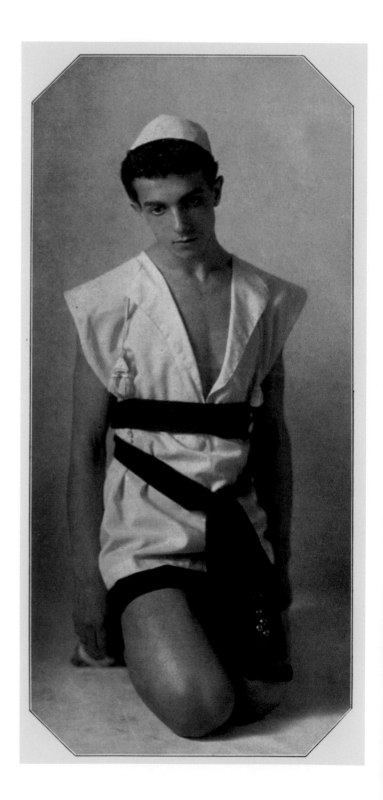

Georges Reinhard
Set model for the décor after a
design by Natalia Goncharova
Gouache on board
55 × 63 × 50 cm
Archives SBM (3031)

Le Coq d'Or

Opera ballet in three acts with music by Nikolai
Rimsky-Korsakov and libretto by Vladimir
Belsky based on a fairy-tale by Alexander
Pushkin adapted by Alexandre Benois.
Produced at the Théâtre National de l'Opéra,
Paris on May 24, 1914 with choreography by
Michel Fokine and designs by Natalia
Goncharova, assisted by Mikhail Larionov.
Stage managers: Serge Grigoriev, Charles Waltz
and Orest Allegri.
Principal performers
• Singers: Aurelia Dobrowolska, Elena Nikolaeva,
Elizaveta Petrenko, Ivan Alchevsky, Aleksandr
Belianin and Vasilii Petrov.
• Dancers: Tamara Karsavina as Queen
Shemakhan, Aleksei Bulgakov as King Dodon,
Enrico Cecchetti as the Astrologer.

Natalia Goncharova
Set design, 1914
Watercolor and gouache on
paper, 68.7 × 100.8 cm
The National Pushkin Museum,
St. Petersburg (KL 2833)

Georges Reinhard
Set model for the décor project
after a design by Natalia
Goncharova
Gouache on board
Archives SBM (3030)

Natalia Goncharova
Set design for Act I, 1914
Watercolor, gouache and
pencil on illustration board
45.1 × 70.1 cm
FAMSF. Theater and Dance
Collection, gift of Mrs. Adolph
B. Spreckels (T&D 1959.36)

Natalia Goncharova
Curtain design for Act III,
Scene 3, 1914
Watercolor, gouache
and pencil on board
37.5 × 53.3 cm
MKMAM, gift of Robert
L. B. Tobin (TL 1998.177)

Costume for the Golden
Cockerel, 1937
Cotton, metallic thread
knit, silk, silk knit, gilded
leather and net
LACMA (M68.51.10a–f)

Natalia Goncharova
Costume design for the Sirin
Bird, 1913–14
Gouache, watercolor, bronze
and pencil on paper
35 × 26.1 cm
STG (R-4511)

Natalia Goncharova
Costume design for Tsar
Dodon, 1914
Watercolor, bronze, graphite
pencil and collage on paper
36.2 × 25.7 cm
SBTM (KP 6350 GKD 1990)

Natalia Goncharova
Costume design for the
Astrologer, 1913–14
Gouache, bronze paint
and graphite pencil on paper
on board, 47.5 × 31.5 cm
STG (R-4513)

Costume for a female subject
of Tsar Dodon, 1937
Cotton, embroidered appliqués
and cotton lace
LACMA (M.68.51.7a–d)

Costume for a Maid, 1937
Lamé, linen, stenciled cotton,
cotton braid, appliqué and
embroidered
LACMA (M68.51.9a–d)

Tamara Karsavina as Queen
Shemakhan, 1914
Photograph by E. O. Hoppé
Vintage silver gelatin print
26 × 18.4 cm
CALA (01515–0016)

Tamara Karsavina as Queen
Shemakhan, 1914
Photograph by E. O. Hoppé
Vintage silver gelatin print
21.9 × 20 cm
CALA (01515–0017)

Alexandre Benois
Costume design for a Blue
Mandarin, 1914
Watercolor, Indian ink,
pencil and silver paint on
paper, 47.3 × 23 cm
CICF (KVP 682/117)

Le Rossignol

Opera in three acts with incidental dances
by Igor Stravinsky and Stepan Mitusov based
on a tale by Hans Christian Andersen.
Produced at the Théâtre National de l'Opéra,
Paris on May 26, 1914 with choreography
by Boris Romanov and designs by Alexandre
Benois.
Staged by Alexandre Benois and Aleksandr
Sanin.
Stage manager: Serge Grigoriev.
Principal performers: Pavel Andreev as the
Emperor, Aurelia Dobrowolska as the
Nightingale, Elizaveta Petrenko as Death.

Alexandre Benois
Décor design for Act III:
"The King's Bedroom," 1914
Gouache and pastel on paper
mounted on canvas
99 × 110 cm
MKMAM, gift of Robert
L. B. Tobin (TL 1998.111)

Alexandre Benois
Décor design for Act I, 1914
Watercolor, gouache and
pencil on paper on canvas
66.7 × 98.7 cm
SRM (R-5825)

Alexandre Benois
Costume design for a Japanese
Ambassador, 1914
Watercolor on board
47.6 × 32.2 cm
CICF (KVP 682/120)

Alexandre Benois
Costume design for a Dancer
in the Chinese March, 1914
Watercolor, Indian ink, ink,
pencil and whitening on paper
47.4 × 30.2 cm
SRM (R-38480)

223

1916

Léon Bakst
Costume design for the
procession of Young Ladies
in Act II, 1916
Graphite pencil with
watercolor and gold paint on
laid paper, 29.5 × 25.3 cm
NMNM (1974.5)
Serge Lifar Collection,
gift of Simone Del Duca

The Sleeping Beauty

Ballet in a prologue and three acts based on
a fairy tale by Charles Perrault, with original
music by Peter Tchaikovsky and original
choreography by Marius Petipa and Ivan
Vsevolozhsky. Abbreviated version produced
by Anna Pavlova at the Hippodrome Theater,
New York, on September 1, 1916 with designs
by Léon Bakst.
Note: *The Sleeping Beauty* was followed
by several versions, e.g., *The Sleeping Princess*
in 1921 (see pp. 258–59).

Acte II

Suite de jeunes filles
costumes fantastiq...

(troupe de...

fleurs de champs avec
minces tiges alternatives de
bleu bluet et blanc.

cheveux longs

en or.

épaule
transparent

fleurs de champs
blancs

corsage

Etoffe de jupe
mousseline avec
nails vertes
leger!

satin...

jupe

transparent

corsage

maillot couleur chair

copiez tout
et continuez les
petites fleurs sur
le nouveau pantalon

225

Natalia Goncharova
Costume design for a Spaniard
with a Shawl, 1916
Gouache, graphite pencil
on watermarked paper
65.8 × 44 cm
STG (R-4426)

Natalia Goncharova
Costume design for a Spanish
Woman with a Fan, 1916
Gouache and pencil on paper
66 × 51 cm
STG (R-4430)

España

Ballet based on Maurice Ravel's music for
Rhapsodie Espagnole with choreography
by Léonide Massine and designs by Natalia
Goncharova. Rehearsed under Sergei Diaghilev
for the Ballets Russes in Rome, fall 1916,
but not produced.
Principal performer: Catherine Devilliers.

227

Bronislava Nijinska as
Kikimora, late 1910s
Photograph by Foulsham
and Banfield, London
Original print
STG (Department
of Manuscripts, f. 180)

Contes Russes

Choreographic miniatures with an epilogue and
danced interludes by Léonide Massine, with
music by Anatolii Liadov and a prelude and
lament orchestrated by Arnold Bax.
The first miniature, entitled *Kikimora* was
produced in San Sebastián on August 25, 1916;
then four miniatures – *Kikimora*, *Baba Yaga*,
Bova-Korolevich and *Round Dance* at the
Théâtre du Châtelet, Paris, on May 11, 1917
with choreography by Léonide Massine assisted
by Mikhail Larionov, and designs by Mikhail
Larionov. On December 23, 1918 the
performance also included the miniature *Swan
Princess*.
Stage manager: Serge Grigoriev.
Principal performers: Lubov Tchernicheva as the
Swan Princess, Léon Woizikovsky and Léonide
Massine as Bova-Korolevich, Bronislava Nijinska
as Kikimora, Stanislas Idzikowski as the Cat.

Attendants of the Swan
Princess (Vera Nemtchinova
is third from left), late 1910s
Photograph by Foulsham
and Banfield, London
Original print
STG (Department
of Manuscripts, f. 180)

Mikhail Larionov
Set design: "The Lake
Fairytale" for the *Swan
Princess* miniature, 1918
Tempera, gouache and
graphite pencil on paper on
board, 35 × 48.8 cm
STG (R-4553)

Mikhail Larionov
Set design: "The Forest"
for the *Baba-Yaga* miniature
1917
Watercolor and pencil on
paper on board, 45.5 × 70 cm
STG (R-3609)

Mikhail Larionov
Costume design for a Wood
Goblin for the *Baba-Yaga*
miniature, 1915
Watercolor, whitening
and graphite pencil on paper
66.8 × 46.4 cm
STG (R-4481)

Mikhail Larionov
Costume design for a Wood
Goblin for the *Baba-Yaga*
miniature, 1915–16
Watercolor, gouache and
graphite pencil on vergé paper
59 × 44.5 cm
STG (R-5692)

Pablo Picasso
Costume design for the
Chinese Conjuror, 1917
Line block print on paper
after the original drawing
26.2 × 16.5 cm
Inscribed "A Georges Michel
/ Souvenir de Rome /
Picasso / 1917".
FAMSF. Theater and Dance
Collection, gift of Mrs. Adolph
B. Spreckels (T&D 1959.50)

Michel Georges-Michel
*The Opening of "La Parade"
at the Théâtre du Châtelet,
Paris, 18 May, 1917*, 1917
Oil on board, 45.8 × 35.7 cm
FAMSF. Theater and Dance
Collection, gift of Mrs. Adolph
B. Spreckels (T&D 1962.13)
Note: From left to right are
Paul Rosenberg, Marie
Laurencin, Sergei Diaghilev,
Misia Sert, Erik Satie, Michel
Georges-Michel, Pablo Picasso
and Jean Cocteau

Parade

Ballet in one act by Jean Cocteau with music
by Erik Satie.
Produced at the Théâtre du Châtelet, Paris
on May 18, 1917 with choreography by Léonide
Massine and designs by Pablo Picasso.
Stage manager: Serge Grigoriev.
Principal performers: Léonide Massine as the
Chinese Conjuror, Lydia Lopukhova and Nicolas
Zverev as the Acrobats, Marie Shabelska as
the Young American Girl.

1918

Lubov Tchernicheva
as Cleopatra, 1918
Photograph by E. O. Hoppé
Vintage gelatin silver print
19 × 13 cm
CALA (14622-B)

Léonide Massine as Amoun
1918
Photograph by E. O. Hoppé
Vintage gelatin silver print
22.8 × 18 cm
CALA (14630-H)

Cleopatra

Choreographic drama in one act based
on Anton Arensky's *Egyptian Nights* with
musical additions by Nikolai Cherepnin,
Aleksandr Glazunov, Mikhail Glinka, Nikolai
Rimsky-Korsakov, and Sergei Taneev.
Produced at the Coliseum Theatre, London
on September 5, 1918 with sets by Robert
Delaunay and costumes by Sonia Delaunay.
Stage manager: Serge Grigoriev.
Principal performers: Lubov Tchernicheva
as Cleopatra, Léonide Massine as Amoun,
Lydia Sokolova as Ta-Hor.

Lubov Tchernicheva
as Cleopatra, 1918
Photograph by E. O. Hoppé
Vintage gelatin silver print
18.4 × 12.7 cm
CALA (14622-E)

Sonia Delaunay
Costume for Cleopatra, 1918
Silk sequins, mirror and beads,
wool yarn, metallic thread
braid and lamé
LACMA (M.68.51.18a–b)

Flora Lion
Lubov Tchernicheva
in Costume for the Role
of Cleopatra, c. 1918
Oil on canvas, 198 × 116.8 cm
Collection of Nilufer Dobra, on
permanent loan at the NMNM
(D.2006.5.1)

Pablo Picasso
Set design for the bullring
1919
Pochoir, 25 × 25 cm
Collection of Nina Lobanov-
Rostovsky

Le Tricorne
(El Sombrero de Tres Picos)

Ballet in one act by Gregorio Martínez Sierra
after a story by Pedro Antonio de Alarcón with
music by Manuel de Falla.

Produced at the Alhambra Theatre, London
on July 22, 1919, and at the Théâtre National
de l'Opéra, Paris on 23 January, 1920 with
choreography by Léonide Massine and designs
by Pablo Picasso.

Stage manager: Serge Grigoriev.

Principal performers: Léonide Massine as the
Miller, Tamara Karsavina as the Miller's Wife,
Léon Woizikovsky as the Corregidor, Stanislas
Idzikowski as the Dandy.

Note: These pochoirs are from: Pablo Picasso,
Le Tricorne (Paris: Rosenberg, 1920), a folio
of thirty-two pochoir reproductions.

Pablo Picasso
Set design with view of a
Spanish town with blue sky
1919
Pochoir, 20 × 25 cm
Collection of Nina Lobanov-
Rostovsky

Pablo Picasso
Costume design for an Old
Woman, 1919
Pochoir, 22 × 15.5 cm
Collection of Nina Lobanov-
Rostovsky

Pablo Picasso
Costume design for
La Sevillana, 1919
Pochoir, 26 × 18 cm
Collection of Nina Lobanov-
Rostovsky

Pablo Picasso
Costume design for the
Corregidor, 1919
Pochoir, 26 × 18 cm
Collection of Nina Lobanov-
Rostovsky

Pablo Picasso
Costume design for a Lady
1919
Pochoir, 26 × 18 cm
Collection of Nina Lobanov-
Rostovsky

The Four Chamberlains
rehearsing on a street
in Monte Carlo, 1920
Modern print, 13 × 18 cm
Archives SBM (1920 06 15)

Le Chant du Rossignol

Ballet in one act based on a tale by Hans
Christian Andersen and adapted from the opera
Le Rossignol by Igor Stravinsky.
Produced at the Théâtre National de l'Opéra,
Paris on February 2, 1920 with choreography by
Léonide Massine and designs by Henri Matisse.
Restaged at the Théâtre de la Gaîté-Lyrique,
Paris on June 17, 1925 with a new choreography
by George Balanchine.
Stage manager: Serge Grigoriev.
Principal performers: Tamara Karsavina as
the Nightingale, Lydia Sokolova as Death, Serge
Grigoriev as the Emperor.

Henri Matisse
Costume for a Mourner, 1920
Felt with velvet appliqués
LACMA (M.68.51.21a–b)

Group rehearsing on a street
in Monte Carlo, 1920
Modern print, 13 × 18 cm
Archives SBM (1920 06 14)

Henri Matisse
Costume for a Warrior, 1920
• Headdress: felt with ink
drawing
• Tunic: felt, velvet with
metallic thread braid, silk
and brass metal trim
• Pantaloons: silk
LACMA (M.68.51.20a–c)

Henri Matisse
Cape for the Emperor, 1920
Silk with metallic embroidery
and studs
MKMAM, gift of The Tobin
Endowment (TL 2001.92)

Pulcinella

Ballet with singing in one act by Igor Stravinsky
after Giovanni Battista Pergolesi.
Produced at the Théâtre National de l'Opéra,
Paris on May 15, 1920 with choreography by
Léonide Massine and designs by Pablo Picasso.
Stage manager: Serge Grigoriev.
Principal performers: Tamara Karsavina
as Pimpinella, Lubov Tchernicheva as Prudenza,
Vera Nemtchinova as Rosetta, Léonide Massine
as Pulcinella, Nicolas Zverev as Florindo,
Enrico Cecchetti as the Doctor.

Pablo Picasso
Set design, c. 1920
Watercolor and gouache on
paper, 32 × 48 cm
MKMAM, gift of The Tobin
Endowment (TL2001.106)

Tamara Karsavina in the
pas de deux, 1920
Photograph by E. O. Hoppé
Digital pigment print
24 × 16.5 cm
CALA (01515-0040-A)

Le Astuzie Femminili

A *dramma giocoso* in four acts by Domenico
Cimarosa rearranged as an opera ballet in three
acts by Ottorino Respighi.
Produced at the Théâtre National de l'Opéra,
Paris on May 27, 1920 with choreography by
Léonide Massine and designs by José-Maria Sert.
Stage manager: Serge Grigoriev.
Principal performers: Mafalda de Voltri
as Bellina, Aurelio Anglada as Filandro,
Zoia Rosovska as Leonora, Gino de Vecchi
as Giampaolo, Tamara Karsavina, Lubov
Tchernicheva.

José-Maria Sert
Costume design for Tamara
Karsavina and Stanislas
Idzikowski in the *pas de deux*
for Scene 3, 1920
Graphite pencil, tempera and
ink on paper, 32.5 × 49.7 cm
WA (1933.539)

Mikhail Larionov
Costume design for the
Soldier, 1915–21
Gouache and pencil on paper
on board, 54 × 37.8 cm
STG (R-4709)

Mikhail Larionov
Costume for a soldier, 1921
Uniform of many different
materials, including a red wax
cloth breastplate, buckram for
the four upright epaulettes and
the painted mask and cap and
blue flannel and cotton fabric
for the jacket, with satin
appliqué and wax cloth cuffs.
Front and back of the trousers
are different as well as left and
right legs which carry appliqué
work on flannel, cotton fabric
and satin
Dansmuseet, Stockholm
(DM 1969-25)

Chout

Choreographic pantomime in six scenes with
music by Sergei Prokofiev based on a legend
interpreted by Mikhail Larionov.
Produced at the Théâtre de la Gaîté-Lyrique,
Paris on May 17, 1921 with choreography
by Mikhail Larionov and Thadée Slavinsky
and designs by Mikhail Larionov.
Stage manager: Serge Grigoriev.
Principal performers: Thadée Slavinsky as the
Buffoon, Lydia Sokolova as the Buffoon's Wife.

Mikhail Larionov
Costume for a buffoon, 1921
Short-sleeved cotton blouse
with knitted white flannel
front and with appliqué
decorations in satin. A long
sleeved shirt decorated with
appliqué white dots and wide
black, yellow cuffs is worn
beneath the blouse. One
trouser leg of white flannel
with stripes of satin and
flannel and the other of satin

with painted fishbone
patterning. Round the waist is
a basque of white buckram on
a cane frame and painted
patterning. Hat in satin.
Dansmuseet, Stockholm
(DM 1969-24)

Two Old Buffoons, 1920s
Photograph by Foulsham
and Banfield, London
Original print
STG (Department
of Manuscripts, f. 180)

Mikhail Larionov
Costume design for the
Old Buffoon, 1915
Watercolor on paper
56 × 38 cm
CICF (KVP 682/375)

M. Larionow. 915

Mikhail Larionov
Costume for the daughter
of the Old Buffoon, 1921
Pink satin bodice with half
the front of white flannel,
bell-shaped sleeves and cuffs
of cotton fabric. Wide skirt
of satin painted with stylized
floral patterns
Dansmuseet, Stockholm
(DM 1969-46)

Mikhail Larionov
Costume design for the
Daughter of the Old Buffoon
1915–21
Gouache and pencil on paper
on board, 45.7 × 35 cm
STG (R-4653)

Jean Jasvinsky as the
Merchant is center stage,
Vera Nemtchinova is the
Matchmaker, 1920s
Photograph by Foulsham
and Banfield, London
Original print
STG (Department of
Manuscripts, f. 180)

Mikhail Larionov
Set design for Scene I, 1921
Gouache on paper, 50 × 69 cm
CICF (KVP 682/385)

Mikhail Larionov
Costume design for the
Matchmaker, 1915–21
Gouache and pencil on paper
on board, 54 × 44.5 cm
STG (R-4652)

Léon Bakst
Costume design for a Duke
1921
Watercolor cut out and applied
to paper, 35.4 × 24.1 cm
LACMA (M68.51.4)

The Sleeping Princess

Ballet in a prologue and three acts based on
a fairy tale by Charles Perrault, *The Sleeping
Beauty*; original music by Peter Tchaikovsky
and original choreography by Marius Petipa and
Ivan Vsevolozhsky.

Produced at the Alhambra Theatre, London
on November 2, 1921 with choreography by
Nicholas Sergeyev and additional choreography
by Bronislava Nijinska, partial reorchestration
by Igor Stravinsky and designs by Léon Bakst.
Stage manager: Serge Grigoriev.

Principal performers: Olga Spessivtseva, Vera
Trefilova, Lubov Egorova and Vera Nemtchinova
as Aurora, Pierre Vladimirov as the Prince,
Carlotta Brianza and Enrico Cecchetti as
the Wicked Fairy Carabosse.

Note: Although the most luxurious of
interpretations, *The Sleeping Princess* was
preceded and followed by several versions, e.g.,
The Sleeping Beauty (produced by Anna Pavlova
at the Hippodrome Theater, New York on
September 1, 1916 with designs by Léon Bakst:
see pp. 224–25) and *Le Mariage d'Aurore*,
produced by Sergei Diaghilev at the Théâtre
National de l'Opéra, Paris on May 18, 1922.

Léon Bakst
Set design for Act IV:
"The Awakening," 1921
Watercolor and pencil
on paper, 48 × 66.8 cm
Thyssen-Bornemisza
Collections (1979.43)

Mikhail Larionov
Costume design for the
Constable cum Sheep, 1922
Watercolor and gouache
on board, 38 × 26.7 cm
STG (R-4681)

Le Renard

Ballet burlesque with voices in one act by Igor
Stravinsky based on a Russian folk tale adapted
by Charles-Ferdinand Ramuz.
Produced at the Théâtre National de l'Opéra,
Paris on May 18, 1922 with choreography by
Bronislava Nijinska and designs by Mikhail
Larionov.
Stage manager: Serge Grigoriev.
Principal performers: Bronislava Nijinska as
the Fox, Stanislas Idzikowski as the Cat,
Jean Jasvinsky as the Cock, Mikhail Fedorov
as the Ram.
Restaged on May 21, 1929 at the Théâtre Sarah-
Bernhardt, Paris with choreography by Serge
Lifar and new designs by Mikhail Larionov.
Principal performers: Nicolas Efimov, Léon
Woizikovsky, Jean Hoyer and Boris Lissanevitch.

Mikhail Larionov
Costume design for the
Captain cum Cat, 1922
Gouache on paper on board
38 × 26.8 cm
STG (R-4494)

Земскій
Котъ
М.922

Scene for the 1929 revival at
the Théâtre Sarah-Bernhardt,
Paris. Léon Woizikovsky is the
Fox, Nicolas Efimov the
Rooster, Jean Hoyer the Cat,
Boris Lissanevitch the Ram
Photograph by Boris Lipnitzki
Original print
STG (Department
of Manuscripts. f. 180)

Scene for the 1929 revival at
the Théâtre Sarah-Bernhardt,
Paris. On stage are the Cat, the
Goat, the Rooster and the Ram
Photograph by Boris Lipnitzki
Original print
STG (Department
of Manuscripts. f. 180)

Mikhail Larionov
Set design: "The Hut," 1922
Gouache and pencil on paper
on board, 26.9 × 36.8 cm
STG (R-4495)

Mavra

Comic opera in one act by Igor Stravinsky with
libretto by Boris Kochno based on Alexander
Pushkin's poem *The Little House in Kolomna*.
Produced at the Hôtel Continental, Paris on May
29, 1922 and at the Théâtre National de l'Opéra,
Paris on June 3, 1922 with choreography by
Bronislava Nijinska and designs by Léopold
Survage.
Stage manager: Serge Grigoriev.
Principal performers: Oda Slobodska as Parasha,
Hélène Sadovène as the Neighbor, Zoia Rosovska
as the Mother, Belina Skoupevsky as the Hussard.

Léopold Survage
Set design, 1922
Tempera on paper
47.5 × 70.4 cm
WA (1933.543)

Les Noces

Choral ballet in four scenes by Igor Stravinsky.
Produced at the Théâtre de la Gaîté-Lyrique,
Paris on June 13, 1923 with choreography by
Bronislava Nijinska and designs by Natalia
Goncharova.
Stage manager: Serge Grigoriev.
Principal performers
• Singers: Elena Smirnova, Maria Davydova.
• Dancers: Félia Doubrowska as the Fiancée,
Léon Woizikovsky, Lubov Tchernicheva.

Natalia Goncharova
Composition with three figures
and motifs in one frame
• Woman, 1915–16
Gouache and pencil on board
38 × 26.5 cm
STG (R-5828)
• Man of the People, 1915–16
Gouache and pencil on board
38 × 26.5 cm
STG (R-5829)
• Courtier, 1915–16
Gouache and pencil on board
38 × 26.5 cm
STG (R-5823)

• Geometric ornament. Design
for upper transverse, 1910s
Gouache and graphite pencil
on paper, 10.5 × 31.8 cm
STG (R-5830)
• Flowers. Design for the
wings, 1910s
Gouache and graphite pencil
on paper, 54.3 × 14.3 cm
STG (R-5831)
• Flowers. Design for the
wings, 1910s
Gouache and graphite pencil
on paper, 54.3 × 14 cm
STG (R-5832)

Natalia Goncharova
Costume design for a peasant
girl carrying fruit, 1916
Gouache, pencil, black ink
and watercolor on laid paper
50.1 × 37.5 cm
NMNM (2006.12.2)

Natalia Goncharova
Set design: composition with
Factory Chimneys, 1916–17
Gouache and pencil on paper
on board, 56 × 78.8 cm
STG (R-4470)

Natalia Goncharova
Curtain design: composition
with Horses and Birds
1915–16
Gouache and graphite pencil on
paper on board, 53 × 73.5 cm
STG (R-6248)

Rehearsal on the roof of the
Opéra, Monte Carlo, 1923
Photograph by Joseph Enrietti
Original print, 13 × 18 cm
Archives SBM (1923 04 94)

Rehearsal on the roof of the
Opéra, Monte Carlo, 1923
Photograph by Joseph Enrietti
Original print, 13 × 18 cm
Archives SBM (1923 04 99)

Rehearsal on the roof of the
Opéra, Monte Carlo, 1923
Photograph by Joseph Enrietti
Original print, 13 × 18 cm
Archives SBM (1923 04 97)

Juan Gris
Design for the front cloth:
Offrandes à la Bergère, 1924
Watercolor, tempera, graphite,
gold and silver paint on paper
24.5 × 30.5 cm
WA (1933.481)

Les Tentations de la Bergère ou l'Amour Vainqueur

Ballet in one act based on the dance interlude
of Peter Tchaikovsky's *Queen of Spades* with
music by Michael de Monteclair reconstructed
and scored by Henri Casadesus.
Produced at the Théâtre de Monte-Carlo on
January 3, 1924 with choreography by Bronislava
Nijinska and designs by Juan Gris.
Stage manager: Serge Grigoriev.
Principal performers: Anton Dolin, Vera
Nemtchinova, Thadée Slavinsky, Anatole Vilzak,
Léon Woizikovsky, Nicolas Zverev.

Juan Gris
Costume design for a Herald
1924
Graphite pencil, tempera,
watercolor, gold and copper
paint with white highlights
on paper, 34.2 × 25.3 cm
WA (1933.483)

Anatole Vilzak as the King
1924
Original print
Archives SBM (1924 00 22)

Les Fâcheux

Ballet in one act by Boris Kochno with music
by Georges Auric, after a comic ballet by Molière.
Produced at the Théâtre de Monte-Carlo
on January 19, 1924 and at the Théâtre
des Champs-Elysées, Paris on June 4, 1924
with choreography by Bronislava Nijinska
and designs by Georges Braque.
Stage manager: Serge Grigoriev.
Principal performers: Lubov Tchernicheva as
Orphise, Anton Dolin as l'Elégant, Anatole Vilzak
as Eraste, Stanislas Idzikowski as Lysandre.

Georges Braque
Series of plates drawn from
Les Fâcheux (Paris: Éditions
du Quatre-Chemins, 1924)
Lithographs with gouache
highlightings on paper,
27.7 × 21.8 cm each
Archives SBM
• Costume design for
La Montagne
• Costume design for the
Première Bavarde
• Costume design for Eraste
• Costume design for the
Deuxième Masque

Anatole Vilzak as Eraste, 1924
Original print
Archives SBM (1924 00 21 bis)

© ARCHIVES MONTE-CARLO SBM

Le Train Bleu

Opérette dansé in one act by Jean Cocteau with
music by Darius Milhaud.
Produced at the Théâtre des Champs-Elysées,
Paris on June 20, 1924 with choreography by
Bronislava Nijinska and set by Henri Laurens,
drop curtain by Pablo Picasso and costumes
by Gabrielle Chanel.
Stage manager: Serge Grigoriev.
Principal performers: Bronislava Nijinska as the
Tennis Champion, Lydia Sokolova as Perlouse,
Anton Dolin as the Beau Gosse, Léon
Woizikovsky as the Golf Player.

Pablo Picasso
Drop curtain, 1924
Oil on canvas, 1000 × 1100 cm
TML (S.316.1978)
Note: So meticulous was
Alexandre Shervashidze's
monumental copy of the
original gouache and so
delighted was Picasso that he
wrote on the canvas: "Dédié
a Diaghilew. Picasso." The
curtain is the largest canvas
ever signed by Picasso. For the
Monaco venue the curtain
hangs in the Salle des Arts du
Sporting d'hiver de la Société
des Bains de Mer

Lydia Sokolova as Perlouse
and Léon Woizikovsky as the
Golf Player, 1924
Photograph by Bassano
Studio, London
Original print, 11.2 × 7.6 cm
Archives SBM (1925 08 03)

Bronislava Nijinska as the
Tennis Champion and Anton
Dolin as the Beau Gosse, 1924
Photograph by Bassano
Studio, London
Original print
Archives SBM (1925 08 05)

Anton Dolin as the Beau Gosse
1924
Photograph by Bassano
Studio, London
Archives SBM (1925 00 08)
Note: The inscription is from
Dolin to his mother on her
birthday

Alexandra Danilova as Flore
and Serge Lifar as Borée, 1925
Original print, 13.4 × 9.5 cm
Archives NMNM
(2002 7 12 C 37 07 0009)
Serge Lifar Collection

Georges Braque
Costume design for the Muses
1925
Pencil, gouache and silver
paint on paper, 33 × 25 cm
MO (Mus K 24)

Zéphyr et Flore

Ballet by Boris Kochno with music by Vladimir
Dukelsky.
Produced at the Théâtre de Monte-Carlo on April
28, 1925 and at the Théâtre de la Gaîté-Lyrique,
Paris on June 15, 1925 with choreography by
Léonide Massine and designs by Georges Braque.
Stage manager: Serge Grigoriev.
Principal performers: Alice Nikitina as Flore,
Anton Dolin as Zéphyr, Serge Lifar as Borée.

Les Matelots

Ballet in five acts by Boris Kochno with music
by Georges Auric.
Produced at the Théâtre de la Gaîté-Lyrique,
Paris on June 17, 1925 with choreography by
Léonide Massine and designs by Pedro Pruna.
Stage manager: Serge Grigoriev.
Principal performers: Vera Nemtchinova
as the Young Girl, Lydia Sokolova as the Friend,
Léon Woizikovsky, Thadée Slavinsky and Serge
Lifar as the Sailors.

Pedro Pruna
Design for the back cloth
of Scene 5, 1925
Watercolor, tempera, gouache
and pencil on paper
36.5 × 42 cm
WA (1933.521)

André Derain
Costume design for the Black
Ballerina, 1926
Graphite, ink and tempera
on paper, 31.5 × 24.5 cm
WA (1933 464)

Alexandra Danilova as the
Black Ballerina and Stanislas
Idzikowski as Jack-in-the-Box
1927
Photograph by Man Ray
Archives SBM (1927 01 59)

Jack-in-the-Box

Ballet in one act by Erik Satie orchestrated
by Darius Milhaud.
Produced at the Théâtre Sarah-Bernhardt, Paris
on June 3, 1926 with choreography by George
Balanchine and designs by André Derain.
Stage manager: Serge Grigoriev.
Principal performers: Alexandra Danilova as the
Black Ballerina, Stanislas Idzikowski as the
Puppet, Lubov Tchernicheva, Félia Doubrowska.

© ARCHIVES MONTE-CARLO SBM

André Derain
Model for set design, 1926
Watercolor and ink on paper
20 × 30 × 40 cm
NMNM (1974.17)
Serge Lifar Collection,
gift of Simone Del Duca

André Derain
Set design with the two
white Ballerinas and the two
black Cloud Carriers, 1926
Graphite, ink, tempera
and watercolor on paper
24.1 × 33 cm
WA (1933.462)

André Derain
Set design with the two
blue Ballerinas and the two
white Cloud Carriers, 1926
Graphite, ink, tempera
and watercolor on paper
24.3 × 32.1 cm
WA (1933.463)

Serge Lifar as the Young Man,
1927
Dedicated to Madame Eugènie
Lalande and signed "Serge
Lifar 1936" bottom left
Photograph by Sasha for
Angelo Photos
Original print, 29 × 21 cm
NMNM

La Chatte

Ballet in one act by Sobeka (a composite pseudonym where So = Sauguet, Be = Balanchine, Ka = Kochno) based on a fable by Aesop reworked by Boris Kochno, with music by Henri Sauguet. Produced at the Théâtre de Monte-Carlo on April 30, 1927 and at the Théâtre Sarah-Bernhardt, Paris on May 27, 1927 with choreography by George Balanchine and designs by Naum Gabo and Antoine Pevsner.
Stage manager: Serge Grigoriev.
Principal performers: Olga Spessivtseva and Alice Nikitina as the Cat, Serge Lifar as the Young Man.

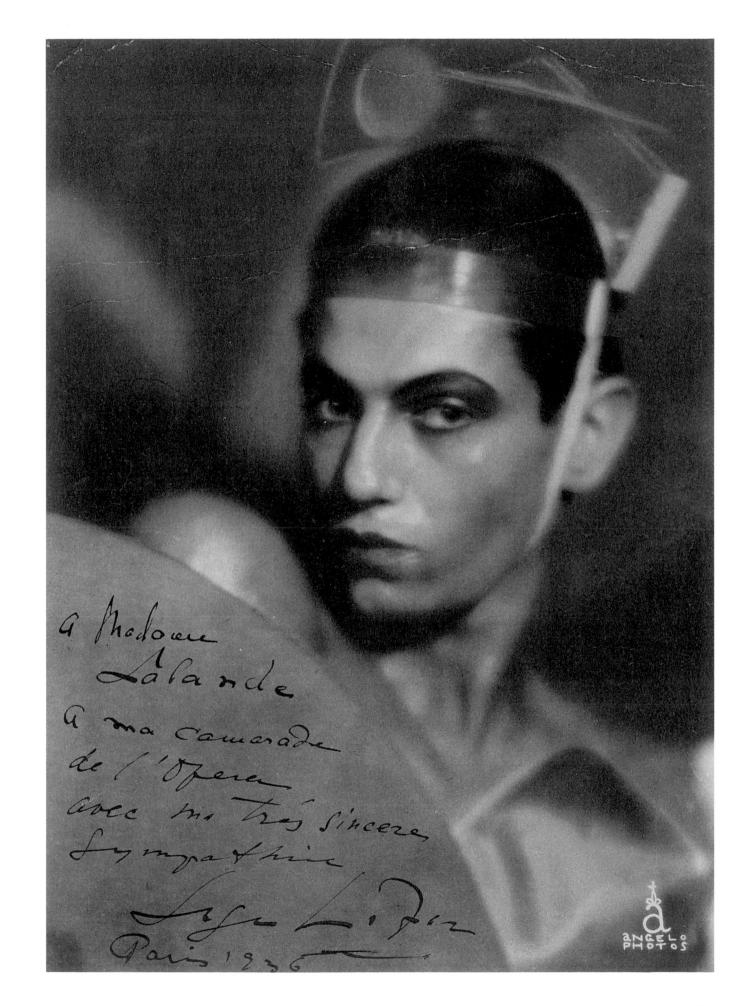

*A Madame
Lalande
A ma camarade
de l'Opéra
avec mes très sincères
sympathies
Serge Lifar
Paris 1936*

Alice Nikitina as the Cat
and Serge Lifar as the Young
Man, 1928
Photograph by Sasha
for Angelo Photos
Reprint
Archives SBM (1928 01 11)

Naum Gabo
Costume design for Serge Lifar
as the Young Man, 1927
Pencil on graph paper
28 × 21.8 cm
WA (1933.475)

Naum Gabo
Costume design for Serge Lifar
as the Young Man, 1927
Pencil on graph paper
27.5 × 21.8 cm
WA (1933.476)

Naum Gabo
Costume design for Serge Lifar
as the Young Man, 1927
Pencil on graph paper
28 × 22 cm
MO (Mus K 31)

Georgii Yakulov
Sketch for an ensemble scene
in Act I: "The Arrival of the
Train," 1927
Pencil, colored pencils and
ink on paper, 21 × 27 cm
MO (Mus K 132)
Boris Kochno Collection

Lubov Tchernicheva and Serge
Lifar, 1927
Photograph by Sasha
Lebrecht / Rue des Archives

Pas d'Acier

Ballet in two scenes by Sergei Prokofiev.
Produced at the Théâtre Sarah-Bernhardt, Paris
on June 7, 1927 with choreography by Léonide
Massine and designs by Georgii Yakulov.
Stage manager: Serge Grigoriev.
Principal performers: Alexandra Danilova, Serge
Lifar, Léonide Massine, Lubov Tchernicheva,
Léon Woizikovsky.

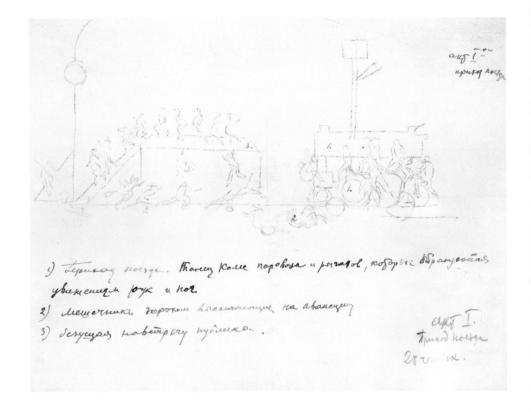

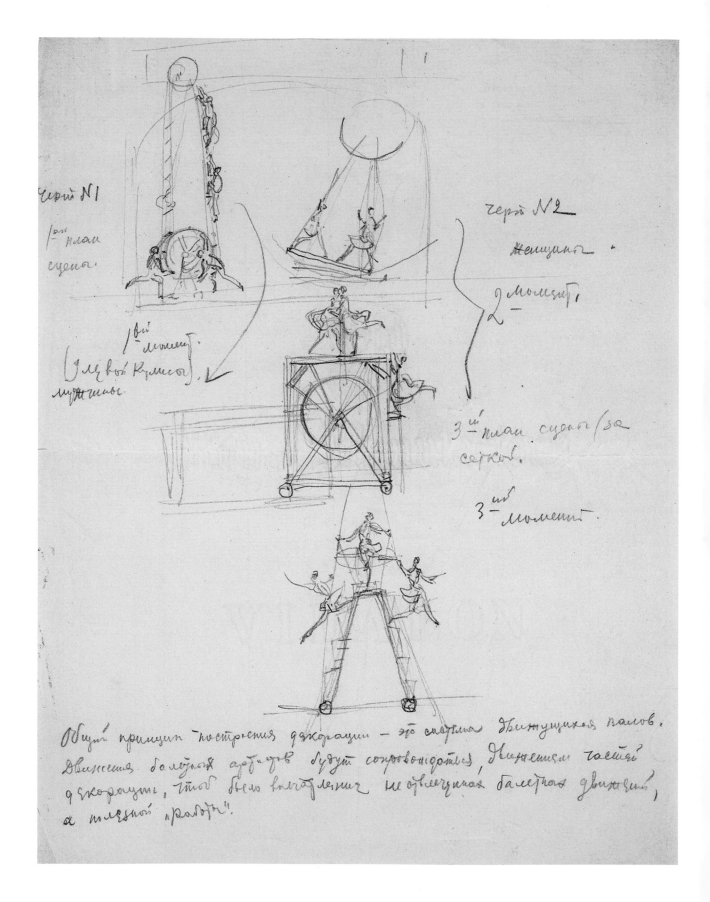

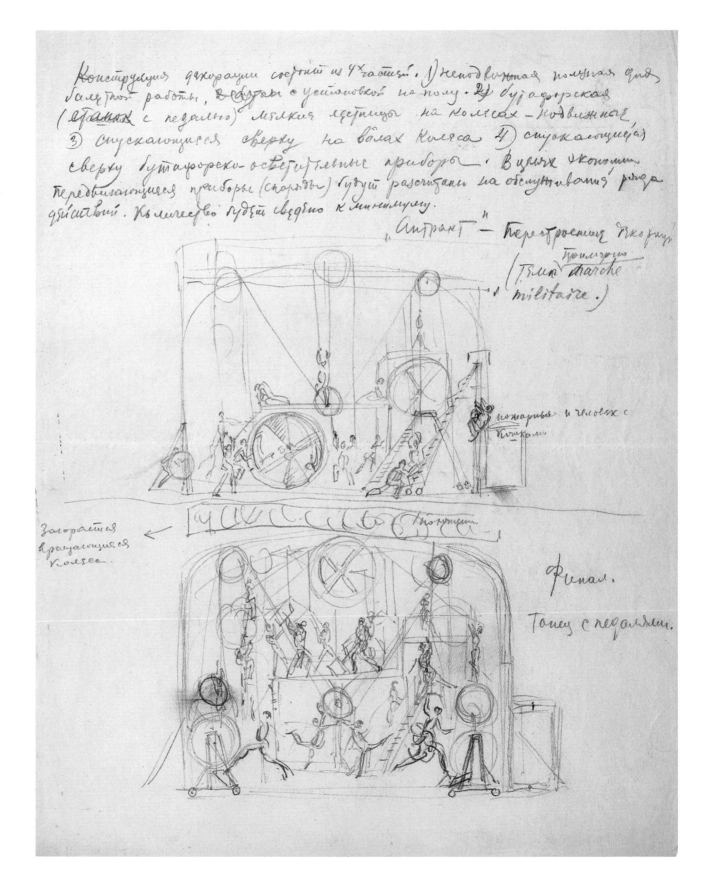

Scene from *Ode*, 1928
Photograph by Boris Lipnitzki,
Paris
11,1 × 8,6 cm
Archives NMNM
(2002 7 12 C 37 07 00 01)
Serge Lifar Collection

Ode

Ballet in two acts with a choir, two solo voices
and a symphony orchestra with music by Nicolas
Nabokov and a libretto based on a poem by
Mikhail Lomonosov.
Produced at the Théâtre Sarah-Bernhardt, Paris
on June 6, 1928 with choreography by Léonide
Massine and designs by Pavel Tchelitchew
assisted by Pierre Charbonnier.
Stage manager: Serge Grigoriev.
Principal performers: Ira Beliankina as Nature,
Serge Lifar as the Pupil, Félia Doubrowska,
Léonide Massine, Constantine Tcherkass.

Pavel Tchelitchew
Set design, 1928
Gouache and pencil on paper
21 × 25 cm
NMNM (1974.7)
Serge Lifar Collection,
gift of Simone Del Duca

Two scenes from *Ode*, 1928
Photographs by Boris Lipnitzki
Reproduced from W. Propert,
The Russian Ballet 1921–1929
(London: Lane, 1931), plate 35

Pavel Tchelitchew
Set design with figures
for Scene 3, 1928
Graphite pencil, ink and
tempera on blue paper
19.8 × 24.8 cm
WA (1933.549)

P. Tchelitchew

Pavel Tchelitchew
Sketch with a dance position
1928
Ink on paper, 27 × 21 cm
MO (Mus K 123)
Boris Kochno Collection

Scene from *Ode*, 1928
Photograph by George
Hoyningen-Huene
Courtesy Staley–Wise Gallery,
New York
Studio Vogue, France

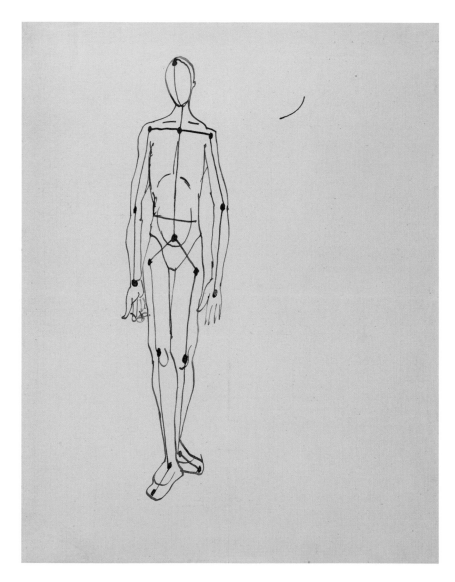

Pavel Tchelitchew
Costume design for Serge Lifar
as the Pupil, 1928
Ink and tempera on card
32 × 24.4 cm
WA (1933.551)

Pavel Tchelitchew
Costume design for the Man
with Phosphorescent
Markings, 1928
Ink on two sheets of paper
35.7 × 20.9 cm
WA (1933.552)

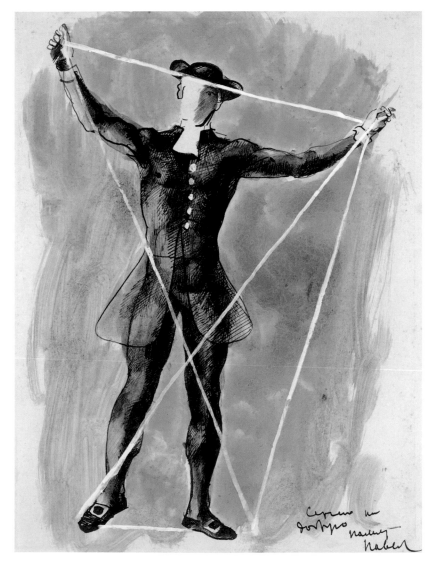

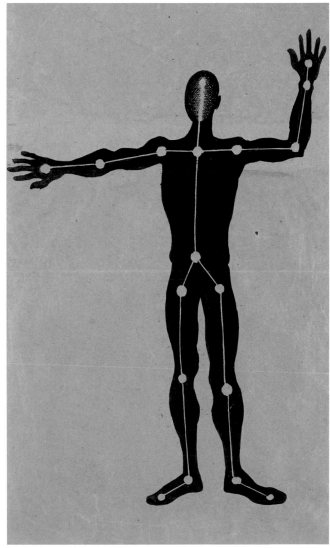

Apollon Musagète

Ballet in two scenes by Igor Stravinsky.
Produced at the Théâtre Sarah-Bernhardt, Paris
on June 12, 1928 with choreography by George
Balanchine and designs by André Bauchant.
Stage manager: Serge Grigoriev.
Principal performers: Serge Lifar as Apollo,
Alice Nikitina as Terpsichore, Lubov
Tchernicheva as Calliope, Félia Doubrowska
as Polumnie.

André Bauchant
Design for the front cloth, 1927
Oil on canvas
101.6 × 132.4 cm
WA (1933.395)

Le Bal

Ballet in two scenes by Boris Kochno after
a novel by Vladimir Sollogub, with music
by Vittorio Rieti.
Produced at the Théâtre de Monte-Carlo
on May 9, 1929 and at the Théâtre Sarah-
Bernhardt, Paris on May 28, 1929 with
choreography by George Balanchine and set
and costumes by Giorgio de Chirico.
Stage manager: Serge Grigoriev.
Principal performers: Anton Dolin as
the Young Man, André Dobrov as the Astrologer,
Alexandra Danilova, Serge Lifar.

Giorgio de Chirico
Design for the cover of the
souvenir program of Sergei
Diaghilev's Ballets Russes
for the 1929 season in Monte
Carlo and Paris
Graphite pencil, tempera
and watercolor on paper
27.5 × 20 cm
WA (1933.438)
The Ella Gallup Sumner
and Mary Catlin Sumner
Collection Fund

Giorgio de Chirico
Costume design for a male
guest, 1929
Tempera, watercolor and
pencil on paper, 34 × 20.7 cm
WA (1933 450)

Giorgio de Chirico
Costume design for Serge Lifar
as the man in the Italian
entrée, 1929
Graphite pencil, tempera
and watercolor on paper
27.5 × 20.2 cm
WA (1933.441)

Giorgio de Chirico
Costume design for a female
guest, 1929
Graphite pencil, tempera
and watercolor on paper
29.2 × 19.9 cm
WA (1933.451)

Alexandra Danilova as
the Young Lady and Serge
Lifar as the Young Man
in Scene 2, 1929
Photograph by Numa Blanc fils
Original print, 16.7 × 11.7 cm
Archives NMNM
(2002 7 12 C 37 07 0033)
Serge Lifar Collection

Alexandra Danilova as the
Young Lady, 1929
Photograph by Numa Blanc fils
Archives SBM (1929 10 05)

Giorgio de Chirico
Costume design for George
Balanchine, 1929
Pencil, watercolor
and gouache on paper
27.8 × 20.3 cm
TML (S 449 1975)

Serge Lifar as the Young Man
1929
Photograph by Numa Blanc fils
Archives SBM (1929 10 14)

Sergei Diaghilev: A Chronology

Oleg Brezgin

On the discrepancies between the Russian and Western calendars please refer to the "Note to the Reader," p. 19

(19) 31 March 1872
Sergei Pavlovich Diaghilev is born at the Selishchensky Barracks of Novgorod Region to Pavel Pavlovich Diaghilev, a noble officer in the Mounted Guardsmen Regiment, and his wife Evgenia Nikolaevna (Evreinova). Following his wife's death, P. P. Diaghilev accepts an appointment to St. Petersburg and marries Elena Valerianovna Panaeva in 1874.

1879
August The Diaghilev family moves to its ancestral estate in Perm Region, first to Bikbarda, then, in the fall of 1880, to a large house in Perm. While in Perm, Sergei starts music lessons with E. Dennemark, a Classical gymnasium school instructor.

1883
Sergei enters the second grade of Perm Gymnasium for Boys.

1887
Fall Sergei composes a romance song to verse by A. Tolstoi, "Do you remember me, Maria…" The song is performed on (14) **26 October** at a family concert.

1890
(7) 19 February Sergei, as part of the Perm Musical Circle, performs "Allegro," the first part of Schumann's *Concerto for Piano*, and also plays accompaniment at a recital at the Mariinskaia Gymnasium for Girls. **May through summer** Sergei graduates from Perm Gymnasium and is admitted to the law school of the University of St. Petersburg. **Fall** St. Petersburg. Along with his cousin Dmitrii Filosofov, he attends a self-education circle at the home of Benois, where he makes the acquaintance of Bakst, Nouvel,

Somov, and others who would later form the core of the World of Art movement.

1891–1895
Diaghilev studies music theory and composition and takes singing lessons from his aunt, singer Panaeva-Kartseva, and professors of the St. Petersburg Conservatory, in particular, A. Cotogna. He hosts music recitals in his apartment and visits L. Tolstoi in Khamovniki (**January 1892**). During his travels abroad, he becomes familiar with the work of Brahms, Verdi, Zola, Wilde, and many prominent painters. A visit to Rimsky-Korsakov (**September 1894**) cools Diaghilev's dreams of a musical career. His interests begin to shift toward the visual arts.

1896
The first publications by Diaghilev include four articles on exhibitions in St. Petersburg and Germany for the newspapers *Novosti* and *Birzhevaia gazeta*. This is the year he graduates from the University.

1897
February St. Petersburg, Baron Stieglitz School. Diaghilev starts his remarkable art promotion career with his first exhibition project: "Exhibition of English and German Watercolorists" (225 entries). **May** Diaghilev ponders the idea of a new artistic group and a new journal in Russia. **October** St. Petersburg, Society for the Encouragement of the Arts, the "Exhibition of Scandinavian Artists" showcases work by over seventy painters from Sweden, Norway and Denmark. Upon Diaghilev's invitation, Zorn attends the opening ceremony.

1898
(15) 27 January through (15) 27 February "Exhibition of Russian and Finnish Artists" held at Baron Stieglitz Museum. **(18) 30 March** Princess Tenisheva and Mamontov sign an agreement to publish a new journal, *Mir iskusstva* [World of Art]. **May through early fall** A smaller version of the Russian–Finnish exhibition visits Munich, Düsseldorf, Cologne, and Berlin. **(10) 22 November** The first double issue of the journal *Mir iskusstva* (1–2) features a manifesto, "Complex Issues," signed by Diaghilev.

1899
(18) 30 January through (22 February) 6 March "International Exhibition of Paintings" sponsored by the *Mir iskusstva* journal held at Baron Stieglitz Museum. The exhibition showcases work by World of Art artists along with art by painters from France, England, Germany, Belgium, Italy, Norway, and Finland. **(10) 22 September** Diaghilev is appointed special projects administrator under Prince Volkonsky, Director of the Imperial Theaters.

1900
(28 January) 10 February through (26 February) 10 March Second "World of Art" exhibition held at Baron Stieglitz Museum. *The Yearbook of Imperial Theaters* for the season 1899–1900 is released under Diaghilev's editorship.

1901
(5) 18 January through (4) 17 February Third "World of Art" exhibition held at the Imperial Academy of Art. **February through March** Diaghilev is fired following his conflict with Volkonsky.

1902
(9) 22 March through (21 April) 4 May Fourth "World of Art" exhibition held at the Passazh [Mall in St. Petersburg]. **April** Diaghilev's monograph *Russian Painting in the Eighteenth Century: D. G. Levitsky* is published, to be granted the Supreme Uvarov Award by the Imperial Academy of Sciences in 1904. **28 (15) November through 14 (1) January 1903** Another "World of Art" exhibition held in Moscow, at the House of Grachev.

1903
(13) 26 February through (25 March) 7 April Fifth "World of Art" exhibition held at the Society for the Encouragement of the Arts in St. Petersburg. **(16) 29 December** The Constitutional Assembly of the Union of Russian Artists in Moscow accepts Diaghilev as its active member.

1904
December Final issue of the *Mir iskusstva* journal.

1905
(6) 19 March through (26 September) 9 October "Exhibition of Russian Historical Portraits" held at the Tauride Palace in St. Petersburg. This is a grandiose show that crowns Diaghilev's quest of many years; it features over 2300 portraits by almost 400 artists on loan from 500 owners. **(24 March) 6 April** Diaghilev honored by art patrons, artists, and collectors at the Metropol Restaurant in Moscow. He delivers an address that is published by *Vesy* journal under the title "The Hour of Reckoning."

Valentin Serov
Portrait of Tamara Karsavina
1909
Pencil on paper, 43 × 26.6 cm
STG (11311)

Dancers and other associates of the Ballets Russes leaving Chicago, 1916. Left to right: Adolph Bolm, Serge Grigoriev, Léonide Massine, Lydia Sokolova, Hilda Buick, Sergei Diaghilev, Lydia Lopukhova, Lubov Tchernicheva, Olga Kokhlova (at that time Pablo Picasso's wife) and Nicolas Kremnev, 1916
Photograph by Mile High Photo Co. Denver
Original print
SPSMTM (GIK 6963/4)

Natalia Goncharova
Portrait of Serge Lifar, 1932
Indian ink and pen on paper
27 × 20.2 cm
STG (R-5443)

1906

(24 February) 9 March through (26 March) 8 April "Exhibition of Contemporary Russian painting" held at the Ekaterininsky Hall in St. Petersburg under the aegis of the World of Art. In addition to the original World of Art members, the exhibition features work by young Moscow artists such as P. Kuznetsov, Larionov, and Sapunov. (2) 15 October through (29 October) 11 November The exhibition "Two Centuries of Russian Painting and Sculpture" is staged at the "Salon d'Automne," Grand Palais, Paris, featuring 750 works by over 100 artists. November The same exhibition shows at the Schulte Salon in Berlin.

1907

April International show (in effect, an abridged version of the Russian exhibition in Paris) held in Venice. (3) 16 – (17) 30 May *Cinq concerts historiques* held at the Grand Opéra in Paris, with participation by Rimsky-Korsakov, Glazunov, Rachmaninoff, Skriabin, and the finest Russian recitalists: soloists Chaliapin, Litvin, Smirnov, and Hofman; and conductors Nikish and Blumenfeld.

1908

(6) 19 May through (22 May) 4 June Mussorgsky's opera *Boris Godunov* featuring Chaliapin is premiered at the Grand Opéra in Paris and runs for a total of seven performances. June Diaghilev and Astruc sign a contract for the first of the "Saisons Russes" in Paris in 1909.

1909

(2) 15 April First ballet rehearsal of *Polovtsian Dances* takes place at the Ekaterininsky Theater in St. Petersburg. 19 May through 19 June The first Russian season runs in Paris at the Théâtre du Châtelet, featuring arias from *Ivan the Terrible* (*The Maid of Pskov*), *Ruslan and Liudmila*, *Judith*, *Prince Igor* and Fokine's ballets *Le Pavillon d'Armide*, *Les Sylphides*, *Cléopâtre*, and *Le Festin*. During the season closing ceremony at the Grand Opéra, the French government bestows the Academic Palm Branch Award upon Pavlova, Karsavina, Fokine, Nijinsky,

and Grigoriev. July through August Diaghilev holds negotiations for the Russian season of 1910, commissions music from Ravel, Debussy, and Ganne and discusses potential collaboration with Cocteau. December Diaghilev commissions Stravinsky to compose music for *L'Oiseau de Feu*.

1910

21–28 May Berlin season runs at the Theater des Westens. 4 June through 7 July Second Russian season runs at the Grand Opéra in Paris. 15, 20 June Two Russian–French gala-performances are given with participation by Grand Opéra actors. Early July The Company stages two shows in Brussels and returns to Paris for additional performances. Fall through December Diaghilev decides to launch a permanent ballet company and signs contracts with Cecchetti, Fokine, Karsavina, Bolm and other dancers.
• This year's premieres include *Carnaval*, *L'Oiseau de Feu*, *Giselle*, *Les Orientales*, and *Schéhérazade*.

1911

January Fired from the Maryinsky Theater, Nijinsky joins Diaghilev's company. 9 April First Monte Carlo season opens at the Casino Grand Théâtre. 15 May Rome season opens at the Teatro Costanzi. 6 June through 17 June Third Paris season runs at the Théâtre du Châtelet. 21 June through 31 July The first London season at the Covent Garden Theatre runs concurrently with Italian opera events (as part of the coronation festivities for George V). September Diaghilev holds negotiations for a St. Petersburg season in February–March 1912 at the new People's House Theater. However, in January 1912 the theater burns to the ground. 16 October through 9 December During the second London season at Covent Garden, Kschessinska makes her debut, and Pavlova participates too. 24–31 December The Paris season continues at the Grand Opéra.
• This year's premieres include: *Aurora and the Prince* (*The Sleeping Beauty*), *Le Coq d'Or*, *Narcisse*, *Sadko* (*The Underwater Kingdom*), *The Battle of Kerzhentz* interlude

(from *The City of Kitège*) with curtains by Roerich, *Petrouchka*, *Le Spectre de la Rose*, *Giselle*, and two acts of *Swan Lake*.

1912

8 January through 2 February Berlin season runs at the Theater des Westens. Diaghilev signs a contract for 53 performances in Berlin in 1912. 14–18 February The troupe performs in Dresden. 19 February through March The Company plays a two-week Vienna season at Hofoper and then tours Budapest. Kschessinska participates. 13 May through 10 June Fourth Paris season at the Théâtre du Châtelet. Nijinsky makes his debut as choreographer. Fokine leaves Diaghilev's company. 12 June through 1 August Third London season at Covent Garden. August The Company tours Deauville. 30 October through November Performances in Cologne, Frankfurt and Munich. 21 November through 19 December Berlin season at the Krolloper. 21 December A performance in Breslau (Wroclaw). 23 December through 6 January 1913 A tour of Budapest.
• This year's premieres include *Le Dieu Bleu*, *Thamar*, *L'Après-midi d'un Faune*, *Daphnis et Chloé*.

1913

8–16 January During the Vienna season musicians of the Vienna Opera initially refuse to play Stravinsky's *Petrouchka*. Diaghilev commissions *La Légende de Joseph* from Richard Strauss. Last ten days of January The company performs in Prague, Leipzig, and Dresden. 4 February through 7 March Fourth London season at Covent Garden. First half of March Performances in Lyon. 9 April through 6 May Monte Carlo season. 15 May through 23 June During this Fifth opera and ballet season in Paris, the lobby at the Théâtre des Champs Élysées features an exposition of 100 studies by Gross dedicated to the Ballets Russes. 24 June through 25 July Fifth opera and ballet season in London at the Royal Theatre, Drury Lane. 11 September through early November The Company embarks on a Latin-American

tour, with a full month of performances at the Teatro Colón in Buenos-Aires, two shows in Montevideo and a Rio-de-Janeiro stint starting on 17 October. December Diaghilev terminates further collaboration with Nijinsky.
• This year's premieres include *Boris Godunov*, *Khovanshchina*, *The Maid of Pskov* (with Chaliapin), *Jeux*, *La Tragédie de Salomé*, and *Le Sacre du Printemps*.

1914

Early in the year Diaghilev signs another contract with Fokine and engages Massine. Late January through early March The Company tours Prague, Stuttgart, Hamburg, Cologne, Leipzig, Hanover, and Breslau. 11–27 March Berlin season at the Theater am Nollendorfplatz. Late March through early April Performances in Zurich. 16 April through 6 May Monte Carlo season. 14 May through 6 June Sixth opera and ballet season in Paris at the Grand Opéra. 30 May through 25 June During the sixth opera and ballet season in London at the Royal Theatre, Drury Lane, Diaghilev makes Prokofiev's acquaintance.
• This year's premieres include *Papillons*, *La Légende de Joseph*, *Schéhérazade* (new adaptation), *Midas*, *Le Coq d'Or* dance cantata, operas *Le Rossignol*, *May Night*, and *Prince Igor*. Due to the war that breaks out in August, the fall tour of Germany is canceled. For all practical purposes, the Company falls apart.

1915

Having settled in Italy for the winter, Diaghilev meets the Italian Futurists. He also invites Prokofiev over from Russia and arranges for his 7 March debut at the Augusteum Hall in Rome. Spring through fall Diaghilev is staying at Villa Bellerive in Ouchy, not far from Lausanne, Switzerland, and during this time contracts for a 1916 American tour with Kahn. Diaghilev is joined by Goncharova, Larionov, Grigoriev, and dancers from Russia and Europe. They rehearse in a small hall, and Massine tries his hand at composing choreography. Diaghilev makes plans for future productions.

Pedro Pruna
Les Trois Graces, 1925
Graphite pencil, ink and
watercolor on the frontispiece
of an unprinted book with
parchment cover
Inscribed top right: "Monte
Carlo 1925"; bottom:
"A Borinska amicalmente
Pruna"
NMNM (1991.4.68)
Collection Boris Kochno

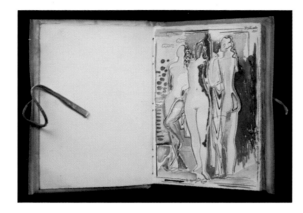

By December, he forms a new troupe without the old stars. **20 and 29 December** Gala-concerts for the benefit of the Red Cross in Geneva and Paris (Grand Opéra) attract participation by Litvine and Stravinsky. Massine makes his choreographic debut with *Soleil de Nuit*.

1916
1 January Along with Diaghilev, Ballets Russes leaves for America. **17 January through 29 April** The USA tour comprises seventeen cities, including Boston, Chicago, Washington, DC, and Philadelphia. The company also performs in New York twice: **17–29 January** at the Century Theater, and **3–29 April** at the Metropolitan Opera. As per the contract, from April 12 on, Nijinsky dances too. Diaghilev signs a contract for the second American tour, to be led by Nijinsky. **6 May** The Company leaves for Cadiz upon invitation from King Alfonso XIII of Spain to come perform in Madrid. **26 May through August** The Spanish season encompasses Madrid (Teatro Real), San Sebastián (Teatro Victoria Eugenia), and Bilbao. **8 September** The Company returns to the USA. Diaghilev takes a small group of dancers to Rome. **16 October through 24 February 1917** The second tour of the USA comprises over fifty cities. Spessivtseva participates.
• This year's premieres include *Las Meninas, Kikimora, Till Eulenspiegel* (New York).

1917
17 February Cocteau and Picasso arrive in Rome to participate in the work on *Parade*. **Mid-March** The bulk of the company returns to Spain from the USA, then moves to Rome. **9–27 April** The Rome season at the Teatro Costanzi is followed by performances in Naples and Florence. **11–26 May** Seventh Paris season at the Théâtre du Châtelet. **2–30 June** Nijinsky participates in the Madrid (Teatro Real) and Barcelona (Teatro Liceo) seasons. Picasso accompanies the troupe on the tour. **July through September** Second Latin-American tour (with Nijinsky, but without Diaghilev) comprises Montevideo, Rio de Janeiro, São Paulo, and Buenos Aires. On **26 September**, Nijinsky performs for the last time with Diaghilev's company. **November** Seasons in Barcelona and Madrid. **December.** The company performs in Lisbon.
• This year's premieres include *Contes Russes, Les Femmes de Bonne Humeur, Parade,* and Stravinsky's orchestral fantasy *Feu d'Artifice* (with light effects by Balla).

1918
31 March through 16 June This Spanish season comprises fourteen cities, including Madrid and Barcelona. **5 September through 29 March 1919** The seventh season in London, at the Coliseum, includes the 1000th performance by the Ballets Russes on 18 November.

1919
First half of April Performances in Manchester. **30 April through 30 July** The London season continues with the premieres of *La Boutique Fantasque* and *Le Tricorne* at Alhambra. **29 September through 20 December** The London season continues at the Empire Theatre. **24–30 December** Eighth season in Paris at the Grand Opéra.

1920
20 January through 16 February The Paris season continues at the Grand Opéra. **Second half of February through March** Performances in Rome and Milan. **13–27 April** Monte Carlo season. **4 May** Sarah Bernhardt participates in a gala-performance at the Grand Opéra in Paris to benefit Russian refugees in France. Rubinstein dances in *Schéhérazade* for the last time. **8 May through 4 June** Ninth season in Paris at the Grand Opéra. **10 June through 30 July** Eighth season in London at the Covent Garden. **3 November through 1 December** A tour of England comprises seven cities. **14 December through 27 December** Tenth (winter) season in Paris at the Théâtre des Champs Elysées includes Picasso and Stravinsky nights.
• This year's premieres include *Le Sacre du Printemps* (Massine), *Pulcinella, Le Astuzie Femminili, Le Chant du Rossignol.*

1921
1 January through 13 February Following the season in Rome, Massine leaves the troupe. **Second half of February** Performances in Lyon. **27 March through 10 April** Performances in Madrid. **Second half of April through May** Monte Carlo season runs. **17–23 May** The eleventh season in Paris is held at the Théâtre de la Gaîté-Lyrique. **26 May through 30 July** Ninth London season at the Princess Theatre. **2 November through 4 February 1922** *The Sleeping Princess* runs for a total of 105 performances at the Alhambra in London.
• This year's premieres include *Cuadro Flamenco, Chout, The Sleeping Princess.*

1922
10 April through 7 May Monte Carlo season. **First half of May** The Company performs in Marseille. **18 May through 13 June** During the twelfth Paris season *Le Mariage d'Aurore, Le Renard* and a short opera bouffe, *Mavra,* premiere at the Grand Opéra. **17 June through 1 July** In the course of its engagement at the Théâtre Mogador in Paris, on **27 June,** the Company stages a benefit gala for The Russian Writer Union in France. **August through fall** The troupe tours Marseille, Geneva, Ostend, San Sebastián, Bayonne, Bordeaux, Brussels, and Liege. Diaghilev reduces the Company to thirty employees and selects Monte Carlo as its winter base.

1923
17 April through May Monte Carlo season. **End of May through early June** The Company performs in Lyon and then tours Switzerland. **13–21 June** The thirteenth season in Paris is held at the Théâtre de la Gaîté-Lyrique. **30 June** The company gives a benefit concert at the Hall of Mirrors at the Palais de Versailles near Paris. **October–November** A tour of Geneva, Lausanne, Bern, and Antwerp. **23 November through February 1924** Opera and ballet season in Monte Carlo.
• This year's premieres include *Danses Russes* and *Les Noces.*

1924
January The troupe collaborates with a group of French composers known as "Le Six" to produce eight new operas and ballets in Monte Carlo. **First half of March** The company tours The Hague, Amsterdam and Rotterdam. **19–30 April** Performances in

Mikhail Larionov
Profile of Sergei Diaghilev
Blue and black ink on paper
27 × 20 cm
NMNM (1997.1.7)

Barcelona. **26 May through 30 June** In the course of its fourteenth season in Paris at the Théâtre des Champs Elysées, the troupe collaborates with Coco Chanel. **15 September through the first half of November** The company tours Munich, Leipzig, Chemnitz, Berlin, Breslau, Hamburg, Mainz, Cologne and Hanover. **24 November through 10 January 1925** The tenth London season runs at the Coliseum.
• This year's premieres include operas *The Dove*, *Le Médicin malgré lui*, *Philémon et Baucis*, and *Une Education manquée*, as well as ballets *Les Biches*, *Cimarosiana*, *Les Fâcheux*, *Le Train Bleu*, *Les Tentations de la Bergère*, and *A Night on the Bare Mountain*.

1925
17 January through 1 February Monte Carlo season. **2–15 May** Performances in Barcelona. **18 May through 1 August** The eleventh London season runs at the Coliseum. **15–20 June** The fifteenth season in Paris is held at the Théâtre de la Gaîté-Lyrique during a break in the London tour. **8–12 October** Performances in Antwerp. **26 October through 19 December** The London season continues at the Coliseum. Nijinska departs the company and Balanchine takes over as ballet master. **21 December through 6 January 1926** Performances in Berlin.
• This year's premieres include *Le Festin*, *Les Contes de Fées*, *Assemblée*, *The Ball* (from *Swan Lake*), *Zéphyr et Flore*, *Les Matelots*, *Barabau*, and Balanchine's version of *Le Chant du Rossignol*.

1926
24 January through 9 May Monte Carlo season. **18 May through 11 June** Sixteenth season in Paris at the Théâtre Sarah-Bernhardt. **14 June through 23 July** Twelfth London season at Her Majesty's Theatre. **Late July through August** Performances in Ostend and Le Touquet. **13 November through 11 December** The London season continues at the Lyceum Theatre. **24 December through 6 January 1927** Performances in Turin.

• This year's premieres include *Roméo et Juliette*, *Pastorale*, *Jack-in-the-Box*, *Le Triomphe de Neptune*, and *L'Oiseau de Feu* with new designs by Goncharova.

1927
10–16 January Performances in Milan at La Scala. **Second half of January through early May** The Monte Carlo season is followed by performances in Marseille. **7–22 May** Barcelona season. **27 May through 11 June** The seventeenth season in Paris at the Théâtre Sarah-Bernhardt. **13 June through 23 July** The thirteenth London season at the Princess Theatre. **October through 22 December** The troupe tours Freiburg, Dresden, Brno, Budapest, Vienna, and Geneva. **27–29 December** Grand Opéra, Paris.
• This year's premieres include *La Chatte*, *Mercure*, *Pas d'Acier*, Massine's version of *Les Fâcheux*, and the opera *Oedipus Rex*.

1928
January A tour of Lyon and Marseille. **End of January through April** The Monte Carlo season is followed by a gala in Nice on **30 March**. **April through May** A tour of Antwerp, Liege, Brussels, and Lausanne. **6-23 June** The eighteenth Paris season at the Théâtre Sarah-Bernhardt. **25 June through 28 July** Fourteenth London season at Her Majesty's Theatre. **29–31 July** Performances in Ostend. **12 November through 15 December** The troupe tours English provincial centers: Manchester, Glasgow, Edinburgh, and Liverpool. **20 December through 3 January 1929** Grand Opéra, Paris.
• This year's premieres include *Ode*, *Apollon Musagète*, and *The Gods Go A-Begging*.

1929
February A tour of Bordeaux and Po. **April through 12 June** Monte Carlo season. **21 May through 12 June** The nineteenth Paris season at the Théâtre Sarah-Bernhardt. **Second half of June** Performances in Berlin and Cologne. **29 June through 26 July** During the fifteenth London season at the Covent Garden, Markevich makes his debut. **End of July through**

4 August Performances in Ostend and Vichy.
• This year's premieres include Lifar's version of *Le Renard*, *Le Fils Prodigue*, and *Le Bal*.

19 August 1929
Diaghilev dies in Venice. He is buried on the island of San Michele.

Sergei Diaghilev: Selected Bibliography
Oleg Brezgin

The literature on Sergei Diaghilev and the centerpiece of his career, the Ballets Russes, is plentiful and diverse, and, certainly, by the end of the 1970s, a wealth of titles on Diaghilev, primarily Western European and American publications, had been accumulated. The classic monographs by Richard Buckle, Lynn Garafola, and other researchers are fully representative of this accomplishment. Fortunately, some of the rare books dating back to the first half of the twentieth century have also been reprinted. Hence, the Selected Bibliography which follows concentrates on books published over the past three decades—when new publications on Diaghilev increased dramatically, especially in Russia which has now rediscovered a prominent fellow citizen long lost from view.

This Bibliography contains three sections:
I. Monographs and collections of articles;
II. Memoirs, diaries and correspondence;
III. Catalogs of exhibitions, collections, and auctions.
Each of the sections lists titles chronologically and in alphabetical order of authors and titles if within a single year.

The author offers his appreciation to the following individuals for their ready assistance and advice: John E. Bowlt, Elena Kharlamova, M. Lourdes Castro Cerón, Gunhild Oberzaucher-Schüller, Anna Mackey, Alexander Schouvaloff, and Elizabeth Souritz.

I. Monographs and Collections of Articles

1980
Buckle, Richard, *Diaghilev*, translated by Tony Mayer (Paris: J.-C. Lattès, 1980).
Kochno, Boris, *Diaghilev and the Ballets Russes* (New York: Books for Libraries, 1980).

1981
Beaumont, Cyril, *Michel Fokine and His Ballets* (New York: Dance Horizons, 1981).

1982
Buckle, Richard, *In the Wake of Diaghilev* (London: Collins, 1982).
Levinson, André, *Ballet Old and New* (New York: Dance Horizons, 1982).
Lifar, Serge, *Serge de Diaghilev* (Monaco: d'Aujourd'Hui, 1982).
Schouvaloff Alexander and Victor Borovsky, *Stravinsky on Stage* (London: Stainer and Bell, 1982).
Sergei Diaghilev i russkoe iskusstvo [Sergei Diaghilev and Russian art], Vols.1–2, compiled by Ilia Zilbershtein and Vladimir Samkov (Moscow: Izobrazitelnoe iskusstvo, 1982).

1984
Buckle, Richard, *Diaghilev* (New York: Atheneum, 1984).
Sternin, Grigorii, *Russkaia khudozhestvennaia kultura vtoroi poloviny 19-go – nachala 20-go veka* [Russian visual art culture of the second half of the nineteenth through early twentieth century] (Moscow: Sovetskii khudozhnik, 1984).
Vlasova, Raisa, *Russkoe teatralno-dekorativnye iskusstvo nachala 20-go veka* [Russian theatrical and decorative art of the early twentieth century] (Leningrad: Russian Federation of Artists, 1984).

1985
Volkov, Solomon, *Balanchine's Tchaikovsky* (New York: Simon and Schuster, 1985).

1986
[Pruzhan, Irina], *Leon Bakst. Set and Costume Designs...* (Leningrad: Aurora, 1986).
Ries, Frank W. D., *The Dance Theatre of Jean Cocteau* (Michigan: UMI Research Press, 1986).

1987
Cooper, Douglas, *Picasso Theatre* (New York: Harry N. Abrams, 1987).

1988
Bowlt, John E., *The Russian Avant-Garde: Theory and Criticism, 1902–1934* (London, Abrams, 1988).
Buckle, Richard, *Nijinsky* (London: Phoenix, 1988).
Buckle, Richard (with John Taras), *George Balanchine, Ballet Master* (New York: Random House, 1988).
Pozharskaia, Militsa, *Russkie sezony v Parizhe* [Russian seasons in Paris] (Moscow: Iskusstvo, 1988).

1989
Sergei Diaghilev i khudozhestvennaia kultura 19–20 vekov [Sergei Diaghilev and artistic culture of the nineteenth and twentieth centuries] (Perm: Book Publishers, 1989).
Shead, Richard, *Ballets Russes* (London: Apple, 1989).

1990
Pozharskaia, Militsa and Tatiana Volodina, *The Art of the Ballets Russes: The Russian Season in Paris, 1908–1929* (London: Aurum, 1990; New York: Abbeville, 1990; Paris: Gallimard, 1990).

1991
Menaker Rothschild, Deborah, *Picasso's "Parade": From Street to Stage* (London: Sotheby's, 1991).
Schouvaloff, Alexander, *Léon Bakst* (Paris: Scala, 1991;

London: Sotheby's, 1991).
The World of Art Movement in Early 20th-Century Russia, introduction by Vsevolod Petrov and Aleksandr Kamensky (Leningrad: Aurora, 1991).

1992
Écrits sur Nijinsky (Paris: Chiron, 1992).
Lev Bakst, compiled by Sergei Golynets (Moscow: Izobrazitelnoe iskusstvo, 1992).

1993
Cocteau, Jean, *Le Coq et l'Arlequin*, new edition (Paris: Stock, 1993).
Grigoriev, Sergei, *Balet Diaghileva, 1909–1929* [Diaghilev's Ballet] (Moscow: ART, 1993).
Parade: genèse d'une creation, text by Dominique Frétard (Paris: Plume, 1993).
Parton, Anthony, *Michail Larionov and the Russian Avant-Garde* (London: Princeton University Press, 1993).

1994
Nestiev, Izrail, *Diaghilev i musykalnyi teatr 20-go veka* [Diaghilev and musical theater of the twentieth century] (Moscow: Muzyka, 1994).

1995
Permskii Ezhegodnik '95. Khoreografiia [Perm 1995 Yearbook. Choreography], compiled by Oleg Levenkov (Perm: Arabesque, 1995).
Spencer, Charles, *Léon Bakst and the Ballets Russes* (London: Academy Editions, 1995).

1996
García-Márquez, Vicente, *Massine* (London: Nick Hern Books, 1996).
Permskii Eezhegodnik '96. Khoreografiia [Perm 1996 Yearbook. Choreography], compiled by Oleg Levenkov and Natalia Chernova (Perm: Arabesque, 1996).

Taper, Bernard, *Balanchine*, second revised edition (Berkeley and Los Angeles: University of California Press, 1996).
Yakovleva, Elena, *Teatralno-dekoratsionnoe iskusstvo N. K. Rerikha* [Theatrical and set paintings by N. K. Roerich] (Samara: Agni, 1996).

1997
Drummond, John, *Speaking of Diaghilev* (London and Boston: Faber and Faber, 1997).
Pastori, Jean-Pierre, *La Danse: Des Ballets russes a l'avant-garde* (Paris: Gallimard, 1997).
Spiegelungen: die Ballets Russes und die Künste, edited by Claudia Jeschke (Berlin: Vorwerk 8, 1997).
V poiskakh Diaghileva [In search of Diaghilev], written and compiled by Aleksandr Laskin (St. Petersburg: St. Petersburg Academy of Culture, 1997).

1998
Benois, Alexandre, *Vozniknoveniye Mira iskusstva* [Founding the World of Art], reprint (Moscow: Iskusstvo, 1998).
Garafola, Lynn, *Diaghilev's Ballets Russes*, second edition (New York: Da Capo, 1998).
Serebryanyi vek v fotografiiakh A. P. Botkinoy [The Silver Age as photographed by A. P. Botkina] (Moscow: Nashe nasledie, 1998).

1999
Davydova, Margarita, *Khudozhnik v teatre nachala 20 veka* [Artist at the early twentieth century theater] (Moscow: Nauka, 1999).
Krasovskaia, Vera, *Pavlova, Nijinsky, Vaganova* (Moscow: Agraf, 1999).
Makovsky, Sergei, *Siluety russkikh khudozhnikov* [Silhouettes of Russian

artists] (Moscow: Republic, 1999).

Smoliarova, Tatiana, *Parizh, 1928: Oda vozvrashchayetsia v teatr* [Paris, 1928: The ode returns to the theater] (Moscow: The Russian State University for Humanities, 1999).

The Ballets Russes and Its World, edited by Lynn Garafola and Nancy van Norman Baer (New Haven and London: Yale University Press, 1999).

Walsh, Stephen, *Igor Stravinsky: A Creative Spring*, Vol. 1 (London: Jonathan Cape, 1999).

2000

Los Ballets Russes de Diaghilev y España, edited by Yvan Nommick and Antonio Álvarez Cañibano (Granada and Madrid: Archivo Manuel de Falla, 2000).

Russkii avangard 1910–1920 godov i teatr [Russian avant-garde of the 1910s–1920s and the theater], under the editorship of Georgii Kovalenko (St. Petersburg: Bulanin, 2000).

2001

Buckle, Richard, *Vatslav Nijinsky* (Moscow: Tsentrpolygraf, 2001).

[Gall, Hugues R.], *Hommage à Boris Kochno* (Paris: Opéra National, 2001).

Huesca, Roland, *Triomphes et scandales: La belle époque des Ballets Russes* (Paris: Hermann, 2001).

Kinkulkina, Natalia, *Aleksandr Sanin* (Moscow: Iskusstvo, 2001).

Rusakova, Aleksandra, *Simvolizm v russkoi zhivopisi* [Symbolism in Russian painting] (Moscow: Belyi gorod, 2001).

Sarabianov, Dmitrii, *Istoriia russkogo iskusstva kontsa 19 – nachala 20 veka* [A history of Russian art of late nineteenth through early twentieth centuries] (Moscow: Act-Press–Galart, 2001).

2002

Fédorovski, Vladimir, *L'Histoire secrète des Ballets Russes* (Monaco: Rocher, 2002).

Paiman, Avril, *Istoriia russkogo simvolizma* [A history of Russian Symbolism], third edition (Moscow: Republic, 2002).

S. Diaghilev i russkoe iskusstvo 19–20 vv. [S. Diaghilev and Russian art of the nineteenth and twentieth centuries], Vols. 1–2 (Perm: Perm Art Gallery, 2002–05).

Volkov, Solomon, *Strasti po Tchaikovskomu: razgovory s Dzhordzhem Balanchinym* [Passionate about Tchaikovsky: Conversations with George Balanchine] (Moscow: Eksmo, 2002).

2003

Cocteau, Jean, *Tiazhest bytiia* [The heavy burden of being] (St. Petersburg: Azbuka–Klassika, 2003).

Dandré, Victor, *Anna Pavlova* (St. Petersburg: Vita Nova, 2003).

Fedorovsky, Vladimir, *Sergei Diaghilev ili zakulisnaia istoriia russkogo baleta* [Sergei Diaghilev or a backstage history of Russian ballet] (Moscow: Exmo, 2003).

Kovalenko, Georgii, *N. Gontcharova, M. Larionov* (Moscow: Nauka, 2003).

Kriuchkova, Valentina, *Picasso: Ot Parada do Gerniki* [Picasso: From Parade to Guernica] (Moscow: Progress–Tradition, 2003).

Laskin, Aleksandr, *Dolgoe puteshestvie s Diagilevym* [A long journey with Diaghilev] (Ekaterinburg: U-Faktoriia, 2003).

Remizov, Aleksei, *Sobranie sochinenii: Peterburgskii buerak* [A ravine of Saint Petersburg] (Moscow: Russkaia kniga, 2003).

Subbotin, E. P. and V. A. Dyldin, *Diaghilevy v Permi: pamiatnye mesta* [The Diaghilevs in Perm: Memorable places] (Perm: Arabesque, 2003).

Vasiliev, Aleksandr, *Krasota v izgnanii* [Beauty in exile], third edition (Moscow: Slovo, 2003).

2004

Asafiev, Boris, *Russkaia zhivopis* [Russian painting] (Moscow: Republic, 2004).

Charles-Roux, Edmonde, *Le Temps Chanel* (Paris: Martinière/Grasset et Fasquelle, 2004).

Dobrovolskaia, Galina, *Mikhail Fokin: russkii period* [Mikhail Fokine: the Russian period] (St. Petersburg: Hyperion, 2004).

Ernst, Sergei, *Alexandre Benois* (Moscow: Terra–Book Club, 2004).

Fédorovski, Vladimir, *Diaghilev et Monaco* (Monaco: Rocher, 2004).

2005

Aleshina, Lilia and Grigorii Sternin, *Obrazy i liudi serebrianogo veka* [Images and people of the Silver Age],

second edition (Moscow: Galart, 2005).

Lifar, Sergei, *Diaghilev i s Diaghilevym* [Diaghilev and with Diaghilev] (Moscow: Vagrius, 2005).

Pospelov, Gleb and Evgenia Iliukhina, *Mikhail Larionov* (Moscow: Galart/RA, 2005).

Tolstoi, Andrei, *Khudozhniki russkoi emigratsii* [Painters of the Russian emigration] (Moscow: Iskusstvo–XXI vek, 2005).

2006

Benois, Alexandre, "Khudozhestvennye pisma 1908–1917" [Artistic letters], in *Rech*, Vol. 1 (St. Petersburg: Sad Iskusstv, 2006).

Gottlieb, Robert, *Balanchine: The Ballet Master* (London: Atlas Books, Harper Press, 2006).

Picasso i okrestnosti [Picasso and thereabouts], under the editorship of M. Busev (Moscow: Progress–Tradition, 2006).

Press, Stephen D., *Prokofiev's Ballets for Diaghilev* (Aldershot, England: Ashgate & Burlington, Vermont, 2006).

Pyman, Avril, *A History of Russian Symbolism* (Cambridge and New York: Cambridge University Press, 2006).

Tomina-Petrova, Elena, *Zhemchuzhina russkogo baleta – Olga Spesivtseva* (The pearl of Russian ballet, Olga Spesivtseva) (St. Petersburg: Logos, 2006).

2007

Brezgin, Oleg, *Persona Diaghileva v khudozhestvennoi kulture Rossii, Zapadnoi Evropy i Ameriki* [Diaghilev's personality in the artistic culture of Russia, Western Europe and America] (Perm: Perm Art Gallery, 2007).

Charles-Roux, Edmonde, *Vremia Chanel* [The time of Chanel] (Moscow: Slovo, 2007).

Ingles, Elizabeth, *Bakst* (Rochester, Kent: Grange Books, 2007).

Levenkov, Oleg, *George Balanchine*, Part 1 (Perm: Knizhnyi mir, 2007).

S. P. Diaghilev i sovremennaia kultura [S. P. Diaghilev and modern culture], under the editorship of Oleg Levenkov (Perm: Knizhnyi mir, 2007).

Sergei Pavlovich Diaghilev, 1872–1929: Materialy k bibliografii [Bibliographic

material], compiled by Irina Kuznetsova and Alla Lapidus, under the editorship of Aleksandr Laskin (St. Petersburg: SPbGUKI, 2007).

2008

Bowlt, John, *Moscow, St. Petersburg: The Russian Silver Age* (New York: Vendome, 2008; London: Thames and Hudson, 2008; Paris: Hazan, 2008).

Elshevskaia, Galina, *Mir Iskusstva* [The World of Art] (Moscow: Belyi Gorod, 2008).

Gaevsky, Vadim, *Khoreograficheskiye portrety* [Choreographic portraits] (Moscow: ART, 2008).

Mackrell, Judith, *Bloomsbury Ballerina: Lydia Lopokova* (London: Weidenfeld & Nicolson, 2008).

II. Memoirs, Diaries, Correspondence

1980

Markevitch, Igor, *Etre et avoir été: Mémoires* (Paris: Gallimard, 1980).

Nijinsky, Romola, *Nijinsky* (New York: Simon and Schuster, 1980).

1981

Fokine, Michel, *Protiv techeniia: Vospominaniia baletmeistera* [Against the current: reminiscences of a ballet master], second edition (Leningrad: Iskusstvo, 1981).

1983

Nijinska, Bronislava, *Mémoires (1891–1914)*, translated by Gérard Mannoni (Paris: Ramsay, 1983).

1985

Cocteau, Jean, *Portrety-Vospominaniia* [Reminiscence portraits] (Moscow: Izvestiya, 1985).

Valentin Serov v perepiske, dokumentakh i interviu [Valentin Serov through correspondence, documents and interviews], Vols. 1–2, compiled by Ilia Zilbershtein and Vladimir Samkov (Leningrad: Khudozhnik RSFSR, 1985–89).

1986

Ansermet, Ernst, *Stati o muzyke i vospominaniia* [Articles on music and Memoirs] (Moscow: Sovetskii kompozitor, 1986).

Danilova, Alexandra, *Choura* (New York: Knopf, 1986).

Markova, Alicia, *Markova Remembers* (Boston: Little, Brown, 1986).

1987

Dobuzhinsky, Mstislav, *Vospominaniia* [Memoirs]

(Moscow: Nauka, 1987).

1988

Karsavina, Tamara, *Theatre Street* (London: Columbus, 1988).

Nijinsky, Vaslav, *Journal*, translated and foreworded by G. S. Solpray (Paris: Gallimard, 1988).

1989

Sokolova, Lydia, *Dancing for Diaghilev: The Memoirs of Lydia Sokolova* (San Francisco: Mercury House, 1989).

1990

Belyi, Andrei, *Nachalo veka* [The beginning of the century] (Moscow: Khudozhestvennaia literatura, 1990).

Konstantin Korovin vspominaet… [Konstantin Korovin remembers], compiled by Ilia Zilbershtein and Vladimir Samkov (Moscow: Izobrazitelnoe iskusstvo, 1990).

1991

Nijinsky, Vaslav, *The Diary of Vaslav Nijinsky*, edited by Romola Nijinsky (London: Quartet Encounters, 1991).

1992

Nijinska, Bronislava, *Early Memoirs* (Durham and London: Duke University Press, 1992).

Volkonsky, Sergei, *Moi vospominaniia* [My memoirs], Vols. 1–2 (Moscow: Iskusstvo, 1992).

1993

Benois, Alexandre, *Moi vospominaniia* [My memoirs], Vols. 1–5 (Moscow: Nauka, 1993).

Lifar, Serge, *Les Mémoires d'Icare* (Lausanne: Sauret, 1993).

1995

Dnevnik Vatslava Nizhinskogo [Diary of Vaslav Nijinsky] (Moscow: ART, 1995).

Lifar, Serge, *Memuary Ikara* [Memories of Icarus] (Moscow: Iskusstvo, 1995).

Natalia Goncharova, Mikhail Larionov. Vospominaniia sovremennikov [Natalia Goncharova and Mikhail Larionov in the memories of their contemporaries] (Moscow: Galart, 1995).

Nijinsky, Vaslav, *Cahiers: le sentiment*, translated by Christian Dumais-Lvowski and Galina Pogojeva (Paris: Actes Sud, 1995).

1997

Massine, Léonide, *Moia zhizn v balete* [My life in the ballet] (Moscow: ART, 1997).

1998

Diaghileva, Elena, *Semeinaia zapis o Diaghilevykh* [Family records on the Diaghilevs] (St. Petersburg and Perm: Bulanin, 1998).

I. F. Stravinsky. Perepiska s russkimi korrespondentami [Russian correspondence], Vols. 1–3, compiled and edited by Viktor Varunts (Moscow: Kompozitor, 1998–2003).

Teliakovsky, Vladimir, *Dnevniki direktora Imperatorskikh teatrov 1898–1906* [Diaries of the director of Imperial Theaters], Vols. 1–3 (Moscow: ART, 1998–2006).

1999

Nijinska, Bronislava, *Rannie vospominaniia* [Early memoirs], part 1–2 (Moscow: ART, 1999).

Nijinsky, Vaslav, *The Diary of Vaslav Nijinsky*, translated by K. Fitz Lyon, edited by Joan Acocella (London: Allen Lane, 1999).

2000

Chaliapin, Fedor, *Vospominaniia: stranitsy iz moei zhizni. Maska i dusha* [Memoirs: pages of my life. The mask and the soul] (Moscow: Lokid, 2000).

Makovsky, Sergei, *Portrety sovremennikov* [Portraits of my contemporaries] (Moscow: Agraf, 2000).

Nijinsky, Vaslav, *Chuvstvo: tetradi* [Feeling: the notebooks], text prepared by Galina Pogozheva (Moscow: Vagrius, 2000).

Shcherbatov, Sergei, *Khudozhnik v ushedshei Rossii* [An artist in the Russia of the past] (Moscow: Soglasie, 2000).

2001

Dobuzhinsky, Mstislav, *Pisma* [Letters] (St. Petersburg: Bulanin, 2001).

Grabar, Igor, *Moia zhizn. Etiudy o khudozhnikakh* [My life. Sketches of the artists] (Moscow: Republic, 2001).

Sert, Misia, *Mizia ili pozhiratelnitsa geniev* [Misia or the devouress of genius] (Moscow: ART, 2001).

2002

Pertsov, Petr, *Literaturnye vospominaniia 1890–1902* [Literary memoirs] (Moscow: NLO [UFO], 2002).

Prokofiev, Sergei, *Dnevniki 1907–1933* [Diaries], part 1–3 (Paris: sprkfv, 2002).

Stravinsky, Igor (with Robert Craft), *Memories and Commentaries* (London: Faber and Faber, 2002).

2003

Aleksandr Nikolaevich Benois i ego adresaty (Alexandre Nikolaevich Benois and his addressees] (St. Petersburg: Sad iskusstv, 2003).

Ignatieva-Trukhanova, Natalia, *Na stsene i za kulisami* [On stage and backstage] (Moscow: Zakharov, 2003).

Nabokov, Nikolai, *Bagazh* (St. Petersburg: Zvezda, 2003).

2004

Gippius, Zinaida, *Nichego ne boius* [I am afraid of nothing] (Moscow: Vagrius, 2004).

Karsavina, Tamara, *Teatralnaia ulitsa* [Theater street], translated by I. Balod (Moscow: Tsentrpolygraf, 2004).

Kschessinska, Mathilde, *Vospominaniia* [Memoirs] (Moscow: Tsentrpolygraf, 2004).

Stravinsky, Igor, *Khronika. Poetika* [Chronicle. Poetics] (Moscow: RossPan, 2004).

2005

Annenkov, Yurii, *Dnevnik moikh vstrech* [The diary of my encounters], under the editorship of R. Gerr (Moscow: Vagrius, 2005).

Nijinska, Romola, *Vaslav Nijinsky* (Moscow: Tsentrpolygraf, 2005).

2006

Tenisheva, Maria, *Vpechatleniia moei zhizni* [The impressions of my life] (Moscow: Molodaia gvardiia, 2006).

2007

Prokofiev, Sergei, *Pisma. Vospominaniia. Stati* [Letters. Memoirs. Articles] (Moscow: Deca–BC, 2007).

Serge Diaghilev: Mémoires suivis de apologie de l'avant-garde (Paris: Hermann, 2007).

Zheverzheeva, Tamara, *Vospominaniia* [Memoirs] (Moscow: SkanRus, 2007).

2008

Semenov, Mikhail, *Vakh i Sireny* [Bacchus and the Sirens] (Moscow: NLO [UFO], 2008).

III. Catalogs of Exhibitions, Collections and Auctions

1979

Diaghilev: Les Ballets Russes, edited by Nicole Wild and Jean-Michel Nectoux (Paris: Bibliothèque nationale, 1979).

Paris–Moscou, 1900–1930 (Paris: Centre Georges Pompidou, 1979).

The Diaghilev Ballet in England, edited by Richard Buckle (Norwich and London, 1979).

1980

Alexandre Benois, 1870–1960: Drawings for the Ballet, edited by Richard Buckle et al. (London: Hazlitt, Gooden & Fox, 1980).

1981

Ballet Designs from the collection of Mr. & Mrs. John Carr Doughty (London: Sotheby's, June 4, 1981).

Moscow–Paris. 1900–1930, Vols. 1–2 (Moscow: Sovetskii khudozhnik, 1981).

Spotlight: Four Centuries of Ballet Costume, edited by Roy Strong et al. (London: Victoria and Albert Museum, 1981).

The Diaghilev Heritage. Selections from the Collection of Robert L. B. Tobin (Houston: Museum of Fine Arts, 1981).

1984

Ballet Material and Manuscripts from the Serge Lifar Collection (London: Sotheby's, May 9, 1984).

1986

Baer, Nancy van Norman, *Bronislava Nijinska: A Dancer's Legacy* (San Francisco: Fine Arts Museum, 1986).

1988

The Art of Enchantment: Diaghilev's Ballets Russes, 1909–1929 (San Francisco: Fine Arts Museum, 1988).

1989

España y los Ballets Russes, edited by Lynn Garafola and Vicente García-Márquez (Madrid: Ministerio de Cultura, 1989).

Nectoux, Jean-Michel, *L'Après-midi d'un Faune: Mallarmé, Debussy, Nijinsky* (Paris, 1989).

Nijinsky (Paris: Musée-Galerie de la Seita, 1989).

1990

Schouvaloff, Alexander, *Theatre on Paper* (London: Sotheby's, 1990).

1991

Collection Boris Kochno (Monaco: Sotheby's, October 11–12, 1991).

1992

Il Simbolismo russo. Sergej Djagilev e l'età d'argento nell'arte, edited by Valerian Dudakov (Milan: Olivetti and Electa, 1992).

Les Ballets Russes à l'Opéra, 1909–1929, edited by Martine Kahane (Paris: Bibliothèque nationale, Hazan, 1992).

Leon Bakst: The Sleeping Beauty, edited by Haviva Carmeli et al. (Tel Aviv: Museum of Art, 1992).

Picasso. Le Tricorne, edited by Brigitte Léal et al. (Lyon: Musée des Beaux-Art, 1992).

1993

Leon Bakst: Sensualismens Triumf, edited by Erik Näslund (Stockholm: Dansmuseet, 1993).

Pastori, Jean-Paul, *De Diaghilev à Béjart: Lausanne danse, 1915–1993* (Lausanne: Musée Historique de Lausanne, 1993).

1994

Barran, Julian, *An Exhibition of Designs for the Russian Ballet* (London: J. Barran, 1994).

Bowlt, John E., *Painters of Russian Theater, 1880–1930: Collection of Nikita and Nina Lobanov-Rostovsky* (Moscow: Iskusstvo, 1994).

Diaghilews Ballets Russes: Aufbruch in die Moderne, edited by S. Dahms and M. Woitas (Salzburg and Munich, 1994).

1995

The Diaghilev and Ballets Russes Costumes from Castle Howard (London: Sotheby's, 1995).

1996

Diaghilev: Creator of the Ballets Russes, edited by Ann Kodicek (London: Barbican Art Gallery, Lund Humphries, 1996).

[Näslund, Erik], *Överdådets konst = The Art of Extravagance: Kostymer från Diaghilews Ryska Baletten i Paris* (Stockholm: Dansmuseet, 1996).

Picasso y el teatro: Parade. Pulcinella. Cuadro Flamenco. Mercure, edited by María Teresa Ocaña (Barcelona: Museu Picasso, 1996).

1997

Parton, Anthony, *Natalia Gontcharova and the Russian Ballet* (London: J. Barran, 1997).

Schouvaloff, Alexander, *The Art of Ballets Russes: the Serge Lifar Collection* (New Haven and London: Yale University Press, 1997).

1998

Bowlt, John E., *L'Avant-garde russe et la scène, 1910–1930. La collection Lobanov-Rostovsky* (Brussels: Musée d'Ixelles, 1998).

Bowlt, John E., *Theater of Reason / Theater of Desire: the Art of Alexandre Benois and Léon Bakst* (Milan: Skira, 1998).

Mir iskusstva: 100 let. Iz chastnykh sobranii moskovskikh kollektsionerov [The World of Art: 100 years. From private collections in Moscow] (Moscow: The State Pushkin Museum of Visual Arts, 1998).

Mir iskusstva: k stoletiiu vystavki russkikh i finliandskikh khudozhnikov 1898 goda [The World of Art: Dedication to the centennial of the exhibition of Russian and Finnish painters of 1898] (St. Petersburg: Palace Editions, 1998).

Russkie sezony Sergeia Diaghileva [Russian seasons of Sergei Diaghilev] (St. Petersburg: Theater Library, Hyperion, 1998).

The World of Art/Mir iskusstva: On the Centenary of the Exhibition of Russian and Finnish Artists 1898 (St. Petersburg: Palace Editions, 1998).

Théâtre et Ballet Russe, 1910–1930 (Milan: Galleria Milano, 1998).

1999

From Russia with Love: Costumes for the Ballets Russes, 1909–1933, edited by R. Leong et al. (Canberra: National Gallery of Australia, 1999).

M. Larionov, N. Goncharova. Parizhskoe nasledie v Tretyakovskoi galeree [Paris legacy at the Tretyakov Gallery] (Moscow: State Tretyakov Gallery, 1999).

Sergei Diaghilev. Perm. Petersburg. Paris, under the editorship of Sergei Golynets (Ekaterinburg: Urals State University Press, 1999).

2000

Nijinsky, 1889–1950, edited by Martine Kahane (Paris: Musée d'Orsay, ADAGP, 2000).

2001

Diaghilev i ego epokha [Diaghilev and his time] (St.Petersburg: State Russian Museum, Palace Editions, 2001).

2002

Music and Ballet: including the papers of Serge Lifar (London: Sotheby's, 2002).

Näslund, Erik, *En guldålder I rysk konst: Alexandre Benois och Konstens värld (Mir iskusstva)* (Stockholm: Dansmuseet, 2002).

2003

Paris russe, 1910–1960 (Bordeaux: Musée des Beaux-

Arts and St. Petersburg: Palace Editions, 2003).

Russkii Parizh, 1910–1960 [Russian Paris] (St. Petersburg: The State Russian Museum, Palace Editions, 2003).

2004

[Näslund, Erik], *Överdådets konst II = The Art of Extravagance II* (Stockholm: Dansmuseet, 2004).

Vek Balanchina (1904–2004) [The century of Balanchine] (St. Petersburg, Aurora–Design, 2004).

Working for Diaghilev, edited by Sjeng Scheijen et al. (Groningen: Groningen Museum, 2004).

2005

Alsteens, Stijn, *Mélange russe. Dessins, estampes et lettres de la Collection Frits Lugt* (Paris: Foundation Custodia, 2005).

La Danza delle Avanguardie: Dipinti, scene e costumi (Milan: Skira, 2005).

Parizhskiye nakhodki. K 100-letiiu so dnia rozhdeniia I. S. Zilbershteina [The Paris discoveries. Dedicated to the centennial of I. S. Zilbershtein] (Moscow: Krasnaia ploshchad, 2005).

2006

Picasso und das Theater = Picasso and the Theater, edited by Olivier Berggruen and Max Hollein (Ostfildern: Hatje Cantz, 2006).

2007

Albom na pamiat. Russkii balet v fotografiiakh iz kollektsii Tony Candeloro, Italiia [Memorial album: Ballets Russes in the photographs collected by Tony Candeloro, Italy] (St. Petersburg: Palace Editions, 2007).

Picasso a Roma, 1917: «Mon atelier de Via Margutta 53/b», edited by Valentina Moncada et al. (Rome: Electa, 2007).

2008

Kniaginia Maria Tenisheva v zerkale Serebrianogo veka [Princess Maria Tenisheva in the mirror of the Silver Age] (Moscow: The State Historical Museum, 2008.

Russland 1900: Kunst und Kultur im Reich des Letzten Zaren, edited by Ralf Beil (Darmstadt: Dumont, [2008]).

Winestein, Anna, *Danser vers la Gloire: l'age d'or des Ballets Russes* (Paris: Sotheby's, 2008).